POKÉMON® STADIUM 2

ULTIMATE BATTLE GUIDE

BY PHILLIP MARCUS

ULTIMATE BATTLE GUIDE

POKÉMON STADIUM 2

2001 Pearson Education

All rights reserved, including the right of reproduction in whole or in part in any form.

BRADY PUBLISHING

An Imprint of Pearson Education

201 West 103rd Street

Indianapolis, Indiana 46290

ISBN: 0-7440-0061-0

Library of Congress Catalog No.: 2001-131206

Printing Code: The rightmost double-digit number is the year of the book's printing; the rightmost single-digit number is the number of the book's printing. For example, 01-1 shows that the first printing of the book occurred in 2001.

04 03 02 01   4 3 2 1

Manufactured in the United States of America.

BRADYGAMES STAFF

Director of Publishing
David Waybright

Editor-In-Chief
H. Leigh Davis

Marketing Manager
Janet Eshenour

Creative Director
Robin Lasek

Licensing Assistant
Mike Degler

CREDITS

Title Manager
Tim Fitzpatrick

Screenshot Editor
Michael Owen

Book Designer
Ann-Marie Deets

Cover Designer
Carol Stamile

Production Designers
Jane Washburne
Tracy Wehmeyer
Lisa England
Bob Klunder

ACKNOWLEDGEMENTS

BradyGAMES would like to sincerely thank everyone at Nintendo of America, especially Cammy Budd, Juana Tingdale, Joy Ashizawa, and the entire NOA Testing Group, especially Randy Shoemake, Jason Mahassa, Joel Simon, and David Santiago. Your generous assistance and expert game knowledge made this guide possible—thank you!

Phillip Marcus: One more run with our little Pokéfriends, and again I'd like to thank Tim Fitzpatrick for braving the trenches with me.

TABLE OF CONTENTS

POKéMON STADIUM 2 TIPS

WELCOME BACK TO THE STADIUM!

Pokémon Stadium 2 takes all of the action from the first game and builds on it, expanding the range of Pokémon to cover all of those found in Gold and Silver. The Mini-Games are new and there are more of them. Plus, you can now earn Game Corner Coins for winning. Another big bonus is the addition of a full-featured library and school that lets you get almost any information you need while you are in the game. The Gym Leader Castle has grown to encompass gyms from both Johto and Kanto.

All of this, plus the addition of the two new Pokémon types, Dark and Steel, means you'll need to build a stronger team than ever before, but even the strongest team won't help you in the new Challenge Cup. This tournament randomly generates your Pokémon team, so you must rely more heavily on your creativity and mastery of the Pokémon battle system to get you through.

From the very beginning of the game, you can access Battle Now! if you want action right away, the Event Battle if you want to face off against a friend, grab a Mystery Gift from a friendly girl, or head into White City and the Pokémon Stadium.

AN OVERVIEW OF THE GAME

THE STADIUM

On the Stadium grounds or "campus," you can visit the Pokémon Stadium itself, which hosts four cups, each with different restrictions on the Pokémon you can bring. The four cups in the Stadium are:

LITTLE CUP

Restricted to baby Pokémon of level 5 only.

CHALLENGE CUP

Forces you to play with a team of random Pokémon.

POKé CUP

Open to Pokémon levels 50 through 55.

PRIME CUP

Open to Pokémon levels 1 through 100.

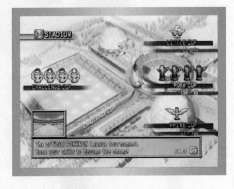

The Challenge Cup and the Poké Cup are divided into four divisions each, ranging from Poké Ball to Master Ball. Each division in the cup consists of eight fights. More extensive coverage of the cups can be found in the Stadium walkthrough later in this book.

THE GYM LEADER CASTLE

The Gym Leader Castle holds all eight gyms from both Johto and Kanto. It also contains the Team Rocket encounter that took place in Goldenrod City in Pokémon Gold and Silver. The Castle is an excellent place to test your Pokémon against every type in the game.

Generally, a gym consists of a few junior trainer fights before you face the leader of that particular gym. Unlike the Stadium, instead of making you restart from the beginning if you are knocked out of a cup, the Castle allows you to save your progress past each gym.

THE POKéMON LABORATORY

Just as it was in the original Pokémon Stadium game, the Lab is a great place to organize your Pokémon, sort your items, use items, TMs, and HMs on your Pokémon, and keep yourself organized. Any time you receive an item or a Pokémon from Pokémon Stadium 2, you can come here to retrieve and store it. The Lab also has special boxes for Red/Blue/Yellow, and Gold/Silver that allow you to store items from those versions.

When you are assembling a new team, much of your time will be spent going between the Lab and the Library, deciding on how you want to train your Pokémon and picking the members for your team.

THE POKéMON ACADEMY

Let Earl give you information on Pokémon, along with tips about what has changed since Red, Blue, and Yellow, advice on what the different status conditions do, specific information about moves, and other useful tidbits. You can take lessons, tests, and finally participate in mock battles against your classmates to show off your new knowledge.

The Academy is also home to the Library, a wonderful resource of information about Pokémon with a complete PokéDex, items listing, type chart, breeding information, and more. Best of all, the data is sorted in several different ways, so you can quickly find the information you're looking for.

THE GB TOWER

The GB Tower returns from the original Pokémon Stadium, and you can play any of the five Game Boy Pokémon titles here. Beating the Stadium or the Gym Leader Castle will unlock the Doduo GB Tower, which allows you to play at double speed. Beating the second will unlock the Dodrio GB Tower, which moves at hyper speed! Note that this will open the accelerated modes only for Red, Blue, and Yellow. To open them for Gold and Silver, you must beat the same areas in Round 2.

The GB Tower is a fantastic tool for playing through the game, building up your team, catching new Pokémon, and transferring everything you accumulate to the Pokémon Lab, where you can use your new resources to train your Pokémon.

YOUR HOUSE

In Gold and Silver, your house could be customized with posters, dolls, and even Nintendo consoles. Now you can see and decorate your room in full 3D!

MINI-GAMES

Twelve new Mini-Games make for a pleasant diversion from training and battling your Pokémon, and if you play a mini-game that features Pokémon that you have on your Game Pak, they will become more happy with you. You can also earn Game Corner Coins as long as you have acquired the Coin Case in your Game Boy game. There is also a Quiz game here that will test your knowledge of Pokémon. For tips on the 12 mini-games, refer to the Mini-Game chapter later in this guide.

FREE BATTLE ARENA

The Arena is the place to be when you have friends over. You can compete in any of the cups straight from the Stadium or use the custom rules editing to make up your own tournament, creating your own Stadium with whatever restrictions you can come up with.

POKéMON ADVICE

CONCERNING THE POKéDEX IN THIS GUIDE

The STATS for any specific Pokémon will never be the same; they will vary even between identical Pokémon. They also change depending on the level. For example, two Pikachu, even if they are the same level, will have stats that differ to some degree. Take this into consideration when you refer to the STATS listed in the PokéDex entries.

Pokémon can learn a variety of different moves depending in part on the moves the male ("father") and female ("mother") Pokémon possess. The BREEDABLE MOVES portion of each PokéDex entry simply lists some of the moves that can be bred into the Pokémon. The levels listed for moves that Pokémon learn through increasing levels are for the Gold and Silver versions, not the Red, Blue, and Yellow versions.

BATTLE ADVICE

You'll face hundreds of battles before you have completely cleared out everything the computer has to offer in the game, but a few simple rules will make those battles much, much easier.

By far the most important thing to remember when you battle is Pokémon type. Match up your types carefully. Never leave too many weaknesses open, and choose your battling team to make the most of the weaknesses in your opponent's lineup. Any team, no matter how well designed, will always have a vulnerability to another team. You must strive to minimize the weaknesses of your team, while giving them attacks to defeat their worst foes.

Spend time looking over the combat type chart at the back of this book and in the Pokémon Stadium 2 Library whenever you decide to build a team, and refer to it constantly during combat when you are choosing which Pokémon to send out. Until you have completely memorized it, these charts will serve you well.

Defensively, a type protects you from certain types of attacks, gives you immunities to others, and weaknesses to still others. Offensively, it determines if you can affect your opponent, and if you can, how much damage you will inflict.

For example, when you use an Electric attack with an Electric Pokémon, it will inflict 1.5X as much damage as an Electric attack from any non-Electric Pokémon. Because Water Pokémon are weak against Electric attacks, Water Pokémon suffer 2X damage. When both types of a dual-type Pokémon are weak against a certain attack type, it will suffer 4X damage. For example, a Water/Flying type Pokémon hit with an Electric attack will take 4X damage—and 6X if the attacking Pokémon is an Electric type!

While type matching is important when it comes to choosing the attacks for your Pokémon, you should also consider giving your Pokémon attacks that don't necessarily match their type. For example, if you give a Ghost attack to your Psychic, you will have an effective attack against other Psychics, and unless they have done the same, you will be strong against their primary form of offense.

The benefit of spreading out your attacks is that it allows a team that may not be powerful in a straight type match-up to use strong attacks. At the same time, it prevents your opponent from doing the same to you. This works extremely well against the computer throughout both rounds of the Stadium and Gym Leader Castle. It also works fairly well against human opponents.

ON TEAMBUILDING

With 17 different types of Pokémon and 251 total Pokémon, choosing just six can be a daunting task. The easiest way to go about team construction is deciding the focus of your team. Are you building it for the Little Cup? You'll need to do some breeding. Poké Cup? You'll need to constrain the levels of your Pokémon to stay within the 155 total level limit and the 50-55 individual limit. Multiplayer? Depends on what your friends typically play with.

Once you've decided on a team to use, spend some time looking over the various Pokémon that qualify for the event you plan to participate in or the friends you plan to play against. Then look at the moves they are capable of learning. Depending on the level range you will be using, some Pokémon that you wouldn't normally consider become much more appealing.

Now you need to look over weaknesses. What Pokémon will you face? Look through the team lists in the walkthrough to get a feel for the types of Pokémon the computer trainers use, and think about what Pokémon your friends like to use a lot. Did you pick too many Pokémon with weaknesses to one type? Do you need more attacks of a certain type? A little preparation will save you a lot of work down the road.

Finally, spend some time training the team. Ideally, you'll want to hatch a baby Pokémon and raise it to whatever level you need. The reason for doing this is stats; the more battles (in the GB Tower or your Game Boy, not in the Stadium) your Pokémon participates in, the more its stats get exercised. Every Pokémon, even identical Pokémon, have different maximum possible stats. A Pokémon raised naturally in fights from level 5 to level 100 will have stats near its maximum possible values and will therefore be much stronger than a wild version of the same Pokémon.

Once you have gone through this process a few times, you should begin to get a feel for how various Pokémon perform in battle. It can take a long, long time to really test out any given set of Pokémon and moves because there are so many possible combinations, but the knowledge you gain while practicing and training is your most valuable asset in creating a strong team.

BEATING POKéMON STADIUM 2

If you're planning to play through the entire game against the computer, here are a few pieces of advice to take with you:

Get hold of a Mewtwo by hook or by crook. If you have Red, Blue, or Yellow, go capture one, raise it up to level 100, and get it in a lot of fights to raise its stats. Test it out, put it in 20 fights against low level Pokémon, put it in the box, then take it out—its stats will have increased.

Failing the ability to acquire Mewtwo, get Lugia, preferably from the Gold version, so that it starts at level 40 and you can raise it up. Aeroblast and Psychic are your friends, and Lugia's incredible defenses allow it to survive many hits that would otherwise knock another Pokémon flat.

Teach your Pokémon the second strongest techniques they can learn of a given type. Teach Thunderbolt instead of Thunder, Surf instead of Hydro Pump. The reason for this is that during the entirety of Round 2, you will find that a single missed move can cost you the entire fight.

Teach your Pokémon lots of type-crossing attacks and don't worry too much about using status moves—focus more on raw offense. With the number of battles you have to fight before you finish the game, using slower tactics can make the fights drag out for a painfully long time. The computer isn't the place to be testing out your more exotic strategies because it rarely behaves the same way a human opponent will.

SECRETS!

There aren't a ton of hidden goodies in Pokémon Stadium 2, but there are a few things you can open up.

When you defeat either the Stadium or the Gym Leader Castle mode for the first time, the GB Tower will be upgraded to the Doduo GB Tower for Pokémon Red, Blue, and Yellow only, which runs at double speed.

Then, when you beat whichever mode you didn't do first, you unlock the Dodrio GB Tower for Pokémon Red, Blue, and Yellow only, which lets you play the game at incredible speed! In order to unlock Doduo and Dodrio GB Tower modes for Gold and Silver, you must beat the Stadium and Gym Leader Castle in Round 2.

Finishing all the cups in the Stadium and both Johto and Kanto castles in the Gym Leader Castle will open up the fight with your Rival. Defeating him will allow you to access Round 2 of Pokémon Stadium 2. This will also change the graphic on the opening screen.

Defeating Round 2 of Pokémon Stadium 2 will change the graphic on the opening screen for a second time.

Finishing Round 1 of Pokémon Stadium 2 will earn you a Farfetch'd equipped with Baton Pass.

Finishing Round 2 of Pokémon Stadium 2 will earn you a Gligar equipped with Earthquake.

POKÉMON STADIUM 2

WALK-THROUGH

STADIUM MODE ROUND 1

If you've played the original Pokémon Stadium game, you'll be pretty familiar with the Stadium Mode in this game. Once again, you make your way through a series of battles, this time with a hundred new faces to challenge you. Again, four tournaments will test your skills, divided up by their rules.

LITTLE CUP
CHALLENGE CUP
POKé CUP
PRIME CUP

The Little and Challenge cups will be new to veterans of Pokémon Stadium. The Poké and Challenge cups are divided into four divisions: Poké Ball, Great Ball, Ultra Ball, and Master Ball. Each division contains eight battles for you to conquer. The Little and Prime cups only require you to defeat eight trainers.

Whether you're competing in a division of a cup tournament or the Little or Prime cups, you'll earn a badge for each of the eight trainers you defeat in the following order:

ROUND 1: ZEPHYRBADGE

ROUND 2: HIVEBADGE

ROUND 3: PLAINBADGE

ROUND 4: FOGBADGE

ROUND 5: STORMBADGE

ROUND 6: MINERALBADGE

ROUND 7: GLACIERBADGE

ROUND 8: RISINGBADGE

Once you've completed all of the tournaments and the Johto and Kanto Gyms, Round 2 of Stadium Mode will open up, and you must defeat all of the tournaments a second time.

To progress past a trainer, you must defeat three of his or her six Pokémon by using three of your six. If you manage a "perfect" battle (none of your Pokémon faint), you will receive an extra continue.

Because you never face all six Pokémon from a trainer, plan your team around the overall types that each trainer possesses, and use your three most effective Pokémon against those types. A well rounded team of six with a minimum of type weaknesses and strong attacks in their own types will get you through each of the cups fairly easily. If you are used to playing with a team of six Pokémon, you'll have to adapt your strategies slightly—being able to use only half of your roster rules out larger combinations.

LITTLE CUP

- Level 5 Tournament

The baby Pokémon cup is restricted to Pokémon of level 5 only, which will heavily limit your selections. The trick here is to breed Pokémon with powerful moves—and with the tiny levels, make sure you have a team with a diverse set of types. Equipping hold items is a useful technique for all cup challenges.

TOURNAMENT RULES

- 86 Different Pokémon are permitted for this tournament; check the list in game.
- Only unevolved Pokémon that can be hatched from eggs *and* can be evolved are legal.
- Six different Pokémon may be used for the team, three can fight.
- All Pokémon must be level 5.
- Items can be used, but each Pokémon must hold a different item.
- No two Pokémon may be asleep or frozen at the same time.
- Self-destructive moves may not be used on your final Pokémon.
- Dragon Rage and Sonicboom will not work.

Round 1: ZEPHYRBADGE
Youngster Bernie

NO.	Pokémon	Type		NO.	Pokémon	Type
175	Togepi	Normal		218	Slugma	Fire
138	Omanyte	Rock/Water		7	Squirtle	Water
191	Sunkern	Grass		56	Mankey	Fighting

Suggested Types: Fire, Water, Electric

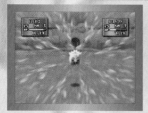

No one type dominates this trainer's Pokémon, but you can use your Fire-type against his Sunkern, Water against his Slugma, Electric against Omanyte and Squirtle, and you should be able to defeat Togepi and Mankey easily enough if they show up.

Round 2: HIVEBADGE
Picnicker Stacy

NO.	Pokémon	Type		NO.	Pokémon	Type
174	Igglybuff	Normal		16	Pidgey	Normal/Flying
209	Snubbull	Normal		19	Rattata	Normal
52	Meowth	Normal		216	Teddiursa	Normal

Suggested Types: Fighting, Rock, Ghost

A set of five Normal-types with a single Flying-type confronts you here. A Ghost will be unaffected by most of their attacks and won't face much risk against the Flying-type. You can use your Fighting-type to clean up against the Normal-types; just be sure to switch it out if the Spearow comes out to play.

Round 3: PLAINBADGE
Camper Grant

NO.	Pokémon	Type		NO.	Pokémon	Type
152	Chikorita	Grass		50	Diglett	Ground
158	Totodile	Water		170	Chinchou	Water/Electric
155	Cyndaquil	Fire		69	Bellsprout	Grass/Poison

Suggested Types: Electric, Flying, Water

You can use your Flying-type against the two Grass and the Ground-types. Use a Water type against the Ground- and Fire-types, and an Electric against the Water, though it won't work as well against Chinchou due to its odd mix of Electric and Water.

Round 4: FOGBADGE
PokéFan Janet

NO.	Pokémon	Type		NO.	Pokémon	Type
236	Tyrogue	Fighting		167	Spinarak	Bug/Poison
46	Paras	Bug/Grass		41	Zubat	Poison/Flying
74	Geodude	Rock/Ground		27	Sandshrew	Ground

Suggested Types: Water, Psychic

You can clean up Geodude and Sandshrew with a Water-type, and Spinarak, Zubat, and Tyrogue with a Psychic. Bring along a third that has any useful status moves or a good defense against their attacks. Janet is fond of using Double Team, and Paras is equipped with Spore, so be careful.

12

Round 5: STORMBADGE
Schoolboy Clark

NO.	Pokémon	Type		NO.	Pokémon	Type
179	Mareep	Electric		58	Growlithe	Fire
23	Ekans	Poison		238	Smoochum	Ice/Psychic
177	Natu	Psychic/Flying		246	Larvitar	Rock/Ground

Suggested Types: Dark, Water, Psychic

You can use a Dark-type against both Psychics effectively. Use Water to deal with the Fire and Ground types. A Psychic will give you power against the Poison; it will also be adequate against the Electric. Watch for a Dig from Clark's Growlithe.

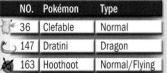

Round 6: MINERALBADGE
Swimmer♀ Cora

NO.	Pokémon	Type		NO.	Pokémon	Type
36	Clefable	Normal		43	Oddish	Grass/Poison
147	Dratini	Dragon		194	Wooper	Water/Ground
163	Hoothoot	Normal/Flying		140	Kabuto	Rock/Water

Suggested Types: Grass, Ice

You can use Grass against both Wooper and Kabuto. Ice will do well against Dratini, Oddish, and Hoothoot. You can fill your remaining slot with a Fighting if you want some extra punch against Clefable, but most any type will do as long as you watch your weaknesses.

Round 7: GLACIERBADGE
Teacher Tina

NO.	Pokémon	Type		NO.	Pokémon	Type
239	Elekid	Electric		133	Eevee	Normal
161	Sentret	Normal		123	Scyther	Bug/Flying
37	Vulpix	Fire		220	Swinub	Ice/Ground

Suggested Types: Water, Psychic, Fighting

A Water type (especially a Wooper) will do nicely against Swinub, Vulpix, and it will provide immunity against Elekid. A Psychic can take care of Scyther, and will do well against the Normal-types. Finally, you can use your Fighting against the Normal-types if necessary.

Round 8: RISINGBADGE
PokéFan Rex

NO.	Pokémon	Type		NO.	Pokémon	Type
172	Pichu	Electric		113	Chansey	Normal
92	Gastly	Ghost/Poison		60	Poliwag	Water
240	Magby	Fire		63	Abra	Psychic

Suggested Types: Rock/Ground, Electric

Your final opponent in the Little Cup boasts a wide selection of Pokémon, but you can defeat him with proper switching. Use a Rock/Ground against his Pichu and Magby, Electric against his Poliwag, and a third of your choice to deal with the others. Be careful with Fighting or Normal-types; they'll have a hard time with his Gastly and Abra.

You'll earn the Little Cup trophy by defeating Rex.

STADIUM MODE ROUND 1

CHALLENGE CUP

- Variable Level Random Pokémon Tournament

This cup will test your skills by forcing you to fight with a team of randomly chosen Pokémon. However, if you decide the team you end up with is too unbalanced toward a single type, you can simply reset and restart until your team is a little more appealing. Each division of the tournament raises the level of the Pokémon that participate, starting at 30 for the Poké Ball and going all the way up to 75 for the Master Ball.

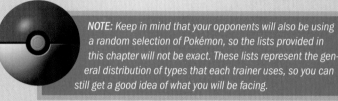

NOTE: Keep in mind that your opponents will also be using a random selection of Pokémon, so the lists provided in this chapter will not be exact. These lists represent the general distribution of types that each trainer uses, so you can still get a good idea of what you will be facing.

This Cup is named appropriately—it will challenge your skills. However, if you pay attention to your types and pick your teams carefully, you'll win!

TOURNAMENT RULES

- Six random Pokémon are provided as your team for each division.
- Three Pokémon are used for each fight.
- No two Pokémon may be asleep or frozen at the same time
- Self-destructive moves may not be used on your final Pokémon.

POKé BALL DIVISION

ROUND 1: ZEPHYRBADGE
Camper Marcus

NO.	Pokémon	Type	NO.	Pokémon	Type
74	Geodude	Rock/Ground	27	Sandshrew	Ground
218	Slugma	Fire	155	Cyndaquil	Fire
194	Wooper	Water/Ground	246	Larvitar	Rock/Ground

Suggested Types: Water, Grass

Water or Grass will easily pummel the vast majority of this trainer's team. You can fill up extra slots with more Grass or Water if you received multiples, or simply pick types that are not weak to his overabundance of Ground-types.

ROUND 2: HIVEBADGE
Rocket Grunt

NO.	Pokémon	Type	NO.	Pokémon	Type
32	Nidoran♂	Poison	43	Oddish	Grass/Poison
167	Spinarak	Bug/Poison	23	Ekans	Poison
41	Zubat	Poison/Flying	69	Bellsprout	Grass/Poison

Suggested Types: Psychic, Fire

A single strong Psychic should put this Team Rocket wannabe out of commission. You may wish to bring along a Fire-type to deal with the Grass-type that he has mixed in.

14

ROUND 3: PLAINBADGE
Picnicker Melissa

NO.	Pokémon	Type		NO.	Pokémon	Type
16	Pidgey	Normal/Flying		163	Hoothoot	Normal/Flying
21	Spearow	Normal/Flying		147	Dratini	Dragon
165	Ledyba	Bug/Flying		102	Exeggcute	Grass/Psychic

Suggested Types: Ice, Electric, Fire

Ice is your friend here—it will take out every Pokémon on Melissa's entire team. If you don't have any Ice attacks handy, you can use Electric against the Flying-types and Fire against any Grass. If a Dragon-type shows up, it is only weak against Ice or Dragon, but just check Dragon's strengths and bring along a Pokémon that can hit it normally and you'll be alright.

ROUND 4: FOGBADGE
Guitarist Daren

NO.	Pokémon	Type		NO.	Pokémon	Type
81	Magnemite	Electric/Steel		172	Pichu	Electric
179	Mareep	Electric		191	Sunkern	Grass
1	Bulbasaur	Grass/Poison		102	Exeggcute	Grass/Psychic

Suggested Types: Water, Grass

Ground will do well against the Electric-types, and you can use Fire to punch through the Steel defenses, as well as bake the Grass-types.

ROUND 5: STORMBADGE
Fisherman Curtis

NO.	Pokémon	Type		NO.	Pokémon	Type
116	Horsea	Water		183	Marill	Water
86	Seel	Water		194	Wooper	Water/Ground
90	Shellder	Water		60	Poliwag	Water

Suggested Types: Electric, Grass

This silly fisherman is just asking to get crisped by an Electric-type. Watch out for a Wooper, though; its half Ground-type gives it complete immunity to Electric attacks. You may want to bring along a Grass-type just to deal with that. Plus, Grass is also quite strong against Water-types.

ROUND 6: MINERALBADGE
Medium Peggy

NO.	Pokémon	Type		NO.	Pokémon	Type
174	Igglybuff	Normal		50	Diglett	Ground
96	Drowzee	Psychic		79	Slowpoke	Water/Psychic
41	Zubat	Poison/Flying		102	Exeggcute	Grass/Psychic

Suggested Types: Dark, Ice, Psychic

Dark-types aren't weak to Psychic, so they'll hold up a lot better than using Bugs. However, if you lack a Dark-type, you can use an Ice-type to take out Flying, Ground, and Grass, and use your own Psychic to fight back against hers.

ROUND 7: GLACIERBADGE
Rocket Grunt

NO.	Pokémon	Type		NO.	Pokémon	Type
132	Ditto	Normal		209	Snubbull	Normal
39	Jigglypuff	Normal		21	Spearow	Normal/Flying
16	Pidgey	Normal/Flying		163	Hoothoot	Normal/Flying

Suggested Types: Fighting, Electric

Again a Team Rocket grunt accosts you with an unbalanced team. Fighting types are effective against this entire team, and Electric against half of it. You can also use a Ghost for immunity to many of the Normal attacks, or use an Ice to freeze the Flying-types.

ROUND 8: RISINGBADGE
Juggler Dwight

NO.	Pokémon	Type		NO.	Pokémon	Type
37	Vulpix	Fire		43	Oddish	Grass/Poison
98	Krabby	Water		236	Tyrogue	Fighting
165	Ledyba	Bug/Flying		235	Smeargle	Normal

Suggested Types: Ice, Psychic

Your final fight in the Poké Ball division puts you up against the most diverse set yet, but it still has a hole. Ice will take out Fire-, Ice-, and Flying-types pretty easily, and with a Psychic to back you up, you should be able to take down any of Dwight's other members, as well.

Once you finish this fight, you'll be awarded with the Poké Ball trophy and you can advance to the Great Ball division.

GREAT BALL DIVISION

ROUND 1: ZEPHYRBADGE
Twins Jan & Jane

NO.	Pokémon	Type	NO.	Pokémon	Type
168	Ariados	Bug/Poison	15	Beedrill	Bug/Poison
166	Ledian	Bug/Flying	100	Voltorb	Electric
12	Butterfree	Bug/Flying	111	Rhyhorn	Ground/Rock

Suggested Types: Fire, Rock/Ground, Water

The first fight in the Great Ball division puts you up against an unbalanced team. Fire will easily dispatch all of the Bug-types, and you can bring along a Rock/Ground and a Water-type to deal with the others.

ROUND 2: HIVEBADGE
Schoolboy Oliver

NO.	Pokémon	Type	NO.	Pokémon	Type
138	Omanyte	Rock/Water	140	Kabuto	Rock/Water
75	Graveler	Rock/Ground	111	Rhyhorn	Ground/Rock
222	Corsola	Water/Rock	95	Onix	Rock/Ground

Suggested Types: Grass, Water

An immense collection of Rock and Ground will challenge you for the HIVEBADGE, so bring along your Grass- and Water-types, which will firmly dispatch all of your opponents.

ROUND 3: PLAINBADGE
Sailor Curt

NO.	Pokémon	Type	NO.	Pokémon	Type
138	Omanyte	Rock/Water	238	Smoochum	Ice/Psychic
8	Wartortle	Water	56	Mankey	Fighting
184	Azumarill	Water	140	Kabuto	Rock/Water

Suggested Types: Electric

Electric is your best bet here, as the bulk of Curt's Pokémon have a Water type with no defense against Electric. Round out the remainder of your team to face off against any extras he brings to the battle—look over the type combat chart and pick out the most appropriate Pokémon for the job.

ROUND 4: FOGBADGE
Swimmer♀ Darcy

NO.	Pokémon	Type	NO.	Pokémon	Type
25	Pikachu	Electric	190	Aipom	Normal
108	Lickitung	Normal	206	Dunsparce	Normal
75	Graveler	Rock/Ground	133	Eevee	Normal

Suggested Types: Fighting, Rock/Ground, Ghost

A bevy of Normal-types oppose your acquisition of the FOGBADGE. You can inflict heavy damage against them with a Fighting-type, or use the resistance of Rock or the immunity of Ghost.

ROUND 5: STORMBADGE
Officer Gerald

NO.	Pokémon	Type	NO.	Pokémon	Type
240	Magby	Fire	219	Magcargo	Fire/Rock
188	Skiploom	Grass/Flying	44	Gloom	Grass/Poison
228	Houndour	Dark/Fire	70	Weepinbell	Grass/Poison

Suggested Types: Water, Fire

Gerald has a fairly even mix of Fire- and Grass-types, which can be washed away and burned up by Water and Fire. Examine the dual types and choose your third member based on what will be strongest against them. After this fight, you're more than half way to the RISING-BADGE and the Great Ball trophy.

ROUND 6: MINERALBADGE
Kimono Girl Emiko

NO.	Pokémon	Type	NO.	Pokémon	Type
240	Magby	Fire	168	Ariados	Bug/Poison
84	Doduo	Normal/Flying	153	Bayleef	Grass
238	Smoochum	Ice/Psychic	140	Kabuto	Rock/Water

Suggested Types: Rock, Flying

The odd mix of types provides you with no obvious strength to utilize, but a Rock-type can do good damage to Flying and Ice, and it is protected against Fire. Flying does well against the Bug and Grass, and you can fill your third slot with a Pokémon you feel is most appropriate against the lineup you face.

16

ROUND 7: GLACIERBADGE
Scientist Roberto

NO.	Pokémon	Type		NO.	Pokémon	Type
137	Porygon	Normal		177	Natu	Psychic/Flying
92	Gastly	Ghost/Poison		47	Parasect	Bug/Grass
228	Houndour	Dark/Fire		202	Wobbuffet	Psychic

Suggested Types: Ice, Dark

Again, a fairly eclectic mix of types opposes you. You can use an Ice to good effect against any Grass-, Flying-, or Fire-types, and a Dark will do well against any Psychic or Ghost you might face. Round out your team with a third that you feel confident using. By this point in the tourney, you should have found some favorites on your team.

ROUND 8: RISINGBADGE
Gentleman Travis

NO.	Pokémon	Type		NO.	Pokémon	Type
137	Porygon	Normal		109	Koffing	Poison
228	Houndour	Dark/Fire		120	Staryu	Water
166	Ledian	Bug/Flying		75	Graveler	Rock/Ground

Suggested Types: Water, Rock/Ground

The final bout for the Great Ball trophy puts you up against a third mixed team. You can use Water to wash out the Fire and Ground, and your own Rock/Ground for protection against some of Travis's types, as well as a good offense against Flying and Fire.

After you defeat Travis, you'll earn the Great Ball championship. The Ultra Ball division will also be accessible.

ULTRA BALL DIVISION

ROUND 1: ZEPHYRBADGE
Camper Marcus

NO.	Pokémon	Type		NO.	Pokémon	Type
247	Pupitar	Rock/Ground		77	Ponyta	Fire
24	Arbok	Poison		105	Marowak	Ground
156	Quilava	Fire		195	Quagsire	Water/Ground

Suggested Types: Water, Grass

You face an unbalanced team for your first fight in the Ultra Ball division. Grass alone will pummel the Water- and Ground-types while taking minimum damage. Should that fail you, your own Water will prove useful against the Ground and Fire.

ROUND 2: HIVEBADGE
Rocket Grunt

NO.	Pokémon	Type		NO.	Pokémon	Type
42	Golbat	Poison/Flying		203	Girafarig	Normal/Psychic
49	Venomoth	Bug/Poison		185	Sudowoodo	Rock
45	Vileplume	Grass/Poison		211	Qwilfish	Water/Poison

Suggested Types: Psychic, Rock/Ground

An over-abundance of Poison is just asking for a Psychic assault, and you can bring along a Rock/Ground if you don't want to deal with Poison techniques hurting you much. Fill your third slot with a Pokémon that you want to test out.

ROUND 3: PLAINBADGE
Picnicker Melissa

NO.	Pokémon	Type		NO.	Pokémon	Type
189	Jumpluff	Grass/Flying		226	Mantine	Water/Flying
227	Skarmory	Steel/Flying		198	Murkrow	Dark/Flying
17	Pidgeotto	Normal/Flying		5	Charmeleon	Fire

Suggested Types: Ice, Electric

Bring along some Ice to freeze all the Flyers and you should be able to sweep Melissa's entire team. You may want to bring an Electric just in case, and for your third, bring along either another test Pokémon or something to match up with any oddball Pokémon Melissa brings out.

ROUND 4: FOGBADGE
Guitarist Daren

NO.	Pokémon	Type		NO.	Pokémon	Type
49	Venomoth	Bug/Poison		26	Raichu	Electric
5	Charmeleon	Fire		189	Jumpluff	Grass/Flying
82	Magneton	Electric/Steel		192	Sunflora	Grass

Suggested Types: Fire, Ice, Rock/Ground

Fire will nicely scorch the Grass, penetrate Steel, and fry Bug. You can also bring along an Ice to frost the Grass if you wish. You can use a Rock/Ground to good effect against the Electric attacks.

ROUND 5: STORMBADGE
Fisherman Curtis

NO.	Pokémon	Type		NO.	Pokémon	Type
195	Quagsire	Water/Ground		119	Seaking	Water
226	Mantine	Water/Flying		211	Qwilfish	Water/Poison
117	Seadra	Water		87	Dewgong	Water/Ice

Suggested Types: Electric, Grass

An Electric assault will bring a host of Water Pokémon to its knees. You can bring along a Grass as well, though you should watch out for any Ice attacks if you do.

ROUND 6: MINERALBADGE
Medium Peggy

NO.	Pokémon	Type		NO.	Pokémon	Type
93	Haunter	Ghost/Poison		64	Kadabra	Psychic
80	Slowbro	Water/Psychic		200	Misdreavus	Ghost
97	Hypno	Psychic		82	Magneton	Electric/Steel

Suggested Types: Dark, Steel, Psychic

Many Psychics and Ghosts challenge you here. Dark will inflict heavy damage, but failing that, you can use Steel to resist the Psychic assault. Remember also that Normal-types are completely unaffected by pure Ghost attacks, and you can use your own Psychics to down the Ghosts.

ROUND 7: GLACIERBADGE
Rocket Grunt

NO.	Pokémon	Type		NO.	Pokémon	Type
53	Persian	Normal		20	Raticate	Normal
113	Chansey	Normal		17	Pidgeotto	Normal/Flying
36	Clefable	Normal		164	Noctowl	Normal/Flying

Suggested Types: Fighting, Rock/Ground

A bevy of Normal types face you. Normals may not be strong against anything, but they tend to have good stats and fairly strong moves. Using your Fighting against them will inflict heavy damage, and you can play defensively by using Rock/Ground, which can also use Rock attacks to good effect against any Flying-types.

ROUND 8: RISINGBADGE
Juggler Dwight

NO.	Pokémon	Type		NO.	Pokémon	Type
199	Slowking	Water/Psychic		213	Shuckle	Bug/Rock
82	Magneton	Electric/Steel		40	Wigglytuff	Normal
148	Dragonair	Dragon		93	Haunter	Ghost/Poison

Suggested Types: Steel, Fighting, Dark

Your final Ultra Ball battle pits you against a spectrum of types. You can play defensively by using Steel, or you can use the excellent offensive power of Fighting to break through. Finally, Dark will serve you well against both Psychic and Ghost.

The Ultra Ball trophy is yours and you can now progress to the final division of the Challenge Cup.

MASTER BALL DIVISION

Round 1: ZEPHYRBADGE
Twins Jan & Jane

NO.	Pokémon	Type	NO.	Pokémon	Type
127	Pinsir	Bug	212	Scizor	Bug/Steel
130	Gyarados	Water/Flying	214	Heracross	Bug/Fighting
38	Ninetales	Fire	123	Scyther	Bug/Flying

Suggested Types: Fire, Rock

An army of Bugs is your first challenge in the Master Ball division. Use Fire to torch them all, and bring along a Rock or an Electric to deal with the hybrid Flying-types.

Round 2: HIVEBADGE
Schoolboy Oliver

NO.	Pokémon	Type	NO.	Pokémon	Type
34	Nidoking	Poison/Ground	232	Donphan	Ground
76	Golem	Rock/Ground	208	Steelix	Steel/Ground
112	Rhydon	Ground/Rock	142	Aerodactyl	Rock/Flying

Suggested Types: Water, Fighting, Steel

Ground- and Rock-types abound on this trainer's roster. Water will wash the vast majority of them away, and you can also use Fighting for the punch and Steel for the defense.

Round 3: PLAINBADGE
Sailor Curt

NO.	Pokémon	Type	NO.	Pokémon	Type
91	Cloyster	Water/Ice	160	Feraligatr	Water
124	Jynx	Ice/Psychic	57	Primeape	Fighting
130	Gyarados	Water/Flying	73	Tentacruel	Water/Poison

Suggested Types: Electric, Grass

Lots of Water types make themselves easy targets for your Electric. You can also use a Grass to good effect; just watch out for a Fighting-type mixed in, and also be wary of the Ice attacks.

Round 4: FOGBADGE
Swimmer♀ Darcy

NO.	Pokémon	Type	NO.	Pokémon	Type
62	Poliwrath	Water/Fighting	242	Blissey	Normal
214	Heracross	Bug/Fighting	128	Tauros	Normal
233	Porygon2	Normal	76	Golem	Rock/Ground

Suggested Types: Fighting, Psychic, Ghost

Fighting will pummel the Normal-types nicely, but you can also use Psychic types to deal with the Fighting and still do good damage against the others. Ghost, of course, will be immune to many attacks. Fill the third slot in your team with a sturdy Pokémon, but remember that Fighting will harm Rock/Ground and Steel badly.

Round 5: STORMBADGE
Officer Gerald

NO.	Pokémon	Type	NO.	Pokémon	Type
102	Exeggcute	Grass/Psychic	229	Houndoom	Dark/Fire
59	Arcanine	Fire	3	Venusaur	Grass/Poison
78	Rapidash	Fire	71	Victreebel	Grass/Poison

Suggested Types: Fire, Water

You can crisp Gerald's Grass types with some Fire Pokémon, but you'll have to change over to Water to deal with the Fire-types. Switching up will be necessary, as Grass and Fire complement each other nicely.

Round 6: MINERALBADGE
Kimono Girl Emiko

NO.	Pokémon	Type	NO.	Pokémon	Type
241	Miltank	Normal	197	Umbreon	Dark
78	Rapidash	Fire	71	Victreebel	Grass/Poison
135	Jolteon	Electric	131	Lapras	Water/Ice

Suggested Types: Steel, Water, Fire

A broad mix of types will force you to choose a team that has been most effective for you up to this point. Spend some time looking over the types and minimize your weaknesses to your opponents' attacks.

ROUND 7: GLACIERBADGE
Scientist Roberto

NO.	Pokémon	Type		NO.	Pokémon	Type
214	Heracross	Bug/Fighting		229	Houndoom	Dark/Fire
121	Starmie	Water/Psychic		94	Gengar	Ghost/Poison
103	Exeggutor	Grass/Psychic		181	Ampharos	Electric

Suggested Types: Rock/Ground, Fire, Dark

Another wide mix of types greets you in the semifinal round. You can use a Rock/Ground-type safely against most of Roberto's Pokémon, a Fire to toast a few, and a Dark against any Psychics that show up.

ROUND 8: RISINGBADGE
Gentleman Travis

NO.	Pokémon	Type		NO.	Pokémon	Type
62	Poliwrath	Water/Fighting		38	Ninetales	Fire
208	Steelix	Steel/Ground		196	Espeon	Psychic
123	Scyther	Bug/Flying		94	Gengar	Ghost/Poison

Suggested Types: Fire, Electric, Steel

The final battle for the Master Ball championship title is against a broad range of strong Pokémon. After the seven previous fights, you should have a pretty good idea of what your team is capable of, so examine Travis's types and choose your team carefully.

Once you have defeated Travis, you will earn the final trophy in the Challenge Cup—congratulations!

STADIUM MODE ROUND 1

POKé CUP

- Level 50-55 Tournament

Mid-level Pokémon are the order of the day here, and you'll need a well-balanced team to defeat all four divisions of this cup. Spend some time looking over the list of Pokémon you will face before you decide on your team selections.

TOURNAMENT RULES

- 246 Different Pokémon are permitted for this tournament, check the list in the game.
- Six different Pokémon may be used for the team, three can fight.
- All Pokémon must be level 50-55.
- The levels of the three battle Pokémon may not add up to more than 155.
- Items can be used, but each Pokémon must hold a different item.
- No two Pokémon may be asleep or frozen at the same time.
- Self-destructive moves may not be used on your final Pokémon.

POKé BALL DIVISION

Round 1: ZEPHYRBADGE
Bug Catcher Nelson

NO.	Pokémon	Type	NO.	Pokémon	Type
165	Ledyba	Bug/Flying	13	Weedle	Bug/Poison
167	Spinarak	Bug/Poison	193	Yanma	Bug/Flying
10	Caterpie	Bug	48	Venonat	Bug/Poison

Suggested Types: Fire, Flying, Rock

Your first encounter in the Poké Cup is a straight Bug team that you can easily put out of commission with any strong Fire, Flying, or Rock Pokémon.

Round 2: HIVEBADGE
Swimmer♂ Bruce

NO.	Pokémon	Type	NO.	Pokémon	Type
118	Goldeen	Water	90	Shellder	Water
86	Seel	Water	223	Remoraid	Water
120	Staryu	Water	61	Poliwhirl	Water

Suggested Types: Electric, Grass

100% Water means 100% beaten by Electric or Grass. A single strong Pokémon of either type should cleanly sweep all of Bruce's Pokémon.

ROUND 3: PLAINBADGE
Hiker Chester

NO.	Pokémon	Type	NO.	Pokémon	Type
66	Machop	Fighting	185	Sudowoodo	Rock
95	Onix	Rock/Ground	111	Rhyhorn	Ground/Rock
75	Graveler	Rock/Ground	231	Phanpy	Ground

Suggested Types: Water, Grass, Fighting

Your third fight puts you up against yet another set of Pokémon skewed toward a single type. Bring along your Water-, Grass-, or Fighting-types to wipe them out, and don't worry too much about Machop showing up.

ROUND 4: FOGBADGE
Super Nerd Clifford

NO.	Pokémon	Type	NO.	Pokémon	Type
81	Magnemite	Electric/Steel	180	Flaaffy	Electric
93	Haunter	Ghost/Poison	23	Ekans	Poison
137	Porygon	Normal	101	Electrode	Electric

Suggested Types: Ground, Psychic

A slightly more diverse group meets you halfway to the trophy, but again, a single type can wipe out the entire team. Bring along something with Ground and a Ground attack and you can take out all of the Electrics, as well as the Poisons. You can use a Psychic to good effect if necessary.

ROUND 5: STORMBADGE
Beauty Alissa

NO.	Pokémon	Type	NO.	Pokémon	Type
241	Miltank	Normal	222	Corsola	Water/Rock
209	Snubbull	Normal	188	Skiploom	Grass/Flying
211	Qwilfish	Water/Poison	113	Chansey	Normal

Suggested Types: Fighting, Electric

A Fighting-type is a good bet to deal with Alissa's Normal types, and you can use an Electric to fry the mixed Water-types. Electric is still even against Skiploom due to it being part Flying, so you can use that to your advantage as well. All of Alissa's Pokémon are female and she's fond of using Attract, so keep gender in mind when you pick your team.

ROUND 6: MINERALBADGE
Burglar Jensen

NO.	Pokémon	Type	NO.	Pokémon	Type
53	Persian	Normal	125	Electabuzz	Electric
5	Charmeleon	Fire	156	Quilava	Fire
228	Houndour	Dark/Fire	207	Gligar	Ground/Flying

Suggested Types: Water, Rock/Ground

The three Fire-types will go down to your Water attacks, and you can defend yourself against almost all of Jensen's Pokémon by using a Rock/Ground. Be warned that many of his Pokémon use Thief to steal your items.

ROUND 7: GLACIERBADGE
Boarder Claude

NO.	Pokémon	Type	NO.	Pokémon	Type
225	Delibird	Ice/Flying	128	Tauros	Normal
215	Sneasel	Dark/Ice	216	Teddiursa	Normal
73	Tentacruel	Water/Poison	134	Vaporeon	Water

Suggested Types: Fighting, Rock

A lot of Ice attacks is Claude's trademark, but you can dispatch most of his Pokémon with a Fighting Pokémon on your side. A Rock-type will do damage against the Ice, but be mindful of Water attacks if you do use Rock.

ROUND 8: MINERALBADGE
Psychic Mason

NO.	Pokémon	Type	NO.	Pokémon	Type
235	Smeargle	Normal	58	Growlithe	Fire
79	Slowpoke	Water/Psychic	177	Natu	Psychic/Flying
26	Raichu	Electric	36	Clefable	Normal

Suggested Types: Dark, Rock/Ground, Fighting

Your final match in the Poké Ball division brings you up against a heavy Psychic user, which is just asking to be abused by Dark. You can also bring along a Rock/Ground to deal with the Electric and Fire and have some punch against Natu.

Fighting will deal with the Normal-types, or you could bring along a Steel, as it has good defense against Psychic attacks.

After you defeat Mason, the Poké Ball trophy is yours.

GREAT BALL DIVISION

ROUND 1: ZEPHYRBADGE

PokéFan Carmen

NO.	Pokémon	Type		NO.	Pokémon	Type
25	Pikachu	Electric		213	Shuckle	Bug/Rock
52	Meowth	Normal		175	Togepi	Normal
35	Clefairy	Normal		122	Mr. Mime	Psychic

Suggested Types: Fighting, Dark

Carmen, a trainer of Normal Pokémon, with a Pikachu, Shuckle, and Mr. Mime thrown in to make things interesting, is your first challenger in the Great Ball division. You can use a Fighting against the Normal-types and Shuckle; just watch out for Mr. Mime using Psychic on you. Your Dark is a good reserve against this and it will probably be fine against Pikachu and Shuckle, as well.

ROUND 2: HIVEBADGE

Youngster Wyatt

NO.	Pokémon	Type		NO.	Pokémon	Type
2	Ivysaur	Grass/Poison		30	Nidorina	Poison
188	Skiploom	Grass/Flying		132	Ditto	Normal
17	Pidgeotto	Normal/Flying		214	Heracross	Bug/Fighting

Suggested Types: Fire, Ice

With the bulk of Wyatt's Pokémon vulnerable to Fire and Ice harming the others, you should be able to take him out pretty easily. Depending on which Pokémon you are using, watch for Ditto—it could cause some problems.

ROUND 3: PLAINBADGE

Firebreather Cliff

NO.	Pokémon	Type		NO.	Pokémon	Type
78	Rapidash	Fire		38	Ninetales	Fire
126	Magmar	Fire		162	Furret	Normal
104	Cubone	Ground		45	Vileplume	Grass/Poison

Suggested Types: Water

While there are a few other types you can use defensively, Water will sweep four of Cliff's six Pokémon. You can fill the remainder of your team with some other types in case his Vileplume pops up. He'll try to use Sunny Day, Confuse Ray, and if possible, trap your Pokémon with Fire Spin. This still won't help him much if you're washing him away with Water.

ROUND 4: FOGBADGE

Biker Dillon

NO.	Pokémon	Type		NO.	Pokémon	Type
70	Weepinbell	Grass/Poison		109	Koffing	Poison
168	Ariados	Bug/Poison		206	Dunsparce	Normal
28	Sandslash	Ground		181	Ampharos	Electric

Suggested Types: Psychic, Fire, Fighting

A Psychic will handily defeat the mixed Poison-types and probably won't have much trouble with the others. You can use a Fire for roughly the same effect, and you may want to bring along a Fighting-type to deal with Sandslash and Dunsparce.

ROUND 5: STORMBADGE

Teacher Molly

NO.	Pokémon	Type		NO.	Pokémon	Type
166	Ledian	Bug/Flying		203	Girafarig	Normal/Psychic
64	Kadabra	Psychic		226	Mantine	Water/Flying
190	Aipom	Normal		148	Dragonair	Dragon

Suggested Types: Ice, Dark, Steel

A good, strong Ice attack will take care of Ledian, Mantine, and Dragonair, while a Dark or Steel will handle Kadabra and Girafarig. Use your third slot to bring along a strong Normal-type, especially if it has some special-based attacks.

ROUND 6: MINERALBADGE
Sage Chen

NO.	Pokémon	Type		NO.	Pokémon	Type
167	Spinarak	Bug/Poison		200	Misdreavus	Ghost
124	Jynx	Ice/Psychic		198	Murkrow	Dark/Flying
93	Haunter	Ghost/Poison		41	Zubat	Poison/Flying

Suggested Types: Psychic, Dark, Steel

A Sage he may be, but Chen is overly reliant on Pokémon that are weak to Psychic. Watch out for Murkrow though, as it is part Dark and will stop you from using a single Psychic to sweep Chen's team. A Dark or a Steel on your team can aid you against him nicely.

ROUND 7: GLACIERBADGE
PokéFan Baxter

NO.	Pokémon	Type		NO.	Pokémon	Type
192	Sunflora	Grass		219	Magcargo	Fire/Rock
108	Lickitung	Normal		224	Octillery	Water
171	Lanturn	Water/Electric		204	Pineco	Bug

Suggested Types: Fire, Grass, Water

A decent selection of types greets your arrival to the semifinals, but Fire will take care of Baxter's Sunflora and Pineco. Grass will counter his Lanturn and Octillery, and Water will douse his Magcargo. Lickitung isn't much trouble if it shows up.

ROUND 8: RISINGBADGE
Pokémaniac Pedro

NO.	Pokémon	Type		NO.	Pokémon	Type
117	Seadra	Water		20	Raticate	Normal
247	Pupitar	Rock/Ground		164	Noctowl	Normal/Flying
34	Nidoking	Poison/Ground		114	Tangela	Grass

Suggested Types: Fighting, Ice, Grass

Your final battle for the Great Ball championship will challenge you with a mixed set, but a Fighting-type can handle Pedro's Pupitar, Raticate, and Noctowl. An Ice-type can also serve double duty. Finally, bring along a Grass to take care of his Seadra.

Your goal of the Master Ball is one step closer once you gain the Great Ball trophy.

ULTRA BALL DIVISION

ROUND 1: ZEPHYRBADGE
Bug Catcher Nelson

NO.	Pokémon	Type		NO.	Pokémon	Type
123	Scyther	Bug/Flying		206	Dunsparce	Normal
12	Butterfree	Bug/Flying		214	Heracross	Bug/Fighting
47	Parasect	Bug/Grass		127	Pinsir	Bug

Suggested Types: Fire, Flying, Rock

A bevy of Bug Pokémon greet your entry to the Ultra Ball division. While Nelson has a single Normal in the form of Dunsparce, you can still pummel all of his Bugs with a single Fire, Flying, or Rock Pokémon.

ROUND 2: HIVEBADGE
Swimmer♂ Bruce

NO.	Pokémon	Type		NO.	Pokémon	Type
87	Dewgong	Water/Ice		82	Magneton	Electric/Steel
62	Poliwrath	Water/Fighting		141	Kabutops	Rock/Water
195	Quagsire	Water/Ground		80	Slowbro	Water/Psychic

Suggested Types: Grass, Electric, Water

A lot of Water-types makes Grass or Electric seem the obvious choice, but watch out for Ice attacks from Dewgong and Quagsire's immunity to Electric, not to mention Magneton. Using your own Water, if it is a hybrid type, can actually be pretty effective. Otherwise, bring along a Grass and Electric, and switch around as necessary.

ROUND 3: PLAINBADGE
Hiker Chester

NO.	Pokémon	Type		NO.	Pokémon	Type
76	Golem	Rock/Ground		138	Omanyte	Rock/Water
232	Donphan	Ground		205	Forretress	Bug/Steel
217	Ursaring	Normal		208	Steelix	Steel/Ground

Suggested Types: Water, Fighting

Chester's stable of Ground-types challenges you here. You can use Water on three of them, Fighting on Ursaring and Omanyte, and you may wish to bring along a Fire-type to deal with Forretress.

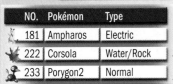

ROUND 4: FOGBADGE
Super Nerd Clifford

	NO.	Pokémon	Type		NO.	Pokémon	Type
	181	Ampharos	Electric		202	Wobbuffet	Psychic
	222	Corsola	Water/Rock		73	Tentacruel	Water/Poison
	233	Porygon2	Normal		227	Skarmory	Steel/Flying

Suggested Types: Grass, Fire

Not too many open points of attack here, but you can use Grass against Ampharos, Corsola, and Tentacruel. The Fire recommendation is for Skarmory if it shows up. You should be able to deal with Porygon2 and Wobbuffet with any of your team.

ROUND 5: STORMBADGE
Beauty Alissa

	NO.	Pokémon	Type		NO.	Pokémon	Type
	241	Miltank	Normal		108	Lickitung	Normal
	189	Jumpluff	Grass/Flying		226	Mantine	Water/Flying
	53	Persian	Normal		40	Wigglytuff	Normal

Suggested Types: Fighting, Electric, Ice

Alissa's Normals will fall to your Fighting-types, and you can use Electric or Ice to take down Jumpluff and Mantine. Again, watch out for her female Pokémon using Attract this round.

ROUND 6: MINERALBADGE
Burglar Jensen

	NO.	Pokémon	Type		NO.	Pokémon	Type
	157	Typhlosion	Fire		51	Dugtrio	Ground
	229	Houndoom	Dark/Fire		234	Stantler	Normal
	219	Magcargo	Fire/Rock		207	Gligar	Ground/Flying

Suggested Types: Water

A single Water-type can easily perform a clean sweep of Jensen's Pokémon, so fill out your second and third slots with any Pokémon that have backup Water moves.

ROUND 7: GLACIERBADGE
Boarder Claude

	NO.	Pokémon	Type		NO.	Pokémon	Type
	215	Sneasel	Dark/Ice		135	Jolteon	Electric
	225	Delibird	Ice/Flying		134	Vaporeon	Water
	9	Blastoise	Water		136	Flareon	Fire

Suggested Types: Electric, Water, Normal

No easy weaknesses are apparent in Claude's team, but you can use Electric against Delibird, Blastoise, and Vaporeon. A hybrid Water-type has good protection against Water and can douse Flareon, and if you have a Normal with some good special-based attacks, bring it along to fill any holes in your lineup.

ROUND 8: RISINGBADGE
Psychic Mason

	NO.	Pokémon	Type		NO.	Pokémon	Type
	115	Kangaskhan	Normal		26	Raichu	Electric
	97	Hypno	Psychic		235	Smeargle	Normal
	59	Arcanine	Fire		178	Xatu	Psychic/Flying

Suggested Types: Water, Grass

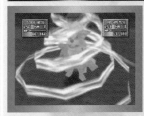

You may face some Psychic power here, but you'll also have to deal with the two Normal-types, as well as an Electric and Fire. A Dark will do nicely against the Psychics, and you can use a Rock/Ground to fight the Fire and the Electric. Failing that, bring along some good Normal-types, but avoid Fighting-types, as Psychic will knock them down fast.

After you defeat Mason, the Ultra Ball trophy is yours. One more division toward the championship.

MASTER BALL DIVISION

ROUND 1: ZEPHYRBADGE
PokéFan Carmen

NO.	Pokémon	Type	NO.	Pokémon	Type
182	Bellossom	Grass	36	Clefable	Normal
184	Azumarill	Water	176	Togetic	Normal/Flying
53	Persian	Normal	26	Raichu	Electric

Suggested Types: Fighting, Grass

A stable of Normal types with Electric, Water, and Grass mixed in is your first challenge in the Master Ball division. Bring along a Fighting to clean up the Normal types, a Grass for the Electric and Water, and you can bring along something with a Fire attack for Bellossom. Carmen's Pokémon are mixed gender and she will attempt to use Attract on you.

ROUND 2: HIVEBADGE
Youngster Wyatt

NO.	Pokémon	Type	NO.	Pokémon	Type
18	Pidgeot	Normal/Flying	20	Raticate	Normal
31	Nidoqueen	Poison/Ground	127	Pinsir	Bug
132	Ditto	Normal	57	Primeape	Fighting

Suggested Types: Fighting, Psychic, Fire

As usual, a hole in this trainer's defenses provides you the opportunity for victory. Use a Fighting-type against Wyatt's Normal-types, Psychic against Nidoqueen and Primeape, and Fire against his Pinsir if it shows up.

ROUND 3: PLAINBADGE
Firebreather Cliff

NO.	Pokémon	Type	NO.	Pokémon	Type
126	Magmar	Fire	229	Houndoom	Dark/Fire
105	Marowak	Ground	103	Exeggutor	Grass/Psychic
85	Dodrio	Normal/Flying	59	Arcanine	Fire

Suggested Types: Water, Ice

Water will douse the majority of Cliff's Pokémon. You may want to bring along something with an Ice attack to freeze up Dodrio and Exeggutor.

ROUND 4: FOGBADGE
Biker Dillon

NO.	Pokémon	Type	NO.	Pokémon	Type
110	Weezing	Poison	112	Rhydon	Ground/Rock
91	Cloyster	Water/Ice	3	Venusaur	Grass/Poison
208	Steelix	Steel/Ground	24	Arbok	Poison

Suggested Types: Psychic, Water, Fire

Psychic will handily defeat Dillon's Weezing, Venusaur, and Arbok, but you'll want to bring along a Water to wash out his Steelix and Rhydon. A Fire type can also be used normally against Cloyster due to its Ice part; it will also be effective against Steelix and Venusaur.

ROUND 5: STORMBADGE
Teacher Molly

NO.	Pokémon	Type	NO.	Pokémon	Type
203	Girafarig	Normal/Psychic	190	Aipom	Normal
122	Mr. Mine	Psychic	171	Lanturn	Water/Electric
131	Lapras	Water/Ice	186	Politoed	Water

Suggested Types: Electric, Grass, Dark

Molly brings up a mix of Water and Psychic-types, but you can deal with most of the Water by using an Electric or a Grass. A Dark will handle the Psychics nicely. She will often try to power up her Pokémon and then pass the abilities to a more effective one with Baton Pass. You can get around this by using attacks that always hit or simply knocking out the Pokémon before she gets a chance to try this trick.

ROUND 6: MINERALBADGE
Sage Chen

NO.	Pokémon	Type		NO.	Pokémon	Type
200	Misdreavus	Ghost		124	Jynx	Ice/Psychic
169	Crobat	Poison/Flying		198	Murkrow	Dark/Flying
94	Gengar	Ghost/Poison		197	Umbreon	Dark

Suggested Types: Fighting, Ice, Psychic

There are few apparent gaps in Chen's defenses, but you can use Fighting against the Dark, Ice against the Flying-types, and Ice or a strong special-based against the Ghosts. You may wish to bring a Psychic, but be careful with the Dark-types in his lineup.

ROUND 7: GLACIERBADGE
PokéFan Baxter

NO.	Pokémon	Type		NO.	Pokémon	Type
160	Feraligatr	Water		210	Granbull	Normal
157	Typhlosion	Fire		242	Blissey	Normal
154	Meganium	Grass		237	Hitmontop	Fighting

Suggested Types: Fighting, Normal

With evolved forms of all three Gold and Silver starting Pokémon, Baxter's only real opening is using a Fighting-type against his Normal-types, but if you bring along a Normal with good special-based attacks, you can take out the starters—just watch out for his Hitmontop if you have your Normal out.

ROUND 8: RISINGBADGE
Pokémaniac Pedro

NO.	Pokémon	Type		NO.	Pokémon	Type
142	Aerodactyl	Rock/Flying		149	Dragonite	Dragon/Flying
68	Machamp	Fighting		248	Tyranitar	Rock/Dark
230	Kingdra	Water/Dragon		6	Charizard	Fire/Flying

Suggested Types: Ice, Fighting

As your final opponent for the Poké Cup championship, Pedro boasts an impressive collection of strong Dragon Pokémon... and an impressive weakness to Ice. Bring along something with a strong Ice attack, as well as a Fighting-type to deal with Aerodactyl and Tyranitar. Fill your third slot with any strong Pokémon you are comfortable using.

Once you've defeated Pedro, the Master Ball trophy and the Poké Cup championship are yours!

PRIME CUP

- Level 1-100 Tournament

The final tournament in the Stadium, the Prime Cup, is a no-holds-barred, ultra-high level Pokémon contest. Bring along your strongest contenders, your legendary Pokémon, and your best tricks, because the computer will present you with lots of challenges.

TOURNAMENT RULES

- All 251 Pokémon are permitted.
- You can use six different Pokémon for the team; three can fight.
- No level restrictions apply.
- You can use items, but each Pokémon must hold a different item.
- You cannot have two Pokémon asleep or frozen at the same time.
- You cannot use self-destructive moves on your final Pokémon.

ROUND 1: ZEPHYRBADGE

Lass Terry

NO.	Pokémon	Type		NO.	Pokémon	Type
182	Bellossom	Grass		162	Furret	Normal
184	Azumarill	Water		40	Wigglytuff	Normal
181	Ampharos	Electric		176	Togetic	Normal/Flying

Suggested Types: Fighting, Psychic

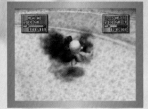

Terry, your first opponent in the Prime Cup, has a stable of three Normal-types (which are vulnerable to your Fighting-types) and a Grass, Electric, and Water. Although you could bring a few dual types to deal with them, you should instead bring along a Psychic and a Normal with special moves.

ROUND 2: HIVEBADGE
Blackbelt Yang

NO.	Pokémon	Type		NO.	Pokémon	Type
202	Wobbuffet	Psychic		106	Hitmonlee	Fighting
57	Primeape	Fighting		237	Hitmontop	Fighting
107	Hitmonchan	Fighting		34	Nidoking	Poison/Ground

Suggested Types: Psychic, Flying

Yang's Fighting Pokémon are strong in spirit, but weak in Psychic defense. You should bring a Psychic powerhouse or a strong Flying-type to deplete his defenses.

ROUND 3: PLAINBADGE

Bird Keeper Adam

NO.	Pokémon	Type		NO.	Pokémon	Type
6	Charizard	Fire/Flying		22	Fearow	Normal/Flying
207	Gligar	Flying/Ground		198	Murkrow	Dark/Flying
142	Aerodactyl	Rock/Flying		85	Dodrio	Normal/Flying

Suggested Types: Electric, Ice

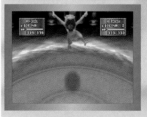

A complete set of Flying-types makes for an Electric paradise. Bring an Ice-type just in case Gligar appears, but other than that, this fight isn't too difficult.

ROUND 4: FOGBADGE
Cooltrainer Floria

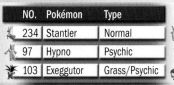

NO.	Pokémon	Type		NO.	Pokémon	Type
234	Stantler	Normal		36	Clefable	Normal
97	Hypno	Psychic		71	Victreebel	Grass/Poison
103	Exeggutor	Grass/Psychic		62	Poliwrath	Water/Fighting

Suggested Types: Dark, Fire, Fighting

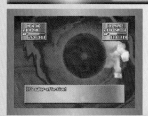

Floria has a few Psychics, a few Normal-types, a few Grass-types. Bring along Dark, Fire, and Fighting for a perfect match up. You could also substitute a Psychic for the Fighting-type to match its defense against Floria's Psychic-types. A Psychic is also effective against the Normal-types and Victreebel.

ROUND 5: STORMBADGE
Fisherman Chase

NO.	Pokémon	Type		NO.	Pokémon	Type
130	Gyarados	Water/Flying		195	Quagsire	Water/Ground
226	Mantine	Water/Flying		87	Dewgong	Water/Ice
171	Lanturn	Water/Electric		149	Dragonite	Dragon/Flying

Suggested Types: Electric, Ice

This is a fairly straightforward match-up. Use your Electric-types against most of the Water-types, with the exception of Quagsire and Lanturn. You should use Ice against those two and Dragonite.

ROUND 6: MINERALBADGE
Scientist Craig

NO.	Pokémon	Type		NO.	Pokémon	Type
205	Forretress	Bug/Steel		215	Sneasel	Dark/Ice
53	Persian	Normal		169	Crobat	Poison/Flying
101	Electrode	Electric		38	Ninetales	Fire

Suggested Types: Fire, Rock/Ground, Psychic

No huge openings present themselves against Craig's team of mixed Pokémon. Use Fire-types against Forretress and Sneasel, Rock/Ground-types against his Electric and Fire, and employ a Psychic for mop-up duty.

ROUND 7: GLACIERBADGE
Skier Kathy

NO.	Pokémon	Type		NO.	Pokémon	Type
124	Jynx	Ice/Psychic		221	Piloswine	Ice/Ground
131	Lapras	Water/Ice		122	Mr. Mime	Psychic
199	Slowking	Water/Psychic		160	Feraligatr	Water

Suggested Types: Steel, Dark, Electric

The semifinal round pits you against a combination of Psychic-, Water-, and Ice-types. You can counter this group by using Steel-, Dark-, and Electric-types. Be careful with how and when you switch your Pokémon in battle and you shouldn't have too much trouble with this fight.

ROUND 8: RISINGBADGE
Cooltrainer Marty

NO.	Pokémon	Type		NO.	Pokémon	Type
151	Mew	Psychic		197	Umbreon	Dark
217	Ursaring	Normal		89	Muk	Poison
121	Starmie	Water/Psychic		248	Tyranitar	Rock/Dark

Suggested Types: Dark, Bug, Steel

Marty, your final opponent in the Prime Cup, brings a mix of Psychic- and Dark-types and a few extras thrown in. Use Dark- and Steel-types for defensive purposes, and utilize Bug-types for offensive strikes against Psychic-types.

Defeat Marty and the Prime Cup championship is yours, thus putting the Round 1 Stadium behind you. Only the Round 1 Gym Leader Castle remains to test your Pokémon skills!

The 16 gyms of Gold and Silver, as well as those of Red, Blue, and Yellow await your Pokémon. In most cases, you must defeat a few trainers from a gym before challenging the gym leader and progressing to the next gym. We'll give you full lists of their teams, just as with the Stadium Mode.

If you have a strong team that you used to defeat the Prime Cup, you can bring it along to go through the entire castle. Otherwise, your Poké Cup team should do well.

GYM LEADER CASTLE RULES

- All 251 Pokémon may enter.
- Six different Pokémon may be used for the team, three can fight.
- No level restrictions apply.
- Gym Leaders will use level 50 Pokémon, but if you use any higher level Pokémon, all of their Pokémon will be raised to the highest level you use.
- Items can be used, but each Pokémon must hold a different item.
- No two Pokémon may be asleep or frozen at the same time.
- Self-destructive moves may not be used on your final Pokémon.

VIOLET GYM, LEADER FALKNER

TRAINER 1:
Bird Keeper Matt

NO.	Pokémon	Type	NO.	Pokémon	Type
16	Pidgey	Normal/Flying	177	Natu	Psychic/Flying
163	Hoothoot	Normal/Flying	84	Doduo	Normal/Flying
21	Spearow	Normal/Flying	17	Pidgeotto	Normal/Flying

Suggested Types: Electric

Violet Gym is home to the ZEPHYR-BADGE for the Pokémon who ride the winds inside. Unfortunately for Matt, the trainer that bars your path to Falkner, a single Electric Pokémon will easily fry all of his Flying-types.

TRAINER 2:
Gym Leader Falkner

NO.	Pokémon	Type	NO.	Pokémon	Type
18	Pidgeot	Normal/Flying	225	Delibird	Ice/Flying
83	Farfetch'd	Normal/Flying	22	Fearow	Normal/Flying
164	Noctowl	Normal/Flying	176	Togetic	Normal/Flying

Suggested Types: Electric

Falkner should learn from his own students: a single exclusive type is not healthy for Pokémon teams. Use your Electric again and take him down.

AZALEA GYM, LEADER BUGSY

TRAINER 1:
Bug Catcher Chaz

NO.	Pokémon	Type		NO.	Pokémon	Type
193	Yanma	Bug/Flying		19	Rattata	Normal
167	Spinarak	Bug/Poison		46	Paras	Bug/Grass
213	Shuckle	Bug/Rock		74	Geodude	Rock/Ground

Suggested Types: Fire, Water

Azalea Gym teaches its students a bit better than Violet Gym, as Chaz has some Rock-types mixed in to help protect against a sweep from a Fire- or Flying-type, but you can bring along a Water to counter that easily enough.

TRAINER 2:
Twins Min&Lyn

NO.	Pokémon	Type		NO.	Pokémon	Type
165	Ledyba	Bug/Flying		187	Hoppip	Grass/Flying
191	Sunkern	Grass		25	Pikachu	Electric
39	Jigglypuff	Normal		35	Clefairy	Normal

Suggested Types: Fire, Fighting

This is an easier fight than the last one, with no strong defense against your Fire this time around. You can also use a Fighting to deal with the Normal-types if you want, but unless Pikachu pops up, you'll likely sweep the field.

TRAINER 3:
Gym Leader Bugsy

NO.	Pokémon	Type		NO.	Pokémon	Type
123	Scyther	Bug/Flying		70	Weepinbell	Grass/Poison
12	Butterfree	Bug/Flying		127	Pinsir	Bug
15	Beedrill	Bug/Poison		247	Pupitar	Rock/Ground

Suggested Types: Fire, Water

Once more, there are lots of soon-to-be-toasted Bug-types to deal with, but bring along a Water-type in case Pupitar shows its face. Once you defeat Bugsy, it's on to the next gym for you.

GOLDENROD GYM, LEADER WHITNEY

TRAINER 1:
Lass Lois

NO.	Pokémon	Type		NO.	Pokémon	Type
216	Teddiursa	Normal		231	Phanpy	Ground
183	Marill	Water		60	Poliwag	Water
52	Meowth	Normal		209	Snubbull	Normal

Suggested Types: Fighting, Grass

A team of super cute Pokémon greet your arrival at the Goldenrod Gym. A Fighting-type will get you through most of them, but you should bring along a Grass-type in case Marill, Poliwag, or Phanpy decide to come out and play.

TRAINER 2:
Beauty Rita

NO.	Pokémon	Type		NO.	Pokémon	Type
190	Aipom	Normal		77	Ponyta	Fire
179	Mareep	Electric		223	Remoraid	Water
50	Diglett	Ground		161	Sentret	Normal

Suggested Types: Grass, Water, Fighting

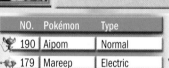

The assault of cute Pokémon continues here, but bring along a Grass, a Water-, and a Fighting-type and you'll be okay. Alternatively, you can simply use a powerful Psychic to sweep the board.

TRAINER 3:
Gym Leader Whitney

NO.	Pokémon	Type		NO.	Pokémon	Type
241	Miltank	Normal		44	Gloom	Grass/Poison
36	Clefable	Normal		85	Dodrio	Normal/Flying
40	Wigglytuff	Normal		234	Stantler	Normal

Suggested Types: Fighting, Fire

Whitney uses almost all Normal-types for her team, making her a prime target for a strong Fighting Pokémon. Bring along a Fire to barbecue Gloom if it makes an appearance.

31

ECRUTEAK GYM, LEADER MORTY

TRAINER 1:
Medium Holly

NO.	Pokémon	Type	NO.	Pokémon	Type
69	Bellsprout	Grass/Poison	132	Ditto	Normal
163	Hoothoot	Normal/Flying	30	Nidorina	Poison
166	Ledian	Bug/Flying	201	Unown	Psychic

Suggested Types: Ice, Steel

An odd collection of Pokémon makes up Holly's team, but you can use Ice to freeze half of them. Steel will give you immunity to Nidorina. Keep in mind that while Unown is Psychic, its attack can be any type, so you should use Bug or Dark offensively against it and don't worry about its offense.

TRAINER 2:
Sage Ty

NO.	Pokémon	Type	NO.	Pokémon	Type
41	Zubat	Poison/Flying	42	Golbat	Poison/Flying
238	Smoochum	Ice/Psychic	200	Misdreavus	Ghost
92	Gastly	Ghost/Poison	93	Haunter	Ghost/Poison

Suggested Types: Dark, Normal, Psychic

A straightforward fight here, the Ghosts are all vulnerable to Dark attacks and Psychic will dispatch the mixed Poison-types. You may want to bring along a Normal-type for its immunity to Ghost attacks, but be sure it has some non-Normal attacks of its own.

TRAINER 3:
Gym Leader Morty

NO.	Pokémon	Type	NO.	Pokémon	Type
94	Gengar	Ghost/Poison	105	Marowak	Ground
168	Ariados	Bug/Poison	203	Girafarig	Normal/Psychic
185	Sudowoodo	Rock	164	Noctowl	Normal/Flying

Suggested Types: Psychic, Water

This gym leader understands the value of diversity, so his team is better rounded. To take him out, bring along a Psychic for the mixed Poison-types and a Water to wash away Sudowoodo and Marowak. If you feel the need, you can bring a Dark- or a Steel-type for Girafarig, but you probably won't need it.

CIANWOOD GYM, LEADER CHUCK

TRAINER 1:
Blackbelt Nick

NO.	Pokémon	Type	NO.	Pokémon	Type
237	Hitmontop	Fighting	106	Hitmonlee	Fighting
33	Nidorino	Poison	119	Seaking	Water
51	Dugtrio	Ground	111	Rhyhorn	Ground/Rock

Suggested Types: Flying, Water

A Flying- and a Water-type will put this trainer in his place. If you're concerned about the Water or Poison, you can bring along a Pokémon specifically to deal with them, but neither Nidorino nor Seaking are particularly powerful, so your others should be able to take them out.

TRAINER 2:
Gym Leader Chuck

NO.	Pokémon	Type		NO.	Pokémon	Type
62	Poliwrath	Water/Fighting		107	Hitmonchan	Fighting
210	Granbull	Normal		28	Sandslash	Ground
67	Machoke	Fighting		57	Primeape	Fighting

Suggested Types: Psychic, Flying, Water

There isn't much to this fight—a single Psychic can drop the hammer on this gym leader's entire team. You can use a Flying-type in its place if you wish (or, say, a Lugia to get the whole package). Bring a Water-type for Sandslash to be fully prepared...

OLIVINE GYM, LEADER JASMINE

TRAINER 1:
Gym Leader Jasmine

NO.	Pokémon	Type		NO.	Pokémon	Type
208	Steelix	Steel/Ground		226	Mantine	Water/Flying
222	Corsola	Water/Rock		227	Skarmory	Steel/Flying
82	Magneton	Electric/Steel		205	Forretress	Bug/Steel

Suggested Types: Fire, Electric

Plenty of Steel Pokémon make a prime target for Fire, but bring along an Electric in case Corsola or Mantine show up—you don't want to get doused.

TEAM ROCKET ENCOUNTER

TRAINER 1:
Rocket Grunt

NO.	Pokémon	Type		NO.	Pokémon	Type
74	Geodude	Rock/Ground		75	Graveler	Rock/Ground
109	Koffing	Poison		110	Weezing	Poison
204	Pineco	Bug		101	Electrode	Electric

Suggested Types: Psychic, Water

Team Rocket never learns. Their interruption of your gym travels will be short lived if you use the right Pokémon. Use your Psychic to deal with their usual Poison-types. A Water-type will wash out the Geodude and Graveler. Be careful of the Electrode popping up while you're using your Water.

TRAINER 2:
Rocket Grunt

NO.	Pokémon	Type		NO.	Pokémon	Type
198	Murkrow	Dark/Flying		206	Dunsparce	Normal
96	Drowzee	Psychic		41	Zubat	Poison/Flying
167	Spinarak	Bug/Poison		228	Houndour	Dark/Fire

Suggested Types: Fighting, Psychic, Dark

You'll need to use a good mix of types to defeat this Rocket Grunt. Use a Fighting for the Dark- and Normal-types, use a Psychic against the Poisons, and if you need too, bring your own Dark to fight the challenger's Psychic.

TRAINER 3:
Rocket Executive

NO.	Pokémon	Type		NO.	Pokémon	Type
215	Sneasel	Dark/Ice		45	Vileplume	Grass/Poison
89	Muk	Poison		20	Raticate	Normal
108	Lickitung	Normal		24	Arbok	Poison

Suggested Types: Psychic, Fighting

Another traditional Team Rocket member, you can easily blast the Poison Pokémon with your Psychic. Keep your Fighting-type in reserve for any Normal-types or Sneasel if it shows up.

TRAINER 4:
Rocket Executive

NO.	Pokémon	Type		NO.	Pokémon	Type
229	Houndoom	Dark/Fire		200	Misdreavus	Ghost
42	Golbat	Poison/Flying		71	Victreebel	Grass/Poison
53	Persian	Normal		202	Wobbuffet	Psychic

Suggested Types: Steel, Psychic, Fighting

Due to this Executive's mix of types, you'll probably have to do a bit of switching to win this battle. After you take out the Exec, you can return to the regular gym progression.

MAHOGANY GYM, LEADER PRYCE

TRAINER 1:
Boarder Alvin

NO.	Pokémon	Type		NO.	Pokémon	Type
86	Seel	Water		238	Smoochum	Ice/Psychic
220	Swinub	Ice/Ground		99	Kingler	Water
90	Shellder	Water		180	Flaaffy	Electric

Suggested Types: Electric, Steel

Electric is your friend here. You can knock out the Water-types. Use a Steel or one of your third Pokémon to deal with Swinub and Flaaffy should either one show up.

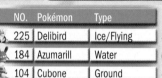

TRAINER 2:
Skier Carol

NO.	Pokémon	Type		NO.	Pokémon	Type
225	Delibird	Ice/Flying		211	Qwilfish	Water/Poison
184	Azumarill	Water		147	Dratini	Dragon
104	Cubone	Ground		117	Seadra	Water

Suggested Types: Electric, Ice

Again, Electric will serve you well. You may wish to bring along an Ice-type to freeze Dratini and Cubone solid, but you can probably get along fine without it—just make sure your Electric doesn't get hammered by Cubone.

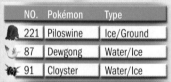

TRAINER 3:
Gym Leader Pryce

NO.	Pokémon	Type		NO.	Pokémon	Type
221	Piloswine	Ice/Ground		217	Ursaring	Normal
87	Dewgong	Water/Ice		232	Donphan	Ground
91	Cloyster	Water/Ice		124	Jynx	Ice/Psychic

Suggested Types: Steel, Fighting

Pryce shifts the focus a little more heavily toward Ice, so you may want to use a Steel-type for defensive purposes. A Fighting-type will do well on offense—just watch that Jynx doesn't blast it with Psychic.

BLACKTHORN GYM, LEADER CLAIR

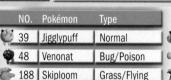

TRAINER 1:
Cooltrainer Gloria

NO.	Pokémon	Type		NO.	Pokémon	Type
39	Jigglypuff	Normal		35	Clefairy	Normal
48	Venonat	Bug/Poison		102	Exeggcute	Grass/Psychic
188	Skiploom	Grass/Flying		43	Oddish	Grass/Poison

Suggested Types: Ice, Fire

Either Ice or Fire will take care of the Grass-types, as well as Venonat. For the Normal-types, you can bring along a Fighting-type or let one of your stronger Pokémon take them out with the others.

TRAINER 2:
Cooltrainer Vince

NO.	Pokémon	Type		NO.	Pokémon	Type
1	Bulbasaur	Grass		152	Chikorita	Grass
7	Squirtle	Water		158	Totodile	Water
4	Charmander	Fire		155	Cyndaquil	Fire

Suggested Types: Fire, Electric, Water

Vince is pretty interesting; he has all of the starter Pokémon from Red, Blue, Yellow and Gold and Silver. Bring along a Dragon-type if you have one, as it will soak up all of the attacks. Otherwise, match up with Fire, Electric, and Water, switching as necessary.

TRAINER 3:
Gym Leader Clair

NO.	Pokémon	Type		NO.	Pokémon	Type
230	Kingdra	Water/Dragon		112	Rhydon	Ground/Rock
181	Ampharos	Electric		59	Arcanine	Fire
148	Dragonair	Dragon		131	Lapras	Water/Ice

Suggested Types: Ice, Psychic, Water

You can bull your way through this gym by using Ice against the Dragons and Psychic against the rest. However, you may wish to bring along a Water-type to wash out Rhydon and Arcanine. Be careful of Ampharos shocking you if you do use a Water-type.

ELITE FOUR

TRAINER 1:
Elite Four Will

NO.	Pokémon	Type	NO.	Pokémon	Type
178	Xatu	Psychic/Flying	36	Clefable	Normal
64	Kadabra	Psychic	103	Exeggutor	Grass/Psychic
203	Girafarig	Normal/Psychic	124	Jynx	Ice/Psychic

Suggested Types: Dark, Steel

A single Dark-type can easily deal with all of Will's Pokémon, but if you are lacking a strong Dark, you can bring along a Steel-type for defense.

TRAINER 2:
Elite Four Koga

NO.	Pokémon	Type	NO.	Pokémon	Type
49	Venomoth	Bug/Poison	207	Gligar	Ground/Flying
168	Ariados	Bug/Poison	101	Electrode	Electric
42	Golbat	Flying/Poison	89	Muk	Poison

Suggested Types: Psychic

Koga still hasn't learned, so bring along a Psychic-type to smash his Poison Pokémon. Any two other strong Pokémon will deal with Gligar and Electrode.

TRAINER 3:
Elite Four Bruno

NO.	Pokémon	Type	NO.	Pokémon	Type
68	Machamp	Fighting	9	Blastoise	Water
76	Golem	Rock/Ground	214	Heracross	Bug/Fighting
115	Kangaskhan	Normal	95	Onix	Rock/Ground

Suggested Types: Psychic, Water

Bruno hasn't learned either; his Pokémon are still heavily unbalanced, and strong as they are, the right team will put them down. Bring along a Psychic-type again, a Water-type, and if you feel the need, a Fighting-type for Kangaskhan and the Rock hybrids.

TRAINER 4:
Elite Four Karen

NO.	Pokémon	Type	NO.	Pokémon	Type
197	Umbreon	Dark	126	Magmar	Fire
71	Victreebel	Grass/Poison	94	Gengar	Ghost/Poison
198	Murkrow	Dark/Flying	45	Vileplume	Grass/Poison

Suggested Types: Psychic, Steel

Karen's lineup isn't quite the team of Dragons you might have been expecting. Your Psychic-type continues its heavy-duty workload with a strong showing against the Poison-types here, and you can also use your Steel-type to good effect against the Poison, as well as the Dark-types. Just watch for Magmar trying to melt down your Steel Pokémon.

FINAL FIGHT, JOHTO CASTLE

JOHTO CHAMPION:
Lance

NO.	Pokémon	Type	NO.	Pokémon	Type
149	Dragonite	Dragon/Flying	142	Aerodactyl	Rock/Flying
248	Tyranitar	Rock/Dark	208	Steelix	Steel/Ground
6	Charizard	Fire/Flying	130	Gyarados	Water/Flying

Suggested Types: Ice, Electric

There's the Dragon! Use your most powerful Pokémon and bring along Ice and Electric attacks to take out his over abundance of Flying-types. He uses fewer Dragon-types than before, perhaps learning that getting completely frozen is no fun, but it doesn't change your strategy much.

With Lance's defeat, the Johto Castle championship is yours and the route to the Kanto trainers is open.

PEWTER GYM

GYM LEADER:
Brock

NO.	Pokémon	Type	NO.	Pokémon	Type
95	Onix	Rock/Ground	127	Pinsir	Bug
76	Golem	Rock/Ground	205	Forretress	Bug/Steel
139	Omastar	Rock/Water	141	Kabutops	Rock/Water

Suggested Types: Water, Grass, Fire

Either Water or Grass will deal nicely with most of Brock's Pokémon, but you may want to bring along a Fire to melt down Forretress.

VERMILION GYM

GYM LEADER:
Lt. Surge

NO.	Pokémon	Type	NO.	Pokémon	Type
26	Raichu	Electric	101	Electrode	Electric
171	Lanturn	Water/Electric	137	Porygon	Normal
125	Electabuzz	Electric	82	Magneton	Electric/Steel

Suggested Types: Ground

A Ground-type will give you complete immunity to almost all of Lt. Surge's Pokémon, though you may want to bring a Grass-type for Lanturn and a Fire type to crisp Magneton.

36

CERULEAN GYM

GYM LEADER:
Misty

NO.	Pokémon	Type	NO.	Pokémon	Type
121	Starmie	Water/Psychic	192	Sunflora	Grass
176	Togetic	Normal/Flying	61	Poliwhirl	Water
55	Golduck	Water	195	Quagsire	Water/Ground

Suggested Types: Electric, Ice

If you use an Electric-type to fry her Water Pokémon and an Ice-type for Sunflora and Quagsire, Misty doesn't stand much of a chance. Either Electric or Ice will put Togetic out of commission, as well.

CELADON GYM

GYM LEADER:
Erika

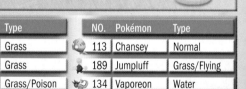

NO.	Pokémon	Type	NO.	Pokémon	Type
182	Bellossom	Grass	113	Chansey	Normal
114	Tangela	Grass	189	Jumpluff	Grass/Flying
3	Venusaur	Grass/Poison	134	Vaporeon	Water

Suggested Types: Fire

Burn the Grass down. This stable of "veggies" is ripe for cooking, though you should consider an Electric-type for Vaporeon in the event it shows up.

FUCHSIA GYM

GYM LEADER:
Janine

NO.	Pokémon	Type
169	Crobat	Poison/Flying
168	Ariados	Bug/Poison
110	Weezing	Poison

NO.	Pokémon	Type
234	Stantler	Normal
207	Gligar	Ground/Flying
73	Tentacruel	Water/Poison

Suggested Types: Psychic

Janine has taken over the gym since Koga graduated to the Elite Four, but he must not have told her about the weakness of Poison to Psychic... Bring along your Psychic-type to teach her this valuable lesson.

CINNABAR GYM

GYM LEADER:
Blaine

NO.	Pokémon	Type
78	Rapidash	Fire
38	Ninetales	Fire
47	Parasect	Bug/Grass

NO.	Pokémon	Type
136	Flareon	Fire
224	Octillery	Water
219	Magcargo	Fire/Rock

Suggested Types: Water

Blaine had his old gym completely destroyed, but he still uses his Fire Pokémon, which you can easily douse with a good Water-type. Fill your other two slots with Pokémon to deal with Parasect and Octillery in case they show up.

SAFFRON GYM

GYM LEADER:
Sabrina

NO.	Pokémon	Type
65	Alakazam	Psychic
122	Mr. Mime	Psychic
97	Hypno	Psychic

NO.	Pokémon	Type
40	Wigglytuff	Normal
162	Furret	Normal
80	Slowbro	Water/Psychic

Suggested Types: Dark, Steel

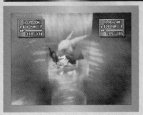

Dark-types will attack the Psychics much more effectively, but you can use Steel-types to good effect defensively. Consider bringing a Fighting-type to use against the Normal-types if you feel the need.

VIRIDIAN GYM

GYM LEADER:
Blue

NO.	Pokémon	Type
18	Pidgeot	Flying
65	Alakazam	Psychic
112	Rhydon	Ground/Rock

NO.	Pokémon	Type
130	Gyarados	Water/Flying
103	Exeggutor	Grass/Psychic
59	Arcanine	Fire

Suggested Types: Ice, Dark, Water

With a more diverse team than any of the other Kanto gym leaders by far, Blue will require you to mix up your team a bit more than you have for quite some time. You can use an Ice-type against his Flying-types, Dark if Alakazam bops up (or Steel if you need too), and a Water-type against Rhydon or Arcanine.

FINAL FIGHT, KANTO CASTLE

???:
Red

NO.	Pokémon	Type	NO.	Pokémon	Type
154	Meganium	Grass	135	Jolteon	Electric
160	Feraligatr	Water	212	Scizor	Bug/Steel
157	Typhlosion	Fire	128	Tauros	Normal

Suggested Types: Psychic, Fire, Grass, Water

Red has a pretty solid team, one of the best you've faced. You can approach this battle one of two ways: go for straight type match-ups and switch Pokémon a lot, or put in your most powerful Psychic and other types and simply out muscle his Pokémon.

RIVAL BATTLE

TRAINER:
Rival

NO.	Pokémon	Type
150	Mewtwo	Psychic
250	Ho-oh	Fire/Flying
249	Lugia	Psychic/Flying

Suggested Types: Dark, Ice, Electric

You can use a full roster of six Pokémon in this fight and it's a no-holds-barred contest for your complete domination of Round 1. Once you've defeated your Rival, Round 2 is open and you are halfway done with the game. Your Rival opposes you with the three strongest legendary Pokémon in the game, Mewtwo, Ho-Oh, and Lugia. But a Dark and a strong Ice and Electric attack will serve you well against them.

Sit back and enjoy the credits—you deserve it!

38

STADIUM MODE ROUND 2

LITTLE CUP

- Level 5 Tournament

Round 2 of the Little Cup is much the same as Round 1, but this time you'll definitely need Pokémon that you've bred yourself to be victorious. Bring along Pokémon that have strong, accurate moves of many different types. Using a Normal type with three different types of attacks will defeat many of the trainers you will encounter here.

Regarding the Suggested Types listed in this chapter, they are mostly aimed at offense rather than defense. That is to say, if you can equip your team of three with major attacks from many different types, you will be able to use a super-effective attack no matter what type your opponent tries to bring against you.

TOURNAMENT RULES

- 86 Different Pokémon are permitted for this tournament, check the list in game.
- Only unevolved Pokémon that can be hatched from eggs *and* can be evolved are legal.
- Six different Pokémon may be used for the team, three can fight.
- All Pokémon must be level 5.
- Items can be used, but each Pokémon must hold a different item.
- No two Pokémon may be asleep or frozen at the same time.
- Self-destructive moves may not be used on your final Pokémon.
- Dragon Rage and Sonicboom will not work.

ROUND 1: ZEPHYRBADGE
Youngster Bernie

NO.	Pokémon	Type
48	Venonat	Bug/Poison
204	Pineco	Bug
100	Voltorb	Electric

NO.	Pokémon	Type
66	Machop	Fighting
102	Exeggcute	Grass/Psychic
111	Rhyhorn	Ground/Rock

Suggested Types: Fire, Ground, Water

Bring out your Fire to roast his Venonat, Pineco, and Exeggcute. You can use a Ground attack for heavy damage against Voltorb or a Ground type for immunity. Water will wash away Rhyhorn, and any of your Pokémon except a Normal should do fine against Machop. Bernie will try to use Light Screen and Reflect to cut down on the damage you inflict, but if your Pokémon are strong, you'll be able to punch through anyway.

ROUND 2: HIVEBADGE
Picnicker Stacy

NO.	Pokémon	Type
116	Horsea	Water
231	Phanpy	Ground
1	Bulbasaur	Grass/Poison

NO.	Pokémon	Type
118	Goldeen	Water
21	Spearow	Normal/Flying
155	Cyndaquil	Fire

Suggested Types: Grass, Electric, Water

A heavy weakness to Grass and Electric Pokémon characterizes this team. You may also wish to bring along a Water attack to deal with Phanpy and Quilava if they decide to visit.

ROUND 3: PLAINBADGE
Camper Grant

NO.	Pokémon	Type		NO.	Pokémon	Type
187	Hoppip	Grass/Flying		216	Teddiursa	Normal
194	Wooper	Water/Ground		52	Meowth	Normal
50	Diglett	Ground		54	Psyduck	Water

Suggested Types: Grass, Fighting, Ice

Grass will take care of most of Grant's Pokémon just fine, though you might want to bring along a baby Machop or Mankey to beat up on his Normal-types. An Ice-type will freeze up Hoppip and work fine against Wooper. Grant likes to use Swagger to confuse your Pokémon and then follow up with a move that lowers your Defense further so that your Pokémon will be hurt badly if it hits itself. Just switch your Pokémon out and he'll waste another turn using Swagger.

ROUND 5: STORMBADGE
Schoolboy Clark

NO.	Pokémon	Type		NO.	Pokémon	Type
172	Pichu	Electric		183	Marill	Water
152	Chikorita	Grass		37	Vulpix	Fire
173	Cleffa	Normal		161	Sentret	Normal

Suggested Types: Grass, Rock, Fighting

Grass will do well against Pichu and Marill. Rock works against Vulpix and Chikorita, and use Fighting for baby Cleffa and Sentret.

ROUND 4: FOGBADGE
PokéFan Janet

NO.	Pokémon	Type		NO.	Pokémon	Type
165	Ledyba	Bug/Flying		228	Houndour	Dark/Fire
81	Magnemite	Electric/Steel		167	Spinarak	Bug/Poison
92	Gastly	Ghost/Poison		86	Seel	Water

Suggested Types: Fire, Grass, Rock/Ground

You can use Fire to melt down Ledian, Magnemite, and Spinarak, using your Grass for defense. Rock/Ground will protect you against Magnemite and Houndour, though you'll need to avoid Seel if you use a Geodude. Janet likes to use Toxic and then play defensively while your Pokémon takes damage. This doesn't work too well when you knock her Pokémon out in two or three turns...

ROUND 6: MINERALBADGE
Swimmer♀ Cora

NO.	Pokémon	Type		NO.	Pokémon	Type
60	Poliwag	Water		104	Cubone	Ground
63	Abra	Psychic		147	Dratini	Dragon
179	Mareep	Electric		4	Charmander	Fire

Suggested Types: Ice, Grass

Dratini can be a pain due to its defenses, so bring along some Ice to freeze it solid, then use a Grass for Poliwag, Mareep, and Cubone. Fill your third slot with any Pokémon you're comfy with at this point. Cora likes to stop your Pokémon from attacking with Attract, Thunder Wave, and the like.

ROUND 7: GLACIERBADGE
Teacher Tina

NO.	Pokémon	Type
133	Eevee	Normal
177	Natu	Psychic/Flying
77	Ponyta	Fire

NO.	Pokémon	Type
19	Rattata	Normal
84	Doduo	Normal/Flying
236	Tyrogue	Fighting

Suggested Types: Fighting, Electric, Water

There isn't much to this team, though in terms of baby Pokémon, Normal-types are a bit stronger than others are. Use Fighting for the Normal-types, Electric for the hybrid Flying-types, and a Water-type to wash up Ponyta. Tina likes to use Curse to power up her Pokémon and then Quick Attack to get around the speed loss from Curse.

ROUND 8: RISINGBADGE
PokéFan Rex

NO.	Pokémon	Type
239	Elekid	Electric
137	Porygon	Normal
95	Onix	Rock/Ground

NO.	Pokémon	Type
79	Slowpoke	Water/Psychic
123	Scyther	Bug/Flying
113	Chansey	Normal

Suggested Types: Fighting, Fire, Water

Scyther and Chansey are two of the strongest Pokémon in the Little Cup, but you can use Fire to burn Scyther or Electric to shock it. Chansey will take heavy damage from Fighting types. Onix is strong, but it's doubly weak to a Water attack. Round up your team and take on Rex for the championship.

With Rex's defeat, another Little Cup trophy is yours and you can move on to the Challenge Cup.

41

CHALLENGE CUP

- Variable Level Random Pokémon Tournament

Round 2 of the Challenge Cup is much the same as Round 1, but the skills you have gained from beating it the first time around should help you more quickly make your Pokémon choices and defeat your opponents.

NOTE: *Again, remember that the opposing Pokémon team lists for the Challenge Cup are simply a sampling of what a given trainer can have. In general, they stay very close to the types laid out, so you can use the lists to get an idea of what you may face. To save yourself time, you can reset the game a couple of times if you are unsatisfied with your team before you begin a division.*

TOURNAMENT RULES

- Six random Pokémon are provided as your team for each division.
- Three Pokémon are used for each fight.
- No two Pokémon may be asleep or frozen at the same time.
- Self-destructive moves may not be used on your final Pokémon.

POKé BALL DIVISION

ROUND 1: ZEPHYRBADGE
Camper Marcus

NO.	Pokémon	Type
218	Slugma	Fire
4	Charmander	Fire
246	Larvitar	Rock/Ground

NO.	Pokémon	Type
50	Diglett	Ground
27	Sandshrew	Ground
194	Wooper	Water/Ground

Suggested Types: Water, Grass

A single Water-type will wash away all of Marcus' Pokémon, though you may wish to bring along a Grass in case he pops a Water-type of his own.

ROUND 2: HIVEBADGE
Rocket Executive

NO.	Pokémon	Type
167	Spinarak	Bug/Poison
41	Zubat	Poison/Flying
48	Venonat	Bug/Poison

NO.	Pokémon	Type
43	Oddish	Grass/Poison
29	Nidoran♀	Poison
69	Bellsprout	Grass/Poison

Suggested Types: Psychic, Flying

Team Rocket never learns. A single Psychic can sweep his team, and failing that, a Flying-type will work well against most of it.

ROUND 3: PLAINBADGE
Picnicker Melissa

NO.	Pokémon	Type		NO.	Pokémon	Type
163	Hoothoot	Normal/Flying		165	Ledyba	Bug/Flying
21	Spearow	Normal/Flying		37	Vulpix	Fire
1	Bulbasaur	Grass/Poison		16	Pidgey	Normal/Flying

Suggested Types: Electric, Fire, Water

An Electric can zap most of Melissa's Pokémon out of the sky, but bring along a Fire and a Water type in case she brings out Grass and Fire.

ROUND 4: FOGBADGE
Guitarist Daren

NO.	Pokémon	Type		NO.	Pokémon	Type
43	Oddish	Grass/Poison		172	Pichu	Electric
187	Hoppip	Grass/Flying		46	Paras	Bug/Grass
81	Magnemite	Electric/Steel		179	Mareep	Electric

Suggested Types: Fire, Grass, Ground

Fire is your friend here. You can melt down most of Daren's team with a single Fire; just bring along a Grass- or a Ground-type for his Electric-types.

ROUND 5: STORMBADGE
Fisherman Curtis

NO.	Pokémon	Type		NO.	Pokémon	Type
7	Squirtle	Water		116	Horsea	Water
194	Wooper	Water/Ground		118	Goldeen	Water
79	Slowpoke	Water/Psychic		183	Marill	Water

Suggested Types: Electric, Grass

Either an Electric- or a Grass-type will deal handily with all of Curtis' Pokémon, as he is extremely fond of using all Water- and mixed Water-types.

ROUND 6: MINERALBADGE
Medium Peggy

NO.	Pokémon	Type		NO.	Pokémon	Type
27	Sandshrew	Ground		96	Drowzee	Psychic
218	Slugma	Fire		79	Slowpoke	Water/Psychic
19	Rattata	Normal		102	Exeggcute	Grass/Psychic

Suggested Types: Dark, Steel, Ghost

All of the types that can effectively fight Psychics are pretty rare, so if you don't have any of them on your team, do a bit of type matching and pick the most effective Pokémon you have available to use.

ROUND 7: GLACIERBADGE
Rocket Executive

NO.	Pokémon	Type		NO.	Pokémon	Type
175	Togepi	Normal		173	Cleffa	Normal
163	Hoothoot	Normal/Flying		21	Spearow	Normal/Flying
39	Jigglypuff	Normal		209	Snubbull	Normal

Suggested Types: Fighting, Electric

Team Rocket has decided to send out an Executive instead of a Grunt, but the tactics that you should use are still the same. Bring along some Fighting moves to deal heavy damage and bring an Electric for her Flying Pokémon.

ROUND 8: RISINGBADGE
Juggler Dwight

NO.	Pokémon	Type		NO.	Pokémon	Type
29	Nidoran♀	Poison		132	Ditto	Normal
66	Machop	Fighting		194	Wooper	Water/Ground
204	Pineco	Bug		152	Chikorita	Grass

Suggested Types: Flying, Psychic

Again, Dwight challenges you with a diverse team. In this match-up, Psychic and Flying can each be used against two of his Pokémon. But examine his setup carefully and pick Pokémon that have no more than two weaknesses and are strong against at least two of his.

With Dwight defeated, the first Round 2 trophy is in your possession and you can move on to the Great Ball division.

GREAT BALL DIVISION

ROUND 1: ZEPHYRBADGE
Twins Jan&Jane

NO.	Pokémon	Type	NO.	Pokémon	Type
138	Omanyte	Water/Rock	193	Yanma	Bug/Flying
47	Parasect	Bug/Grass	12	Butterfree	Bug/Flying
166	Ledian	Bug/Flying	104	Cubone	Ground

Suggested Types: Fire, Grass

A bundle of Bugs is in Jan & Jane's bag, and they're all burnable with a Fire Pokémon. Bring along a Grass-type for any Rock- or Ground-types that show up.

ROUND 2: HIVEBADGE
Schoolboy Oliver

NO.	Pokémon	Type	NO.	Pokémon	Type
95	Onix	Rock/Ground	140	Kabuto	Rock/Water
104	Cubone	Ground	222	Corsola	Water/Rock
231	Phanpy	Ground	75	Graveler	Rock/Ground

Suggested Types: Water, Grass

Oliver has lots of Ground, Rock, and some Water, which is easily defeated by your own Water and Grass Pokémon. Remember that your Water-type is normally effective against Rock/Water and you'll have better defense against his Water attacks.

ROUND 3: PLAINBADGE
Sailor Curt

NO.	Pokémon	Type	NO.	Pokémon	Type
120	Staryu	Water	170	Chinchou	Water/Electric
159	Croconaw	Water	8	Wartortle	Water
238	Smoochum	Ice/Psychic	44	Gloom	Grass/Poison

Suggested Types: Electric, Fire

Sailors are fond of their Water Pokémon, so you should be fond of your Electric. Watch for some Water-types that aren't as weak to Electric (or immune, in the case of Wooper) and bring along a few extra types to deal with the other Pokémon.

ROUND 4: FOGBADGE
Swimmer♀ Darcy

NO.	Pokémon	Type	NO.	Pokémon	Type
52	Meowth	Normal	240	Magby	Fire
83	Farfetch'd	Normal/Flying	44	Gloom	Grass/Poison
17	Pidgeotto	Normal/Flying	137	Porygon	Normal

Suggested Types: Fighting, Water, Fire

A lot of Normal-types are a good target for Fighting-types (or a Ghost if you happen to have one). Other than that, the few oddballs mixed into your challenger's roster will require you to spread out your types a little.

ROUND 5: STORMBADGE
Officer Gerald

NO.	Pokémon	Type	NO.	Pokémon	Type
153	Bayleef	Grass	188	Skiploom	Grass/Flying
58	Growlithe	Fire	2	Ivysaur	Grass/Poison
240	Magby	Fire	219	Magcargo	Fire/Rock

Suggested Types: Fire, Water

A split mix of Grass and Fire means you need a split between Fire and Water. If you wish, you can use Ice to freeze the Grass-types, assuming you have a Pokémon with an Ice attack.

ROUND 6: MINERALBADGE
Kimono Girl Emiko

NO.	Pokémon	Type	NO.	Pokémon	Type
228	Houndour	Dark/Fire	239	Elekid	Electric
12	Butterfree	Bug/Flying	111	Rhyhorn	Ground/Rock
206	Dunsparce	Normal	120	Staryu	Water

Suggested Types: Water, Electric, Grass

A good mix of Pokémon make up Emiko's team, so divide your three Pokémon over Water, Electric, and Grass to deal with her types. You'll probably need to do a lot of switching to deal with her, but she'll go down eventually.

ROUND 7: GLACIERBADGE
Scientist Roberto

NO.	Pokémon	Type		NO.	Pokémon	Type
180	Flaaffy	Electric		228	Houndour	Dark/Fire
92	Gastly	Ghost/Poison		202	Wobbuffet	Psychic
177	Natu	Psychic/Flying		206	Dunsparce	Normal

Suggested Types: Dark, Steel, Rock/Ground

Roberto's team is spread over many types, but he has a few holes you can exploit. A Dark- or Steel-type will help against the Psychics, and a Rock/Ground gives you immunity to Electric and should perform well against most of his team.

ROUND 8: RISINGBADGE
Gentleman Travis

NO.	Pokémon	Type		NO.	Pokémon	Type
238	Smoochum	Ice/Psychic		166	Ledian	Bug/Flying
30	Nidorina	Poison		240	Magby	Fire
222	Corsola	Water/Rock		56	Mankey	Fighting

Suggested Types: Rock/Ground, Water

Not much has changed with Travis' team; he still has a wide mix of Pokémon spread over many types. A Rock/Ground and a Water will do well against most, and you can fill your third slot with any Pokémon that counters at least two of his.

With Travis defeated, the Great Ball trophy is yours and the Ultra Ball is open.

ULTRA BALL DIVISION

ROUND 1: ZEPHYRBADGE
Camper Marcus

NO.	Pokémon	Type		NO.	Pokémon	Type
205	Forretress	Bug/Steel		77	Ponyta	Fire
105	Marowak	Ground		221	Piloswine	Ice/Ground
207	Gligar	Ground/Flying		156	Quilava	Fire

Suggested Types: Water, Fire

A single Fire will get you most of the way through Marcus' team again this round, but you may wish to bring a Water-type depending on the type of Pokémon he decides to field against you. Fill your third slot with a Pokémon you want to test out.

45

ROUND 2: HIVEBADGE
Rocket Executive

NO.	Pokémon	Type		NO.	Pokémon	Type
110	Weezing	Poison		49	Venomoth	Bug/Poison
24	Arbok	Poison		203	Girafarig	Normal/Psychic
211	Qwilfish	Water/Poison		215	Sneasel	Dark/Ice

Suggested Types: Psychic

Another Rocket Grunt upgraded to Executive level and you know the drill. Bring along your Psychic Pokémon to deal with all of his Poison types, and you can fill your other slots with any Pokémon that match up nicely against any extras he brings along.

ROUND 3: PLAINBADGE
Picnicker Melissa

NO.	Pokémon	Type		NO.	Pokémon	Type
22	Fearow	Normal/Flying		198	Murkrow	Dark/Flying
213	Shuckle	Bug/Rock		164	Noctowl	Normal/Flying
189	Jumpluff	Grass/Flying		226	Mantine	Water/Flying

Suggested Types: Electric, Ice

A whole lotta Flying-types means an easy victory for your Electric Pokémon or any Pokémon with some Ice attacks handy. Again, fill your extra slots with backup Pokémon or any that you want to test out.

ROUND 4: FOGBADGE

Guitarist Daren

NO.	Pokémon	Type		NO.	Pokémon	Type
182	Bellossom	Grass		122	Mr. Mime	Psychic
171	Lanturn	Water/Electric		20	Raticate	Normal
26	Raichu	Electric		189	Jumpluff	Grass/Flying

Suggested Types: Fire, Grass, Dark

Daren has a good mix of Pokémon, but as is usual with the computer trainers, he has a hole or two to exploit. Use a Fire to burn his Grass, a Grass for his Electric, and a Dark or Steel for defense against his others.

ROUND 5: STORMBADGE

Fisherman Curtis

NO.	Pokémon	Type		NO.	Pokémon	Type
171	Lanturn	Water/Electric		119	Seaking	Water
211	Qwilfish	Water/Poison		195	Quagsire	Water/Ground
87	Dewgong	Water/Ice		117	Seadra	Water

Suggested Types: Electric, Grass

Curtis still uses pure Water Pokémon, which you can zap with Electric or soak up with Grass, but watch for Lanturn or Quagsire showing up; either one can cause problems for your Electric-type.

ROUND 6: MINERALBADGE

Medium Peggy

NO.	Pokémon	Type		NO.	Pokémon	Type
200	Misdreavus	Ghost		122	Mr. Mime	Psychic
97	Hypno	Psychic		93	Haunter	Ghost/Poison
203	Girafarig	Normal/Psychic		226	Mantine	Water/Flying

Suggested Types: Dark, Steel

The only truly effective types against Peggy's lineup are Dark or Steel. If you've got either, use 'em. Otherwise, bring your strongest Pokémon that are not weak to Psychic attacks.

ROUND 7: GLACIERBADGE

Rocket Executive

NO.	Pokémon	Type		NO.	Pokémon	Type
113	Chansey	Normal		210	Granbull	Normal
162	Furret	Normal		203	Girafarig	Normal/Psychic
36	Clefable	Normal		20	Raticate	Normal

Suggested Types: Fighting, Steel, Ghost

Another upgraded Rocket Executive with the same batch of Normal-types from before. Bring your Fighting to pound them or a Steel or Ghost for sheer defense. Other than that, any strong Pokémon will do well here.

ROUND 8: RISINGBADGE

Juggler Dwight

NO.	Pokémon	Type		NO.	Pokémon	Type
182	Bellossom	Grass		171	Lanturn	Water/Electric
198	Murkrow	Dark/Flying		28	Sandslash	Ground
162	Furret	Normal		49	Venomoth	Bug/Poison

Suggested Types: Steel, Fire, Grass

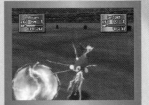

Your final opponent in the Ultra Ball division is Dwight and he hasn't changed his methods much. He still has a wide spectrum of Pokémon, so you'd be well advised to carefully examine his types. Try to bring Pokémon that are good against at least two of his types and strong defensively, as well.

With Dwight's defeat, the Ultra Ball trophy is yours.

MASTER BALL DIVISION

ROUND 1: ZEPHYRBADGE
Twins Jan&Jane

NO.	Pokémon	Type	NO.	Pokémon	Type
212	Scizor	Bug/Steel	123	Scyther	Bug/Flying
214	Heracross	Bug/Fighting	59	Arcanine	Fire
130	Gyarados	Water/Flying	178	Xatu	Psychic/Flying

Suggested Types: Fire, Electric, Water

Some impressive Pokémon bar your entry to the Master Ball division, but there are large holes in Jan & Jane's defense that you can use to your advantage. Bring a Fire for the Bug-types and any Steel that shows up, an Electric for the Flying-types, and a Water if a Fire-type pops up.

ROUND 2: HIVEBADGE
Schoolboy Oliver

NO.	Pokémon	Type	NO.	Pokémon	Type
212	Scizor	Bug/Steel	27	Sandshrew	Ground
208	Steelix	Steel/Ground	155	Cyndaquil	Fire
232	Donphan	Ground	246	Larvitar	Rock/Ground

Suggested Types: Water, Fire

Lots of Water will wash away Oliver's team, just as it did in Round 1. You may consider brining a Fire to melt the Steel-types down. Ice is also good against the Ground-types.

ROUND 3: PLAINBADGE
Sailor Curt

NO.	Pokémon	Type	NO.	Pokémon	Type
230	Kingdra	Water/Dragon	241	Miltank	Normal
124	Jynx	Ice/Psychic	131	Lapras	Water/Ice
9	Blastoise	Water	141	Kabutops	Rock/Water

Suggested Types: Electric, Fighting, Ice

This time, lots of Water composes your opponent's team. Bring Electric to crisp most of them, but be wary of the Ice- or Dragon-types that can show up. Fighting, Rock, or Steel are all decent against Ice, and you can use Ice of your own against Rock or Dragon hybrids. Because most Ice users are part Water, you'll be protected against Curt's Water attacks, as well.

ROUND 4: FOGBADGE
Swimmer♀ Darcy

NO.	Pokémon	Type	NO.	Pokémon	Type
94	Gengar	Ghost/Poison	217	Ursaring	Normal
242	Blissey	Normal	62	Poliwrath	Water/Fighting
233	Porygon2	Normal	214	Heracross	Bug/Fighting

Suggested Types: Psychic, Fighting, Steel

Lots of Pokémon are effective here, but you can use Psychic well against any mixed Fighting-types or Poison-types that show up. Your own Fighting and Steel will help take out the Normal-types. Really, any team of your strongest Pokémon is effective here.

ROUND 5: STORMBADGE
Officer Gerald

NO.	Pokémon	Type	NO.	Pokémon	Type
6	Charizard	Fire/Flying	3	Venusaur	Grass/Poison
71	Victreebel	Grass/Poison	103	Exeggutor	Grass/Psychic
59	Arcanine	Fire	157	Typhlosion	Fire

Suggested Types: Water, Fire, Ice, Psychic

A split mix of Fire and Grass means your team needs a mix of Water and Fire attacks to take them out. You can also bring along Ice to use against the Grass, meaning a single Water/Ice Pokémon can be used against his entire team. Finally, a Psychic is useful against the Poison hybrids.

ROUND 6: MINERALBADGE
Kimono Girl Emiko

NO.	Pokémon	Type	NO.	Pokémon	Type
181	Ampharos	Electric	68	Machamp	Fighting
229	Houndoom	Dark/Fire	121	Starmie	Water/Psychic
169	Crobat	Poison/Flying	115	Kangaskhan	Normal

Suggested Types: Electric, Steel

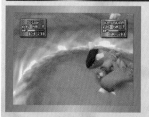

Not a lot of openings here, but you can use Electric against some of Emiko's Pokémon. Use Steel defensively, and examine her types carefully to decide your third Pokémon.

Round 7: GLACIERBADGE

Scientist Roberto

NO.	Pokémon	Type		NO.	Pokémon	Type
94	Gengar	Ghost/Poison		142	Aerodactyl	Rock/Flying
197	Umbreon	Dark		121	Starmie	Water/Psychic
38	Ninetales	Fire		124	Jynx	Ice/Psychic

Suggested Types: Steel, Electric, Water

Here we have another broad mix of types. Bring a Steel for defense and an Electric and Water for offense. Due to Roberto's spread out team, you may not have exactly the types you need to defeat him cleanly, so try to pick Pokémon that are strong against at least two of his.

Round 8: RISINGBADGE

Gentleman Travis

NO.	Pokémon	Type		NO.	Pokémon	Type
154	Meganium	Grass		181	Ampharos	Electric
131	Lapras	Water/Ice		31	Nidoqueen	Poison/Ground
78	Rapidash	Fire		123	Scyther	Bug/Flying

Suggested Types: Electric, Water, Fire

A lot of the elemental-type Pokémon show up on his team. You can use your own mix of Water, Fire, and Electric to take Travis down. A lot of switching will be required and expect your opponent to do the same.

When Travis is defeated, the Challenge Cup championship is in your hands and you're one step closer to defeating Round 2 of Stadium Mode.

48

STADIUM MODE ROUND 2

POKé CUP

- Level 50-55 Tournament

The Poké Cup is a bit tougher this time around, but it is nowhere near as frustrating as the Challenge Cup because you get to use your own team. If you have any difficulty with it, spend some time in the GB Tower raising your Pokémon a bit.

TOURNAMENT RULES

- 246 Different Pokémon are permitted for this tournament, check the list in game.
- Six different Pokémon may be used for the team, three can fight.
- All Pokémon must be level 50-55.
- The levels for the three battle Pokémon may not add up to more than 155.
- Items can be used, but each Pokémon must hold a different item.
- No two Pokémon may be asleep or frozen at the same time.
- Self-destructive moves may not be used on your final Pokémon.

POKé BALL DIVISION

 ### ROUND 1: ZEPHYRBADGE
Bug Catcher Nelson

NO.	Pokémon	Type
193	Yanma	Bug/Flying
123	Scyther	Bug/Flying
165	Ledyba	Bug/Flying

NO.	Pokémon	Type
14	Kakuna	Bug/Poison
168	Ariados	Bug/Poison
70	Weepinbell	Grass/Poison

Suggested Types: Fire, Electric

Nelson's unhealthy fascination with Bug-types continues into Round 2, and while a few of his Pokémon have grown up, you can still burn them all with Fire and zap the Flying-types with Electric.

 ### ROUND 2: HIVEBADGE
Swimmer♂ Bruce

NO.	Pokémon	Type
119	Seaking	Water
184	Azumarill	Water
171	Lanturn	Water/Electric

NO.	Pokémon	Type
211	Qwilfish	Water/Poison
87	Dewgong	Water/Ice
117	Seadra	Water

Suggested Types: Grass, Electric

Bruce's Pokémon have also evolved, but he's still vulnerable to a Grass and Electric assault. You may want to keep your Grass in reserve in case his Lanturn comes out, and let your Electric zap the rest of his Pokémon.

ROUND 3: PLAINBADGE
Hiker Chester

NO.	Pokémon	Type		NO.	Pokémon	Type
28	Sandslash	Ground		12	Butterfree	Bug/Flying
192	Sunflora	Grass		75	Graveler	Rock/Ground
141	Kabutops	Rock/Water		107	Hitmonchan	Fighting

Suggested Types: Water, Fire, Psychic

Chester seems to have learned his lesson a bit better. While Water will still sweep most of his Pokémon, you'll need to bring along some extras with the possibility of them doing more than warming the bench.

ROUND 4: FOGBADGE
Super Nerd Clifford

NO.	Pokémon	Type		NO.	Pokémon	Type
137	Porygon	Normal		247	Pupitar	Rock/Ground
204	Pineco	Bug		241	Miltank	Normal
101	Electrode	Electric		200	Misdreavus	Ghost

Suggested Types: Fighting, Grass, Fire

You can use a Grass-type against two of his Pokémon and a Fire-type against his Pineco. Bring along any strong Pokémon for your third and you'll be fine against his team. He'll try to use Swagger and then paralyze you to prevent you from attacking at all, but this can often backfire—Swagger will cause you to inflict even more damage and you can switch out if you don't like the odds.

ROUND 5: STORMBADGE
Beauty Alissa

NO.	Pokémon	Type		NO.	Pokémon	Type
185	Sudowoodo	Rock		176	Togetic	Normal/Flying
40	Wigglytuff	Normal		17	Pidgeotto	Normal/Flying
225	Delibird	Ice/Flying		105	Marowak	Ground

Suggested Types: Electric, Water

Three Flying-types means Electric is the order of the day. You can use a Water-type to sweep away Sudowoodo and Marowak. Use another strong Pokémon or bring a Fighting-type to deal with Wigglytuff and the half Normal hybrids.

ROUND 6: MINERALBADGE
Burgler Jensen

NO.	Pokémon	Type		NO.	Pokémon	Type
207	Gligar	Ground/Flying		38	Ninetales	Fire
206	Dunsparce	Normal		78	Rapidash	Fire
156	Quilava	Fire		208	Steelix	Steel/Ground

Suggested Types: Water

Extremely vulnerable to Water, you can wash out Jensen's entire team pretty easily. He's fond of using Thief, as his burglar title implies, but otherwise, there's not much to worry about here.

ROUND 7: GLACIERBADGE
Boarder Claude

NO.	Pokémon	Type		NO.	Pokémon	Type
215	Sneasel	Dark/Ice		148	Dragonair	Dragon
115	Kangaskhan	Normal		36	Clefable	Normal
113	Chansey	Normal		122	Mr. Mime	Psychic

Suggested Types: Steel, Water

Claude will use a lot of Ice attacks against you. Both Steel and Water are strong against Ice attacks, and you can bring any tough Pokémon you feel will do well to knock his out.

ROUND 8: RISINGBADGE
Psychic Mason

NO.	Pokémon	Type		NO.	Pokémon	Type
80	Slowbro	Water/Psychic		195	Quagsire	Water/Ground
234	Stantler	Normal		154	Meganium	Grass
57	Primeape	Fighting		235	Smeargle	Normal

Suggested Types: Grass, Psychic, Fire

A good Grass-type will deal with Mason's Slowbro and Quagsire. You can use a powerful Psychic of your own to deal with his Normal-types and Primeape. Bring a Fire-type if you want to torch Meganium.

With the defeat of Mason, the first Round 2 Poké Cup trophy is yours.

GREATBALL DIVISION

ROUND 1: ZEPHYRBADGE
PokéFan Carmen

NO.	Pokémon	Type	NO.	Pokémon	Type
192	Sunflora	Grass	211	Qwilfish	Water/Poison
114	Tangela	Grass	164	Noctowl	Normal/Flying
213	Shuckle	Bug/Rock	224	Octillery	Water

Suggested Types: Fire, Electric

An almost even split between Grass and Electric-vulnerable Pokémon means your team choices are pretty clear. Shuckle is only affected normally by Fire due to its Rock-type and it has a really high Defense, so you may wish to bring a Water or a strong Psychic to deal with it.

ROUND 2: HIVEBADGE
Youngster Wyatt

NO.	Pokémon	Type	NO.	Pokémon	Type
210	Granbull	Normal	132	Ditto	Normal
168	Ariados	Bug/Poison	22	Fearow	Normal/Flying
99	Kingler	Water	111	Rhyhorn	Ground/Rock

Suggested Types: Fighting, Psychic, Electric

There isn't much to Wyatt's team. You can use a Fighting-type or a strong Psychic against his Normal-types (which will also take care of Ariados), and bring along an Electric for Kingler and Fearow if you wish.

ROUND 3: PLAINBADGE
Firebreather Cliff

NO.	Pokémon	Type	NO.	Pokémon	Type
126	Magmar	Fire	38	Ninetales	Fire
219	Magcargo	Fire/Rock	237	Hitmontop	Fighting
108	Lickitung	Normal	182	Bellossom	Grass

Suggested Types: Water, Psychic

Firebreather Cliff lives up to his name, fielding half of a team that's vulnerable to Water. Bring a Psychic to deal with Hitmontop, Lickitung, and Bellossom if you feel the need.

ROUND 4: FOGBADGE
Biker Dillon

NO.	Pokémon	Type	NO.	Pokémon	Type
110	Weezing	Poison	181	Ampharos	Electric
227	Skarmory	Steel/Flying	91	Cloyster	Water/Ice
34	Nidoking	Poison/Ground	47	Parasect	Bug/Grass

Suggested Types: Psychic, Fire, Electric

You'll find a mix of types here. You can use Psychic against the Poison, Fire against the Steel and Bug, and Electric for the Water. Any of your three Pokémon should be able to take Ampharos as long as they aren't weak against Electric-types. Dillon likes to use Toxic and then use Protect while Toxic deals damage. However, if you keep attacking, Protect will fail and your attacks will go through anyway. You can also switch out when you know he'll waste a round using Protect.

ROUND 5: STORMBADGE
Teacher Molly

NO.	Pokémon	Type	NO.	Pokémon	Type
122	Mr. Mime	Psychic	28	Sandslash	Ground
203	Girafarig	Normal/Psychic	234	Stantler	Normal
49	Venomoth	Bug/Poison	235	Smeargle	Normal

Suggested Types: Dark, Water, Psychic

Any of your strong Pokémon can defeat this team pretty easily. If you want to do a bit of matching, bring a Dark- or Steel-type for defense and use Water- and Psychic-types to wipe out the rest of Molly's team. Avoid letting her have time to use Double Team repeatedly, or you could quickly find yourself in an untenable situation.

ROUND 6: MINERALBADGE
Sage Chen

NO.	Pokémon	Type
200	Misdreavus	Ghost
42	Golbat	Poison/Flying
73	Tentacruel	Water/Poison

NO.	Pokémon	Type
87	Dewgong	Water/Ice
89	Muk	Poison
197	Umbreon	Dark

Suggested Types: Psychic, Electric

Chen's team could be completely taken out with a Psychic and an Electric-type, but watch out for Umbreon showing up to spoil your Psychic fun.

ROUND 7: GLACIERBADGE
PokéFan Baxter

NO.	Pokémon	Type
3	Venusaur	Grass/Poison
226	Mantine	Water/Flying
82	Magneton	Electric/Steel

NO.	Pokémon	Type
113	Chansey	Normal
64	Kadabra	Psychic
141	Kabutops	Rock/Water

Suggested Types: Electric, Fire, Psychic

Use an Electric to take out Baxter's Mantine and Kabutops. Bring Fire to burn down his Venusaur and Magneton, and use a Psychic of your own to take care of Kadabra and Chansey.

ROUND 8: RISINGBADGE
Pokémaniac Pedro

NO.	Pokémon	Type
149	Dragonite	Dragon/Flying
134	Vaporeon	Water
232	Donphan	Ground

NO.	Pokémon	Type
103	Exeggutor	Grass/Psychic
106	Hitmonlee	Fighting
217	Ursaring	Normal

Suggested Types: Ice, Electric, Psychic

Your final opponent in the Great Ball division sports a Dragonite, but this just makes him even more vulnerable to Ice because you can use it against Dragonite, Donphan, and Exeggutor. Bring along an Electric and a Psychic for mop up work.

With Pedro's defeat, you are halfway through the Poké Cup.

52

ULTRA BALL DIVISION

ROUND 1: ZEPHYRBADGE
Bug Catcher Nelson

NO.	Pokémon	Type	NO.	Pokémon	Type
166	Ledian	Bug/Flying	193	Yanma	Bug/Flying
139	Omastar	Rock/Water	49	Venomoth	Bug/Poison
85	Dodrio	Normal/Flying	15	Beedrill	Bug/Poison

Suggested Types: Fire, Electric

Lots of Bug-types for Nelson, which can be handily burned by your Fire Pokémon. He also has three split Flying-types and Omastar, all of which are vulnerable to Electric.

ROUND 2: HIVEBADGE
Swimmer♂ Bruce

NO.	Pokémon	Type	NO.	Pokémon	Type
226	Mantine	Water/Flying	206	Dunsparce	Normal
222	Corsola	Water/Rock	91	Cloyster	Water/Ice
26	Raichu	Electric	119	Seaking	Water

Suggested Types: Electric, Grass

A very typical swimmer, Bruce brings along four Water-types and Raichu just to cause you problems. If you use a Grass against his Water-types, watch out for Ice attacks.

ROUND 3: PLAINBADGE

Hiker Chester

NO.	Pokémon	Type	NO.	Pokémon	Type
162	Furret	Normal	36	Clefable	Normal
108	Lickitung	Normal	184	Azumarill	Water
199	Slowking	Water/Psychic	78	Rapidash	Fire

Suggested Types: Electric, Water

Electric and Water will deal with half of Chester's team, and you can bring along a Fighting Pokémon or a strong Psychic to deal with the rest of his Normal Pokémon.

ROUND 4: FOGBADGE
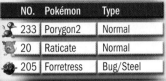
Super Nerd Clifford

NO.	Pokémon	Type	NO.	Pokémon	Type
233	Porygon2	Normal	171	Lanturn	Water/Electric
20	Raticate	Normal	82	Magneton	Electric/Steel
205	Forretress	Bug/Steel	51	Dugtrio	Ground

Suggested Types: Grass, Fire

The Normal-types shouldn't put up much of a fight, but you should bring along a Grass to deal with Lanturn, Dugtrio, and Magneton. Lastly, Fire will completely melt Forretress.

ROUND 5: STORMBADGE

Beauty Alissa

NO.	Pokémon	Type	NO.	Pokémon	Type
40	Wigglytuff	Normal	45	Vileplume	Grass/Poison
136	Flareon	Fire	189	Jumpluff	Grass/Flying
31	Nidoqueen	Poison/Ground	186	Politoed	Water

Suggested Types: Fire, Ground, Electric

A slightly better balanced team greets you at the halfway mark, but you can still deal with Alissa's team by using Fire for the Grass, Ground on Flareon and Nidoqueen, and Electric if Politoed drops in. You may also wish to bring an Ice for Nidoqueen and the Grass types. Alissa still uses Attract.

ROUND 6: MINERALBADGE

Burglar Jensen

NO.	Pokémon	Type	NO.	Pokémon	Type
53	Persian	Normal	127	Pinsir	Bug
208	Steelix	Steel/Ground	130	Gyarados	Water/Flying
198	Murkrow	Dark/Flying	146	Moltres	Fire/Flying

Suggested Types: Electric, Water

Jensen brings the Legendary Bird Moltres along with him, but you can wipe that out pretty easily with Electric or Water. Three of his team members are weak to Electric, and you can bring a third to deal with Pinsir and Persian.

ROUND 7: GLACIERBADGE
Boarder Claude

NO.	Pokémon	Type		NO.	Pokémon	Type
215	Sneasel	Dark/Ice		55	Golduck	Water
144	Articuno	Ice/Flying		115	Kangaskhan	Normal
242	Blissey	Normal		145	Zapdos	Electric/Flying

Suggested Types: Rock, Electric, Psychic

The other two Legendary Birds show up here, and both of Claude's Normal Pokémon are quite strong, so you'll need to use powerful Pokémon on your side. Electric will crisp Golduck and Articuno, Rock can be used well against Zapdos or Articuno, and a strong Psychic should be able to down Blissey and Kangaskhan.

ROUND 8: RISINGBADGE
Psychic Mason

NO.	Pokémon	Type		NO.	Pokémon	Type
178	Xatu	Psychic/Flying		9	Blastoise	Water
196	Espeon	Psychic		214	Heracross	Bug/Fighting
135	Jolteon	Electric		56	Mankey	Fighting

Suggested Types: Dark, Steel, Psychic, Grass

Mason has a strong team this time around, but he has a lot of weaknesses. Dark or Steel will serve you well against his Psychics. Psychic will take out his Fighting-types (just be careful with Heracross). Grass will do well against Jolteon and Blastoise.

With Mason defeated, you have only one division left in the Poké Cup.

MASTER BALL DIVISION

ROUND 1: ZEPHYRBADGE
PokéFan Carmen

NO.	Pokémon	Type		NO.	Pokémon	Type
221	Piloswine	Ice/Ground		71	Victreebel	Grass/Poison
97	Hypno	Psychic		76	Golem	Rock/Ground
87	Dewgong	Water/Ice		36	Clefable	Normal

Suggested Types: Water, Ice, Dark

Carmen's team doesn't have any easy openings to use at all. Indeed, if you have certain hybrid Pokémon, you'll have a much easier time of it. Bring a Water/Ice for resistance to some of her attacks and to use Ice against her Ground and Grass. A Dark will protect you from the Psychic and if you have Houndoom, you can use its Fire against Victreebel as well.

ROUND 2: HIVEBADGE
Youngster Wyatt

NO.	Pokémon	Type		NO.	Pokémon	Type
210	Granbull	Normal		22	Fearow	Normal/Flying
168	Ariados	Bug/Poison		112	Rhydon	Ground/Rock
160	Feraligatr	Water		128	Tauros	Normal

Suggested Types: Fighting, Grass, Electric

Bring along a Fighting or a strong Pokémon to deal with the Normal-types, a Grass for Rhydon and Feraligatr, with an Electric-type for backup against Feraligatr and Fearow.

ROUND 3: PLAINBADGE
Firebreather Cliff

NO.	Pokémon	Type		NO.	Pokémon	Type
6	Charizard	Fire/Flying		242	Blissey	Normal
157	Typhlosion	Fire		31	Nidoqueen	Poison/Ground
199	Slowking	Water/Psychic		103	Exeggutor	Grass/Psychic

Suggested Types: Water, Dark, Steel

A single Water Pokémon is effective against half of Cliff's team, but you may want to bring along a Dark or a Steel for defense against the Psychics. You'll also need a strong Fighting or other Pokémon to take out Blissey.

ROUND 4: FOGBADGE
Biker Dillon

NO.	Pokémon	Type		NO.	Pokémon	Type
241	Miltank	Normal		227	Skarmory	Steel/Flying
134	Vaporeon	Water		89	Muk	Poison
110	Weezing	Poison		181	Ampharos	Electric

Suggested Types: Psychic, Electric

Bring a Psychic and an Electric to deal with four parts of Dillon's team. Use an Electric to zap Vaporeon and Skarmory. You may wish to bring a Grass- or a Ground-type to take care of Ampharos.

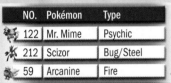

ROUND 5: STORMBADGE
Teacher Molly

NO.	Pokémon	Type		NO.	Pokémon	Type
122	Mr. Mime	Psychic		203	Girafarig	Normal/Psychic
212	Scizor	Bug/Steel		20	Raticate	Normal
59	Arcanine	Fire		195	Quagsire	Water/Ground

Suggested Types: Dark, Fire, Grass

A Dark type can handle the Psychics. Fire will work against her friendly Scizor, and a Grass can take care of Quagsire. Watch out for her evasion tactics—she's still fond of Double Team.

ROUND 6: MINERALBADGE
Sage Chen

NO.	Pokémon	Type		NO.	Pokémon	Type
169	Crobat	Poison/Flying		124	Jynx	Ice/Psychic
197	Umbreon	Dark		200	Misdreavus	Ghost
244	Entei	Fire		131	Lapras	Water/Ice

Suggested Types: Electric, Steel, Water

The Legendary Cat Entei appears in Chen's lineup; you may want to bring a Water (or a Rock-type) to fight it. For Lapras and Crobat, you can use an Electric, and Steel will deal with Umbreon and Jynx quite nicely.

ROUND 7: GLACIERBADGE
PokéFan Baxter

NO.	Pokémon	Type		NO.	Pokémon	Type
78	Rapidash	Fire		142	Aerodactyl	Rock/Flying
245	Suicune	Water		105	Marowak	Ground
65	Alakazam	Psychic		101	Electrode	Electric

Suggested Types: Water, Grass

Despite the appearance of the second Legendary Cat, Suicune, you can take out Baxter's whole team with a Water- and a Grass-type. Bring along a third Pokémon of your choice that matches up well against his Pokémon.

ROUND 8: RISINGBADGE
Pokémaniac Pedro

NO.	Pokémon	Type		NO.	Pokémon	Type
94	Gengar	Ghost/Poison		125	Electabuzz	Electric
121	Starmie	Water/Psychic		68	Machamp	Fighting
143	Snorlax	Normal		149	Dragonite	Dragon/Flying

Suggested Types: Ice, Grass, Psychic

No third cat here, but you do get an appearance by Dragonite, which really isn't much of a threat as long as you bring an Ice attack. Snorlax, on the other hand, can be much more annoying, so make sure you have a very powerful Pokémon to deal with it. Finally, a Psychic will put Gengar and Machamp in their place. Bring a Grass for Starmie and Electabuzz.

Once Pedro is defeated, the Poké Cup championship is in your hands and only one Cup remains for the entire Round 2 Stadium!

PRIME CUP

- Level 1-100 Tournament

Round two of the Prime Cup is guaranteed to hit you with every powerful Pokémon in the game, but you can finally cut loose with your own powerhouse team, so not much will be different. Other than that, you can expect the computer to use status-affecting attacks heavily and it will switch Pokémon much more often.

TOURNAMENT RULES

- All 251 Pokémon are permitted.
- Six different Pokémon may be used for the team, three can fight.
- No level restrictions apply.
- Items can be used, but each Pokémon must hold a different item.
- No two Pokémon may be asleep or frozen at the same time.
- Self-destructive moves may not be used on your final Pokémon.

ROUND 1: ZEPHYRBADGE
Lass Terry

NO.	Pokémon	Type		NO.	Pokémon	Type
182	Bellossom	Grass		208	Steelix	Steel/Ground
242	Blissey	Normal		189	Jumpluff	Grass/Flying
232	Donphan	Ground		241	Miltank	Normal

Suggested Types: Fire, Ice

Terry has pretty much swapped out her team and now she's quite vulnerable to Fire and Ice. Bring along strong attackers of each type, as well as your token overpowered Psychic to deal with her others.

ROUND 2: HIVEBADGE
Blackbelt Yang

NO.	Pokémon	Type		NO.	Pokémon	Type
202	Wobbuffet	Psychic		57	Primeape	Fighting
9	Blastoise	Water		214	Heracross	Bug/Fighting
73	Tentacruel	Water/Poison		62	Poliwrath	Water/Fighting

Suggested Types: Psychic, Electric

Half a team of Water and three total Fighting-types give you an easy opening with Psychic and Electric of your own. You can bring along a Dark for Wobbuffet, but given that it normally uses reaction moves, you don't really need a specific type against it.

ROUND 3: PLAINBADGE
Bird Keeper Adam

NO.	Pokémon	Type		NO.	Pokémon	Type
149	Dragonite	Dragon/Flying		146	Moltres	Fire/Flying
178	Xatu	Psychic/Flying		145	Zapdos	Electric/Flying
142	Aerodactyl	Rock/Flying		144	Articuno	Ice/Flying

Suggested Types: Ice, Electric

Adam has certainly upgraded his team, and while he is sporting some of the most powerful Flying-types in the game, he is still extremely vulnerable to Ice and Electric. Bring along both to knock him out of the skies.

ROUND 5: STORMBADGE
Fisherman Chase

NO.	Pokémon	Type		NO.	Pokémon	Type
139	Omastar	Rock/Water		110	Weezing	Poison
160	Feraligatr	Water		195	Quagsire	Water/Ground
171	Lanturn	Water/Electric		80	Slowbro	Water/Psychic

Suggested Types: Electric, Grass

Again, you'll see a lot of powerful Pokémon, but nearly all Water-types, making them quite vulnerable to either your Electric or Grass Pokémon. Grass is especially useful against both Lanturn and Quagsire because their types make Electric a poor choice with which to fight.

57

ROUND 4: FOGBADGE
Cooltrainer Floria

NO.	Pokémon	Type		NO.	Pokémon	Type
97	Hypno	Psychic		186	Politoed	Water
103	Exeggutor	Grass/Psychic		122	Mr. Mime	Psychic
78	Rapidash	Fire		196	Espeon	Psychic

Suggested Types: Dark, Steel, Electric

Floria has a much more Psychic-slanted team this time around. A Dark or a Steel-type is almost a necessity to defeat her. If you do use a Steel-type, be wary of her Rapidash. You can use an Electric to get rid of Politoed and fight evenly with Rapidash.

ROUND 6: MINERALBADGE
Scientist Craig

NO.	Pokémon	Type		NO.	Pokémon	Type
121	Starmie	Water/Psychic		234	Stantler	Normal
197	Umbreon	Dark		169	Crobat	Poison/Flying
200	Misdreavus	Ghost		101	Electrode	Electric

Suggested Types: Dark, Steel, Psychic

A Dark- or Steel-type can deal with Starmie, Umbreon, and Misdreavus. You may want your own Psychic for Crobat and the others. You can type match a bit more if you feel the need, but Craig's team isn't quite the same caliber as the others you've faced up to this point.

ROUND 7: GLACIERBADGE
Skier Kathy

NO.	Pokémon	Type		NO.	Pokémon	Type
245	Suicune	Water		230	Kingdra	Water/Dragon
248	Tyranitar	Dark/Rock		212	Scizor	Bug/Steel
143	Snorlax	Normal		135	Jolteon	Electric

Suggested Types: Ice, Water, Fire

Kathy has a very powerful team here. You can use Grass defensively against Suicune, Kingdra, and Jolteon. Ice will serve you well against Kingdra, and you can use Water on Tyranitar and Scizor. Because she tends to use a lot of Ice attacks, your Grass may have problems against some of her team, so you may want to match up your Pokémon against hers more specifically and avoid using Grass altogether if you have a strong enough team.

ROUND 8: RISINGBADGE
Cooltrainer Marty

NO.	Pokémon	Type		NO.	Pokémon	Type
251	Celebi	Grass/Psychic		68	Machamp	Fighting
53	Persian	Normal		131	Lapras	Water/Ice
94	Gengar	Ghost/Poison		243	Raikou	Electric

Suggested Types: Dark, Psychic, Electric

Celebi! The little Grass/Psychic Pokémon is cute, but it's rather vulnerable to either Dark or Fire. You can also bring along a Psychic type for Gengar and Machamp, and send an Electric-type to fry Lapras. For Raikou, either bring a specific Pokémon to use against it or let a Pokémon that isn't weak deal with it.

With Marty down, Round 2 of the Stadium is done and only the Gym Leader Castle is between you and your final victory!

GYM LEADER CASTLE ROUND 2

Again, you must go through the Johto and Kanto castles. This time, the trainers and gym leaders will have upgraded their Pokémon. You can still use your Prime Cup team to good effect through both castles and failing that, your Poké Cup team may be good enough to handle it.

GYM LEADER CASTLE RULES

- All 251 Pokémon may enter.
- Six different Pokémon may be used for the team, three can fight.
- No level restrictions apply.
- Gym Leaders will use level 50 Pokémon, but if you use any higher level Pokémon, all of their Pokémon will be raised to the highest level you use.
- Items can be used, but each Pokémon must hold a different item.
- No two Pokémon may be asleep or frozen at the same time.
- Self-destructive moves may not be used on your final Pokémon.

VIOLET GYM, LEADER FALKNER

TRAINER 1:
Bird Keeper Matt

NO.	Pokémon	Type
17	Pidgeotto	Normal/Flying
176	Togetic	Normal/Flying
22	Fearow	Normal/Flying

NO.	Pokémon	Type
83	Farfetch'd	Normal/Flying
164	Noctowl	Normal/Flying
198	Murkrow	Dark/Flying

Suggested Types: Electric

While Matt has evolved all of his Pokémon, he still hasn't learned his lesson. Bring an Electric Pokémon and zap all of his birds again.

TRAINER 2:
Gym Leader Falkner

NO.	Pokémon	Type
18	Pidgeot	Normal/Flying
85	Dodrio	Normal/Flying
207	Gligar	Ground/Flying

NO.	Pokémon	Type
6	Charizard	Fire/Flying
227	Skarmory	Steel/Flying
145	Zapdos	Electric/Flying

Suggested Types: Electric, Ice

With the exception of Zapdos and Gligar, you can still fry the majority of Falkner's team with an Electric. Use your second and third slots to deal with Zapdos and Gligar, preferably with an Ice attack.

TRAINER 1:
Bug Catcher Chaz

NO.	Pokémon	Type		NO.	Pokémon	Type
15	Beedrill	Bug/Poison		27	Sandshrew	Ground
192	Sunflora	Grass		193	Yanma	Bug/Flying
12	Butterfree	Bug/Flying		206	Dunsparce	Normal

Suggested Types: Fire, Ice

Chaz has changed his team around a little since the Round 1 fight, but it's still not much of a match for some good Fire and Ice attacks to burn and freeze his Pokémon.

TRAINER 2:
Twins Min&Lyn

NO.	Pokémon	Type		NO.	Pokémon	Type
166	Ledian	Bug/Flying		204	Pineco	Bug
133	Eevee	Normal		209	Snubbull	Normal
77	Ponyta	Fire		30	Nidorina	Poison

Suggested Types: Fire, Water

A little Fire and Water will take care of most of Min & Lyn's team, and you can bring any strong Pokémon to deal with the Normal-types and Nidorina.

TRAINER 3:
Gym Leader Bugsy

NO.	Pokémon	Type		NO.	Pokémon	Type
123	Scyther	Bug/Flying		195	Quagsire	Water/Ground
214	Heracross	Bug/Fighting		185	Sudowoodo	Rock
127	Pinsir	Bug		20	Raticate	Normal

Suggested Types: Fire, Water

What would a battle against Bugsy be without lots of Bug-types to cook with Fire? You may want to bring along a Water-type for Quagsire and Sudowoodo.

TRAINER 1:
Lass Lois

NO.	Pokémon	Type		NO.	Pokémon	Type
162	Furret	Normal		189	Jumpluff	Grass/Flying
137	Porygon	Normal		222	Corsola	Water/Rock
51	Dugtrio	Ground		190	Aipom	Normal

Suggested Types: Water, Electric, Fighting

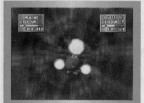

Water- and Electric-types can be used against Dugtrio, Jumpluff, and Corsola. You can bring a Fighting-type to deal with Lois' Normal Pokémon if you feel the need, but any strong Pokémon should do.

TRAINER 2:
Beauty Rita

NO.	Pokémon	Type		NO.	Pokémon	Type
25	Pikachu	Electric		40	Wigglytuff	Normal
176	Togetic	Normal/Flying		184	Azumarill	Water
36	Clefable	Normal		225	Delibird	Ice/Flying

Suggested Types: Electric, Fighting

An Electric will zap Delibird and Togetic, and you can use any strong Pokémon to deal with the rest. A Fighting-type will do well against the Normal-types of course; just watch that you don't bring anything weak against Pikachu.

TRAINER 3:
Gym Leader Whitney

NO.	Pokémon	Type		NO.	Pokémon	Type
241	Miltank	Normal		232	Donphan	Ground
55	Golduck	Water		122	Mr. Mime	Psychic
53	Persian	Normal		128	Tauros	Normal

Suggested Types: Dark, Steel, Grass

Dark and Steel are both handy against Mr. Mime, and Steel is good defensively against all but Donphan and Golduck; use a Grass-type against those two.

ECRUTEAK GYM, LEADER MORTY

TRAINER 1:
Medium Holly

NO.	Pokémon	Type	NO.	Pokémon	Type
92	Gastly	Ghost/Poison	211	Qwilfish	Water/Poison
164	Noctowl	Normal/Flying	119	Seaking	Water
70	Weepinbell	Grass/Poison	132	Ditto	Normal

Suggested Types: Psychic, Electric

Holly's team is very similar to her team in Round 1, but with a few evolutions. The lineup is quite weak to Psychic- and Electric-types due to all the Poison and Water. Bring both and move on to the next trainer.

TRAINER 2:
Sage Ty

NO.	Pokémon	Type	NO.	Pokémon	Type
93	Haunter	Ghost/Poison	42	Golbat	Poison/Flying
88	Grimer	Poison	89	Muk	Poison
124	Jynx	Ice/Psychic	198	Murkrow	Dark/Flying

Suggested Types: Psychic

A single Psychic can take out most of Ty's team, but if you're worried about Jynx or Murkrow, bring a Rock-type for both of them, or bring a Fire-type for Jynx and an Electric for Murkrow.

TRAINER 3:
Gym Leader Morty

NO.	Pokémon	Type	NO.	Pokémon	Type
94	Gengar	Ghost/Poison	131	Lapras	Water/Ice
226	Mantine	Water/Flying	200	Misdreavus	Ghost
210	Granbull	Normal	103	Exeggutor	Grass/Psychic

Suggested Types: Electric, Dark

For the leader of a haunted gym, Morty has a pretty strange team, though he does have Gengar and Misdreavus present. You can use Electric to take care of his Water Pokémon and Dark for the rest.

CIANWOOD GYM, LEADER CHUCK

TRAINER 1:
Blackbelt Nick

NO.	Pokémon	Type	NO.	Pokémon	Type
67	Machoke	Fighting	24	Arbok	Poison
75	Graveler	Rock/Ground	148	Dragonair	Dragon
99	Kingler	Water	127	Pinsir	Bug

Suggested Types: Psychic, Ice, Grass

A good variety of Pokémon makes up Nick's team. You can use Psychic against Machoke and Arbok. Pit Ice against Graveler and Dragonair. Send Grass against Graveler and Kingler. Most of your team should be able to handle Pinsir.

61

TRAINER 2:
Gym Leader Chuck

NO.	Pokémon	Type	NO.	Pokémon	Type
62	Poliwrath	Water/Fighting	181	Ampharos	Electric
28	Sandslash	Ground	107	Hitmonchan	Fighting
217	Ursaring	Normal	97	Hypno	Psychic

Suggested Types: Psychic, Grass

Chuck has a bit less emphasis on Fighting-types this time around, but he's still vulnerable to Psychic. You can use Grass against Sandslash and Ampharos. You might want to bring a Dark or a Steel against Hypno.

OLIVINE GYM, LEADER JASMINE

TRAINER 1:
Gym Leader Jasmine

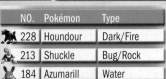

NO.	Pokémon	Type	NO.	Pokémon	Type
208	Steelix	Steel/Ground	80	Slowbro	Water/Psychic
234	Stantler	Normal	78	Rapidash	Fire
9	Blastoise	Water	212	Scizor	Bug/Steel

Suggested Types: Fire, Electric, Water

Jasmine is still using a few Steel Pokémon, but less focus is placed there and she has a slightly broader team. Use a Fire to melt her Steel-types down, Electric for the Water, and a Water of your own for Rapidash.

62

TEAM ROCKET ENCOUNTER

TRAINER 1:
Rocket Grunt

NO.	Pokémon	Type	NO.	Pokémon	Type
110	Weezing	Poison	185	Sudowoodo	Rock
101	Electrode	Electric	205	Forretress	Bug/Steel
91	Cloyster	Water/Ice	76	Golem	Rock/Ground

Suggested Types: Grass, Water

No tremendous reliance on Poison makes this Rocket Grunt a better challenger than usual. You can use Grass against Electrode, Sudowoodo, and Golem. Send Water against Sudowoodo, Forretress, and Golem. Finally, you may wish to bring an Electric of your own for Cloyster.

TRAINER 2:
Rocket Grunt

NO.	Pokémon	Type	NO.	Pokémon	Type
228	Houndour	Dark/Fire	90	Shellder	Water
213	Shuckle	Bug/Rock	95	Onix	Rock/Ground
184	Azumarill	Water	87	Dewgong	Water/Ice

Suggested Types: Electric, Water

A split mix of types leaves this Grunt wide open to an Electric and Water assault from your Pokémon.

TRAINER 3:
Rocket Executive

NO.	Pokémon	Type	NO.	Pokémon	Type
45	Vileplume	Grass/Poison	141	Kabutops	Rock/Water
24	Arbok	Poison	71	Victreebel	Grass/Poison
219	Magcargo	Fire/Rock	42	Golbat	Poison/Flying

Suggested Types: Psychic, Water

This executive would do well to learn from her underlings—lots of Poison is not healthy for you. Bring along your Psychic to deal with the Poison Pokémon, and bring a Water-type to wash out Magcargo and Kabutops.

TRAINER 4:
Rocket Executive

NO.	Pokémon	Type	NO.	Pokémon	Type
229	Houndoom	Dark/Fire	97	Hypno	Psychic
224	Octillery	Water	47	Parasect	Bug/Grass
202	Wobbuffet	Psychic	248	Tyranitar	Rock/Dark

Suggested Types: Dark, Water, Fire

Your last Team Rocket opponent holds a fairly strong lineup. You can use Dark to chew up his Psychic members, Water for Houndoom and Tyranitar, and Fire for Parasect. If you have the right Pokémon, you can mix in some Electric for Octillery.

MAHOGANY GYM, LEADER PRYCE

TRAINER 1:
Boarder Alvin

	NO.	Pokémon	Type		NO.	Pokémon	Type
	86	Seel	Water		82	Magneton	Electric/Steel
	64	Kadabra	Psychic		3	Venusaur	Grass/Poison
	225	Delibird	Ice/Flying		215	Sneasel	Dark/Ice

Suggested Types: Fire, Electric

There isn't much to Alvin's squad this time around. He's using slightly different Pokémon, and now he's pretty badly vulnerable to Fire and Electric.

TRAINER 2:
Skier Carol

	NO.	Pokémon	Type		NO.	Pokémon	Type
	117	Seadra	Water		105	Marowak	Ground
	20	Raticate	Normal		61	Poliwhirl	Water
	139	Omastar	Rock/Water		53	Persian	Normal

Suggested Types: Electric, Water

Lots of Water and Carol's fondness for Ice attacks means Electric will be your primary offense. You can use a Water-type against Omastar and Marowak to good effect. Bring along any strong Pokémon to fill out your team against the others.

TRAINER 3:
Gym Leader Pryce

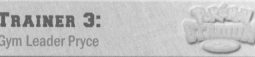

	NO.	Pokémon	Type		NO.	Pokémon	Type
	221	Piloswine	Ice/Ground		73	Tentacruel	Water/Poison
	195	Quagsire	Water/Ground		203	Girafarig	Normal/Psychic
	237	Hitmontop	Fighting		144	Articuno	Ice/Flying

Suggested Types: Water, Psychic, Electric

Minus an upgrade to Articuno, Pryce's team isn't that much more dangerous. You can use Water against Piloswine and Quagsire just fine. Send a Psychic to do your bidding against Hitmontop and Tentacruel. Finally, an Electric will crisp Articuno.

BLACKTHORN GYM, LEADER CLAIR

TRAINER 1:
Cooltrainer Gloria

	NO.	Pokémon	Type		NO.	Pokémon	Type
	235	Smeargle	Normal		55	Golduck	Water
	114	Tangela	Grass		93	Haunter	Ghost/Poison
	124	Jynx	Ice/Psychic		38	Ninetales	Fire

Suggested Types: Fire, Electric, Water

An odd mix of types meets you at the entrance to Blackthorn Gym. Bring a Fire to toast Tangela and melt Jynx. Use a Water type to wash out Ninetales.

TRAINER 2:
Cooltrainer Vince

	NO.	Pokémon	Type		NO.	Pokémon	Type
	2	Ivysaur	Grass/Poison		153	Bayleef	Grass
	8	Wartortle	Water		159	Croconaw	Water
	5	Charmeleon	Fire		156	Quilava	Fire

Suggested Types: Fire, Electric, Water

Vince has evolved his Pokémon one step, but you can still use the same match-ups to take all of his Pokémon down. You'll need to do a bit of switching unless you have multiple effective moves on a single Pokémon.

TRAINER 3:
Gym Leader Clair

	NO.	Pokémon	Type		NO.	Pokémon	Type
	230	Kingdra	Water/Dragon		112	Rhydon	Ground/Rock
	181	Ampharos	Electric		6	Charizard	Fire/Flying
	34	Nidoking	Poison/Ground		130	Gyarados	Water/Flying

Suggested Types: Electric, Ice, Water

Using very close to the same team she did in Round 1, Clair will fall to a good mix of Electric for her Flying Pokémon, Ice for the Dragon and Ground, and Water as insurance against the Ground-based Pokémon.

ELITE FOUR

TRAINER 1:
Elite Four Will

NO.	Pokémon	Type	NO.	Pokémon	Type
178	Xatu	Psychic/Flying	136	Flareon	Fire
125	Electabuzz	Electric	113	Chansey	Normal
226	Mantine	Water/Flying	97	Hypno	Psychic

Suggested Types: Dark, Electric, Water

Apparently, Will has decided he is no longer the master of Psychic Pokémon. This time around, he has mixed in a bunch of other types. You don't really need to use a Dark for his Psychics, but you can, or use a Steel if you want. An Electric will crisp Xatu and Mantine, and a Water will wash out Flareon. You can use any strong Pokémon against Electabuzz, though you could bring a Ground if you want.

TRAINER 2:
Elite Four Koga

NO.	Pokémon	Type	NO.	Pokémon	Type
49	Venomoth	Bug/Poison	234	Stantler	Normal
126	Magmar	Fire	171	Lanturn	Water/Electric
131	Lapras	Water/Ice	168	Ariados	Bug/Poison

Suggested Types: Fire, Electric, Water

Koga is also all over the board with his Pokémon team. Bring a Fire for his few Bug types. An Electric will work well against Lapras and Lanturn, and a Water-type is a good match for Magmar if it shows up.

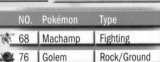

TRAINER 3:
Elite Four Bruno

NO.	Pokémon	Type	NO.	Pokémon	Type
68	Machamp	Fighting	210	Granbull	Normal
76	Golem	Rock/Ground	103	Exeggutor	Grass/Psychic
57	Primeape	Fighting	217	Ursaring	Normal

Suggested Types: Psychic, Water, Fire

Bruno has not spread out his team as well as his companions have, and you can use a Psychic to good effect against most of his squad. A Water-type will firmly wash out Golem, and a Fire-type will torch Exeggutor.

TRAINER 4:
Elite Four Karen

NO.	Pokémon	Type	NO.	Pokémon	Type
197	Umbreon	Dark	80	Slowbro	Water/Psychic
53	Persian	Normal	200	Misdreavus	Ghost
198	Murkrow	Dark/Flying	101	Electrode	Electric

Suggested Types: Electric, Dark

While Karen has two Dark types and a Psychic; they really aren't strong enough to worry about too much. You can bring an Electric to zap Murkrow, a Dark of your own for Misdreavus and Slowbro, and a Grass or Ground for Electrode. If you have them, Bug- or Fighting-types are also strong against Dark if you're worried about Umbreon.

FINAL FIGHT, JOHTO CASTLE

JOHTO CHAMPION:
Lance

NO.	Pokémon	Type	NO.	Pokémon	Type
149	Dragonite	Dragon/Flying	115	Kangaskhan	Normal
142	Aerodactyl	Rock/Flying	59	Arcanine	Fire
160	Feraligatr	Water	248	Tyranitar	Rock/Dark

Suggested Types: Ice, Electric, Water

Lance's team isn't much different from Round 1 of the Gym Leader Castle, and while Ice and Electric are still useful, you may wish to bring along a Water type to help wash out Aerodactyl, Arcanine, and Tyranitar.

Once Lance is down the second time, you have only the Kanto Gym Leaders and your Rival before your ultimate victory!

PEWTER GYM

GYM LEADER:
Brock

NO.	Pokémon	Type	NO.	Pokémon	Type
208	Steelix	Steel/Ground	80	Slowbro	Water/Psychic
214	Heracross	Bug/Fighting	217	Ursaring	Normal
112	Rhydon	Ground/Rock	213	Shuckle	Bug/Rock

Suggested Types: Water, Electric, Psychic

Brock has swapped Pokémon around somewhat, but he's still very vulnerable to Water. If you want extra type-matching against him, bring an Electric for Slowbro and a fast Psychic to blast Heracross before he gets a move in.

VERMILION GYM

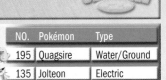

GYM LEADER:
Lt. Surge

NO.	Pokémon	Type	NO.	Pokémon	Type
26	Raichu	Electric	195	Quagsire	Water/Ground
71	Victreebel	Grass/Poison	135	Jolteon	Electric
233	Porygon2	Normal	85	Dodrio	Normal

Suggested Types: Ground, Ice

The trend of mixing in Pokémon that are invulnerable to the gym's weakness continues here. Lt. Surge brings a Victreebel and a Quagsire to the party. You can get rid of both with Ice. Use Ground or Grass of your own against the Electric attacks, and bring any strong Pokémon for the Normal-types.

CERULEAN GYM

GYM LEADER:
Misty

NO.	Pokémon	Type	NO.	Pokémon	Type
121	Starmie	Water/Psychic	181	Ampharos	Electric
40	Wigglytuff	Normal	148	Dragonair	Dragon
31	Nidoqueen	Poison/Ground	186	Politoed	Water

Suggested Types: Electric, Ice

Apparently, being a Water-focused gym leader means training an Electric Pokémon. But Misty is just trying to throw a wrench into your plans of using all Electric-types. You can still get away with it; just bring an Ice-type for Nidoqueen and Dragonair.

CELADON GYM

GYM LEADER:
Erika

NO.	Pokémon	Type	NO.	Pokémon	Type
182	Bellossom	Grass	226	Mantine	Water/Flying
105	Marowak	Ground	242	Blissey	Normal
38	Ninetales	Fire	103	Exeggutor	Grass/Psychic

Suggested Types: Ice, Electric, Water

This is another gym with Pokémon types all over the place. Ice will do well against the Grass-types and Marowak. A good Electric attack will put Mantine down. Sending your own Water to douse Ninetales and Marowak is advisable.

FUCHSIA GYM

GYM LEADER:
Janine

NO.	Pokémon	Type	NO.	Pokémon	Type
169	Crobat	Poison/Flying	134	Vaporeon	Water
154	Meganium	Grass	205	Forretress	Bug/Steel
89	Muk	Poison	203	Girafarig	Normal/Psychic

Suggested Types: Psychic, Fire, Electric

A little less Poison makes Janine's team less vulnerable to a clean sweep from a Psychic, but you can still bring one along. A Fire-type will totally melt Forretress and torch Meganium, and an Electric-type will help with Vaporeon.

CINNABAR GYM

GYM LEADER:
Blaine

NO.	Pokémon	Type	NO.	Pokémon	Type
59	Arcanine	Fire	36	Clefable	Normal
122	Mr. Mime	Psychic	45	Vileplume	Grass/Poison
113	Chansey	Normal	146	Moltres	Fire/Flying

Suggested Types: Water, Psychic

Learning from his fellow gym leaders, Blaine has diversified his team, so while you can still use Water, you may wish to bring a strong Psychic for Vileplume and the Normal-types. Given how annoying Chansey and Clefable can be at times, an extremely strong physical Pokémon is also an asset in this fight.

SAFFRON GYM

GYM LEADER:
Sabrina

NO.	Pokémon	Type	NO.	Pokémon	Type
65	Alakazam	Psychic	106	Hitmonlee	Fighting
212	Scizor	Bug/Steel	28	Sandslash	Ground
157	Typhlosion	Fire	199	Slowking	Water/Psychic

Suggested Types: Fire, Water, Electric

Fire, Water, and Electric will take care of most of Sabrina's Pokémon, though you may wish to bring a Dark- or Steel-type specifically for her Psychics. However, given that she's using only two, you may not need heavy defense.

VIRIDIAN GYM

GYM LEADER:
Blue

NO.	Pokémon	Type	NO.	Pokémon	Type
123	Scyther	Bug/Flying	229	Houndoom	Dark/Fire
241	Miltank	Normal	221	Piloswine	Ice/Ground
94	Gengar	Ghost/Poison	230	Kingdra	Water/Dragon

Suggested Types: Ice, Water, Psychic

Blue's lineup is one of the better teams you have faced as far as type diversity is concerned, but the individual Pokémon aren't especially strong. Bring an Ice-type for Scyther, Kingdra, and Piloswine. Send a Water-type against Houndoom and Piloswine, and include a Psychic-type for Gengar and anyone but Houndoom.

66

???:
Red

NO.	Pokémon	Type		NO.	Pokémon	Type
243	Raikou	Electric		149	Dragonite	Dragon/Flying
244	Entei	Fire		143	Snorlax	Normal
245	Suicune	Water		196	Espeon	Psychic

Suggested Types: Water/Ice, Electric, Ground

All three of the Legendary Cats are on Red's team, but you can still type match to take them out. Dragonite is as vulnerable to Ice as it always has been. Espeon can be battered down or you can use Dark or Steel, and Snorlax will fall to any very strong physical Pokémon.

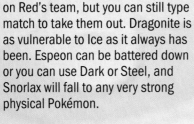

TRAINER:
Rival

NO.	Pokémon	Type
150	Mewtwo	Psychic
250	Ho-oh	Fire/Flying
249	Lugia	Psychic/Flying

Suggested Types: Dark, Ice, Electric

Nothing has changed on your Rival's team. While he has arguably three of the strongest Pokémon in the game, you get to use a full team of six, and he's still weak against Dark, Ice, Electric, and even Water if you want to use it.

You're done! You've conquered both rounds of the Stadium and Gym Leader Castle, and you've proven your skills against every challenger in the land, under every condition possible! Enjoy the credits for the last time. Victory is yours, and there are always more Pokémon to catch and teams to train!

67

MINI-GAMES

GUTSY GOLBAT

DESCRIPTION

Press the A Button repeatedly to go up. Use the Control Stick to move from side to side. The one who collects the most hearts wins. Your hearts will scatter for others to collect if you hit a Magnemite or get hit hard by an opponent.

TIPS

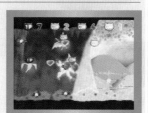

- It helps to keep your distance from opposing players.
- There are often a lot of Magnemite near the bottom of the screen, so venture there at your own risk.
- Stay at the right side of the screen near the beginning of the game to quickly grab some hearts as the game begins. Once you have a few, back off to avoid getting hit.
- If you're desperate for hearts near the end of the game, jump into the melee with your opponents in the hope of stealing some of theirs.

TOPSY-TURVY

DESCRIPTION

Use the Control Stick to guide your path. Bump into opponents to knock them out of the ring. Knock your opponent out of the ring five times to win. Press the A Button to use Rapid Spin. Use this move to knock your opponent out of the ring.

TIPS

- Be careful with the Control Stick—you can accidentally steer yourself out of the ring! However, this is not detrimental.
- Try to stay near the center of the ring.
- Build momentum before you attempt to bump an opponent out of the ring.
- Swinging from one side of the ring to the other builds momentum quickly.
- Don't forget to press the A Button when you bump!

CLEAR CUT CHALLENGE

DESCRIPTION

Press the A Button to cut falling logs as close to the white line as possible. There are five logs in all. Time your cuts—if you cut above the white line, you'll lose points. The one with the highest total score wins.

TIPS

- It's better to cut early than late.
- You'll get bonus points if you cut exactly on the white line.
- Try to cut the log even if you know you're late (above the white line). If you don't cut at all, you lose ten points!
- The above tip does not apply to the first log—since everyone starts with zero points, you can't lose any by making an inaccurate cut.

FURRET'S FROLIC

DESCRIPTION

Press the + Control Pad to control your position on the grass. Release it to move back to the center. Press the A Button to shoot the ball forward. Get the most points to win.

TIPS

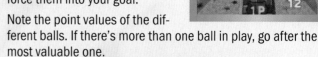

- You're trying to shoot as many balls into your goal as possible.
- Don't bother trying to defend other players' goals—just go to where the balls are and try to force them into your goal.
- Note the point values of the different balls. If there's more than one ball in play, go after the most valuable one.

1 Point   2 Points   3 Points   5 Points

68

BARRIER BALL

DESCRIPTION

Use the Control Stick to move and hit the ball back. Press the A Button to hit a smash. Earn a point for getting the ball in an opponent's court, and lose a point when your court is scored on. Get five points to win.

TIPS

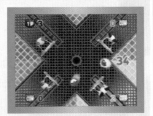

- More balls are put into play even if previous balls have not been cleared from the screen—stay alert!

- If you're moving while you hit the ball, your motion will put "English" on the ball, making it more difficult for opponents to track and return.

- Focus on defending your court, and always press the A Button for a smash every time you deflect a ball.

PICHU'S POWER PLANT

DESCRIPTION

When an electrode pops out, press and hold the + Control Pad in the same direction. If the lamp is blue, repeatedly tap the A Button. If the lamp is green, tap the B Button. The first to fully charge wins.

TIPS

- Using an alternate grip on the controller can improve your chances in this mini-game.

- Instead of thinking in terms of "A Button" and "B Button," think in terms of "blue" and "green." Start the game with your finger poised above one of the buttons. If the first electrode matches that button's color, start tapping! Otherwise, quickly move to the other button before you start tapping. In this manner, you can concentrate on simply switching back and forth between buttons whenever the electrode's color changes.

RAMPAGE ROLLOUT

DESCRIPTION

Use the + Control Pad to run around the track. The first to complete nine laps wins. Press the A Button to leave a dust cloud. You can earn and save up to three dust clouds per lap, depending on your rank.

TIPS

- Avoid touching the dust clouds; they'll make you spin out.

- Stay to the inside of the track unless you have to avoid a dust cloud.

- If you have more than one dust cloud saved up, quickly place two in adjacent lanes; this will make it harder for your opponents to avoid hitting one of them.

- If an opponent is directly behind you, leave a dust cloud directly in his or her face!

STREAMING STAMPEDE

DESCRIPTION

Press the A Button to count the Pokémon visiting the studio. There are five questions (waves of Pokémon to count). Even if you don't get the right answer, you could earn points for getting close. Get the highest score to win.

TIPS

- Press the A Button once for every Pokémon that you have to count. Your presses will register only when Pokémon are crossing the screen.

- Be sure to count only the Pokémon shown at the beginning of each wave. Sometimes other Pokémon will be mixed in to throw you off.

- Questions are worth more points as the game progresses. Point values are 10, 10, 20, 20, and 40. Definitely try to get a perfect on the last question!

TUMBLING TOGEPI

DESCRIPTION

Run downward, using the Control Stick to avoid flowers, boulders, and logs. Step on a blue arrow to speed up. You can jump over logs, but you will slow down. The first one to the goal wins.

TIPS

- Consecutive speed-boosting arrows will often appear on opposites sides of your lane—always be ready to change direction to step on them!

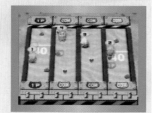

- Instead of watching your Togepi, watch the leading edge of your lane so that you can plan your path before it's too late to avoid an obstacle.

EGG EMERGENCY

DESCRIPTION

Catch the falling eggs! Use the L and R Buttons to move from side to side. Avoid the Voltorb, or you'll lose some of your eggs. There are 100 eggs in all. The player who catches the most eggs wins!

TIPS

- Stay relaxed, and remember that you have to release both Buttons to return to center.

- Instead of watching your Chansey, watch the top of the screen to see what's falling.

- If you're uncomfortable trying to go for an egg that's immediately in front of or behind a Voltorb, let it go rather than lose some of your eggs.

DELIBIRD'S DELIVERY

DESCRIPTION

Fill the sack with up to five gifts using the Control Stick and carry it to the top. Highest score wins. Earn extra points for picking up the same items in a row.

TIPS

- The object of this game is very similar to the Sushi-Go-Round Mini-Game in the original Pokémon Stadium game.

- Note that each gift has a different point value—when you have a choice, go after the more valuable gifts!

| 1000 | 600 | 350 | 250 | 100 | 50 | 20 |

- The more gifts in your sack, the slower your Delibird will move, so be careful when you're heading back to deposit your gifts—if a Swinub hits you, you'll lose the gifts in your sack!

- Pay heed to the tip in the game's description—you'll earn bonus multipliers if you pick up more than one of the same item in succession—that is, assuming you successfully deposit your load.

EAGER EEVEE

DESCRIPTION

When Aipom opens the lid, dash to the fruit by pressing the A Button. Press the B Button to fake a dash. The race is run five times. Get the highest score to win.

TIPS

- Aipom will sometimes feint opening the lid. Make sure the lid is lifted before you dash. If you hit the closed lid, it'll take a few moments for you to recover.

- Note that the fruits have different point values. If you accidentally dash into the Pineco, you'll have to sit out the next round.

| 1000 | 500 | 100 X ? | Penalty |

- If you tie for being the fastest to the fruit, both players get credit.

- Faking a dash (B Button) can sometimes lure opponents into dashing toward the closed lid, especially if you're playing against the computer.

COMPLETE POKéDEX

#1 BULBASAUR

TYPE: Grass/Poison

STATS	HP	Attack	Defense	Speed	SpAttack	SpDefense
	45	49	49	45	65	65

BREEDABLE MOVES: Razor Wind, Safeguard, Petal Dance, Light Screen, Skull Bash

ABLE TO LEARN:
TM: 2, 3, 6, 10, 11, 12, 13, 17, 19, 20, 21, 22, 27, 31, 32, 34, 35, 40, 44, 45, 49
HM: 1, 5

TECHNIQUES:

Name	Level	Type	Power	Name	Level	Type	Power	Name	Level	Type	Power	Name	Level	Type	Power
Tackle	0	Normal	35	Vine Whip	10	Grass	35	Razor Leaf	20	Grass	55	Synthesis	39	Grass	-
Growl	0	Normal	-	Poisonpowder	15	Poison	-	Sweet Scent	25	Normal	-	Solarbeam	46	Grass	120
Leech Seed	7	Grass	-	Sleep Powder	15	Grass	-	Growth	32	Normal	-				

#2 IVYSAUR

TYPE: Grass/Poison

STATS	HP	Attack	Defense	Speed	SpAttack	SpDefense
	60	62	63	60	80	80

BREEDABLE MOVES: Razor Wind, Safeguard, Petal Dance, Light Screen, Skull Bash

ABLE TO LEARN:
TM: 2, 3, 6, 10, 11, 12, 13, 17, 19, 20, 21, 22, 27, 31, 32, 34, 35, 40, 44, 45, 49
HM: 1, 5

TECHNIQUES:

Name	Level	Type	Power	Name	Level	Type	Power
Razor Leaf	22	Grass	55	Synthesis	47	Grass	-
Sweet Scent	29	Normal	-	Solarbeam	56	Grass	120
Growth	38	Normal	-				

#3 VENUSAUR

TYPE: Grass/Poison

STATS	HP	Attack	Defense	Speed	SpAttack	SpDefense
	80	82	83	80	100	100

BREEDABLE MOVES: Razor Wind, Safeguard, Petal Dance, Light Screen, Skull Bash

ABLE TO LEARN:
TM: 2, 3, 5, 6, 10, 11, 12, 13, 15, 17, 19, 20, 21, 22, 27, 31, 32, 34, 35, 40, 44, 45, 49
HM: 1, 5

TECHNIQUES:

Name	Level	Type	Power
Growth	41	Normal	-
Synthesis	53	Grass	-
Solarbeam	65	Grass	120

#4 CHARMANDER

TYPE: Fire

STATS	HP	Attack	Defense	Speed	SpAttack	SpDefense
	39	52	43	65	60	50

BREEDABLE MOVES: Rock Slide, Bite, Outrage, Ancientpower, Belly Drum, Beat Up

ABLE TO LEARN:
TM: 1, 2, 3, 6, 8, 10, 11, 13, 17, 20, 21, 23, 24, 27, 28, 31, 32, 34, 35, 38, 39, 40, 44, 45, 48, 49
HM: 1, 4

TECHNIQUES:

Name	Level	Type	Power	Name	Level	Type	Power	Name	Level	Type	Power	Name	Level	Type	Power
Scratch	0	Normal	40	Smokescreen	13	Normal	-	Flamethrower	31	Fire	95	Fire Spin	49	Fire	15
Growl	0	Normal	-	Rage	19	Normal	-	Slash	37	Normal	70				
Ember	7	Fire	40	Scary Face	25	Normal	-	Dragon Rage	43	Dragon	40				

#5 CHARMELEON

TYPE: Fire

STATS	HP	Attack	Defense	Speed	SpAttack	SpDefense
	58	64	58	80	80	65

BREEDABLE MOVES: Rock Slide, Bite, Outrage, Ancientpower, Belly Drum, Beat Up

ABLE TO LEARN:
TM: 1, 2, 3, 6, 8, 10, 11, 13, 17, 20, 21, 23, 24, 27, 28, 31, 32, 34, 35, 38, 39, 40, 44, 45, 48, 49
HM: 1, 4

TECHNIQUES:

Name	Level	Type	Power	Name	Level	Type	Power
Rage	20	Normal	-	Slash	41	Normal	70
Scary Face	27	Normal	-	Dragon Rage	48	Dragon	40
Flamethrower	34	Fire	95	Fire Spin	55	Fire	15

#6 CHARIZARD

TYPE: Fire

STATS	HP	Attack	Defense	Speed	SpAttack	SpDefense
	78	84	78	100	109	85

BREEDABLE MOVES: Rock Slide, Bite, Outrage, Ancientpower, Belly Drum, Beat Up

ABLE TO LEARN:
TM: 1, 2, 3, 5, 6, 8, 10, 11, 13, 15, 17, 20, 21, 23, 24, 26, 27, 28, 31, 32, 34, 35, 37, 38, 39, 40, 44, 45, 47, 48, 49
HM: 1, 2, 4

TECHNIQUES:

Name	Level	Type	Power
Slash	44	Normal	70
Dragon Rage	54	Dragon	40
Fire Spin	64	Fire	15

#7 SQUIRTLE

TYPE: Water

STATS	HP	Attack	Defense	Speed	SpAttack	SpDefense
	44	48	65	43	50	64

BREEDABLE MOVES: Haze, Mist, Foresight, Flail, Confusion, Mirror Coat

ABLE TO LEARN:
TM: 1, 2, 3, 4, 6, 8, 10, 13, 14, 16, 17, 18, 20, 21, 23, 27, 28, 31, 32, 33, 34, 35, 40, 44, 45
HM: 3, 4, 6, 7

TECHNIQUES

Name	Level	Type	Power	Name	Level	Type	Power	Name	Level	Type	Power	Name	Level	Type	Power
Tackle	0	Normal	35	Withdraw	10	Water	-	Rapid Spin	23	Normal	20	Skull Bash	40	Normal	100
Tail Whip	4	Normal	-	Water Gun	13	Water	40	Protect	28	Normal	-	Hydro Pump	47	Water	120
Bubble	7	Water	20	Bite	18	Dark	60	Rain Dance	33	Water	-				

#8 WARTORTLE

TYPE: Water

STATS	HP	Attack	Defense	Speed	SpAttack	SpDefense
	59	63	80	58	65	80

BREEDABLE MOVES: Haze, Mist, Foresight, Flail, Confusion, Mirror Coat

ABLE TO LEARN:
TM: 1, 2, 3, 4, 6, 8, 10, 13, 14, 16, 17, 18, 20, 21, 23, 27, 28, 31, 32, 33, 34, 35, 40, 44, 45
HM: 3, 4, 6, 7

TECHNIQUES

Name	Level	Type	Power	Name	Level	Type	Power
Bite	19	Dark	60	Rain Dance	37	Water	-
Rapid Spin	25	Normal	20	Skull Bash	45	Normal	100
Protect	31	Normal	-	Hydro Pump	53	Water	120

#9 BLASTOISE

TYPE: Water

STATS	HP	Attack	Defense	Speed	SpAttack	SpDefense
	79	83	100	78	85	105

BREEDABLE MOVES: Haze, Mist, Foresight, Flail, Confusion, Mirror Coat

ABLE TO LEARN:
TM: 1, 2, 3, 4, 5, 6, 8, 10, 13, 14, 15, 16, 17, 18, 20, 21, 23, 26, 27, 28, 31, 32, 33, 34, 35, 40, 44, 45
HM: 3, 4, 6, 7

TECHNIQUES

Name	Level	Type	Power
Rain Dance	42	Water	-
Skull Bash	55	Normal	100
Hydro Pump	68	Water	120

#10 CATERPIE

TYPE: Bug

STATS	HP	Attack	Defense	Speed	SpAttack	SpDefense
	45	30	35	45	20	20

BREEDABLE MOVES: None

ABLE TO LEARN:
TM: None
HM: None

TECHNIQUES

Name	Level	Type	Power
Tackle	0	Normal	35
String Shot	0	Bug	-

#11 METAPOD

TYPE: Bug

STATS	HP	Attack	Defense	Speed	SpAttack	SpDefense
	50	20	55	30	25	25

BREEDABLE MOVES: None

ABLE TO LEARN:
TM: None
HM: None

TECHNIQUES

Name	Level	Type	Power
Harden	7	Normal	-

#12 BUTTERFREE

TYPE: Bug/Flying

STATS	HP	Attack	Defense	Speed	SpAttack	SpDefense
	60	45	50	70	80	80

BREEDABLE MOVES: None

ABLE TO LEARN:
TM: 3, 6, 10, 11, 12, 13, 15, 17, 19, 20, 21, 22, 27, 29, 32, 34, 35, 39, 44, 45, 50
HM: 5

TECHNIQUES

Name	Level	Type	Power	Name	Level	Type	Power	Name	Level	Type	Power
Confusion	10	Psychic	50	Sleep Powder	15	Grass	-	Gust	28	Flying	40
Poisonpowder	13	Poison	-	Supersonic	18	Normal	-	Psybeam	34	Psychic	65
Stun Spore	14	Grass	-	Whirlwind	23	Normal	-	Safeguard	40	Normal	-

#13 WEEDLE

TYPE: Bug/Poison

STATS	HP	Attack	Defense	Speed	SpAttack	SpDefense
	40	35	30	50	20	20

BREEDABLE MOVES: None

ABLE TO LEARN:
TM: None
HM: None

TECHNIQUES

Name	Level	Type	Power
Poison Sting	0	Poison	15
String Shot	0	Bug	-

#14 KAKUNA

TYPE: Bug/Poison

STATS	HP	Attack	Defense	Speed	SpAttack	SpDefense
	45	25	50	35	25	25

BREEDABLE MOVES: None

ABLE TO LEARN
TM: None
HM: None

TECHNIQUES

Name	Level	Type	Power	Name	Level	Type	Power	Name	Level	Type	Power	Name	Level	Type	Power
Harden	7	Normal	-												

#15 BEEDRILL

TYPE: Bug/Poison

STATS	HP	Attack	Defense	Speed	SpAttack	SpDefense
	65	80	40	75	45	80

BREEDABLE MOVES: None

ABLE TO LEARN
TM: 3, 6, 10, 11, 12, 13, 15, 17, 19, 20, 21, 27, 32, 34, 35, 36, 39, 44, 45, 49
HM: 1

TECHNIQUES

Name	Level	Type	Power	Name	Level	Type	Power	Name	Level	Type	Power	Name	Level	Type	Power
Fury Attack	10	Normal	15	Rage	25	Normal	20	Agility	40	Psychic	-				
Focus Energy	15	Normal	-	Pursuit	30	Dark	40								
Twineedle	20	Bug	25	Pin Missile	35	Bug	14								

#16 PIDGEY

TYPE: Normal/Flying

STATS	HP	Attack	Defense	Speed	SpAttack	SpDefense
	40	45	40	56	35	35

BREEDABLE MOVES: Pursuit, Foresight, Faint Attack

ABLE TO LEARN
TM: 3, 6, 10, 11, 13, 17, 20, 21, 27, 31, 32, 34, 35, 39, 43, 44, 45, 46, 47
HM: 2

TECHNIQUES

Name	Level	Type	Power	Name	Level	Type	Power	Name	Level	Type	Power	Name	Level	Type	Power
Tackle	0	Normal	35	Quick Attack	15	Normal	40	Agility	37	Psychic	-				
Sand-Attack	5	Ground	-	Whirlwind	21	Normal	-	Mirror Move	47	Flying	-				
Gust	9	Flying	40	Wing Attack	29	Flying	60								

#17 PIDGEOTTO

TYPE: Normal/Flying

STATS	HP	Attack	Defense	Speed	SpAttack	SpDefense
	63	60	55	71	50	50

BREEDABLE MOVES: Pursuit, Foresight, Faint Attack

ABLE TO LEARN
TM: 3, 6, 10, 11, 13, 17, 20, 21, 27, 31, 32, 34, 35, 39, 43, 44, 45, 46, 47
HM: 2

TECHNIQUES

Name	Level	Type	Power	Name	Level	Type	Power	Name	Level	Type	Power	Name	Level	Type	Power
Quick Attack	15	Normal	40	Agility	43	Psychic	-								
Whirlwind	23	Normal	-	Mirror Move	55	Flying	-								
Wing Attack	33	Flying	60												

#18 PIDGEOT

TYPE: Normal/Flying

STATS	HP	Attack	Defense	Speed	SpAttack	SpDefense
	83	80	75	91	70	70

BREEDABLE MOVES: Pursuit, Foresight, Faint Attack

ABLE TO LEARN
TM: 3, 6, 10, 11, 13, 15, 17, 20, 21, 27, 31, 32, 34, 35, 39, 43, 44, 45, 46, 47
HM: 2

TECHNIQUES

Name	Level	Type	Power	Name	Level	Type	Power	Name	Level	Type	Power	Name	Level	Type	Power
Agility	46	Psychic	-												
Mirror Move	61	Flying	-												

#19 RATTATA

TYPE: Normal

STATS	HP	Attack	Defense	Speed	SpAttack	SpDefense
	30	56	35	72	25	35

BREEDABLE MOVES: Screech, Flame Wheel, Reversal, Counter, Bite, Fury Swipes

ABLE TO LEARN
TM: 2, 3, 6, 8, 10, 11, 13, 14, 16, 17, 20, 21, 23, 25, 27, 28, 30, 31, 32, 34, 35, 39, 40, 44, 45, 46
HM: None

TECHNIQUES

Name	Level	Type	Power	Name	Level	Type	Power	Name	Level	Type	Power	Name	Level	Type	Power
Tackle	0	Normal	35	Hyper Fang	13	Normal	80	Super Fang	34	Normal	-				
Tail Whip	0	Normal	-	Focus Energy	20	Normal	-								
Quick Attack	7	Normal	40	Pursuit	27	Dark	40								

#20 RATICATE

TYPE: Normal

STATS	HP	Attack	Defense	Speed	SpAttack	SpDefense
	55	81	60	97	50	70

BREEDABLE MOVES: Screech, Flame Wheel, Reversal, Counter, Bite, Fury Swipes

ABLE TO LEARN
TM: 2, 3, 5, 6, 8, 10, 11, 13, 14, 15, 16, 17, 20, 21, 23, 25, 27, 28, 30, 31, 32, 34, 35, 39, 40, 44, 45, 46
HM: 1, 4

TECHNIQUES

Name	Level	Type	Power	Name	Level	Type	Power	Name	Level	Type	Power	Name	Level	Type	Power
Hyper Fang	13	Normal	80	Super Fang	40	Normal	-								
Scary face	20	Normal	-												
Pursuit	30	Dark	40												

#21 SPEAROW

TYPE: Normal/Flying

STATS	HP	Attack	Defense	Speed	SpAttack	SpDefense
	40	60	30	70	31	31

BREEDABLE MOVES: Scary Face | Quick Attack | False Swipe | Faint Attack | Tri Attack

ABLE TO LEARN: TM: 3, 6, 10, 11, 13, 17, 20, 21, 27, 31, 32, 34, 35, 39, 43, 44, 45, 46, 47
HM: 2

Name	Level	Type	Power	Name	Level	Type	Power	Name	Level	Type	Power	Name	Level	Type	Power
Peck	0	Flying	35	Fury Attack	13	Normal	15	Drill Peck	37	Flying	80				
Growl	0	Normal	-	Pursuit	25	Dark	40	Agility	43	Psychic	-				
Leer	7	Normal	-	Mirror Move	31	Flying	-								

#22 FEAROW

TYPE: Normal/Flying

STATS	HP	Attack	Defense	Speed	SpAttack	SpDefense
	65	90	65	100	61	61

BREEDABLE MOVES: Scary Face | Quick Attack | False Swipe | Faint Attack | Tri Attack

ABLE TO LEARN: TM: 3, 6, 10, 11, 13, 15, 17, 20, 21, 27, 31, 32, 34, 35, 39, 43, 44, 45, 46, 47
HM: 2

Name	Level	Type	Power	Name	Level	Type	Power	Name	Level	Type	Power	Name	Level	Type	Power
Pursuit	26	Dark	40	Agility	47	Psychic	-								
Mirror Move	32	Flying	-												
Drill Peck	40	Flying	80												

#23 EKANS

TYPE: Poison

STATS	HP	Attack	Defense	Speed	SpAttack	SpDefense
	35	60	44	55	40	54

BREEDABLE MOVES: Spite | Slam | Pursuit | Beat Up

ABLE TO LEARN: TM: 2, 3, 6, 10, 11, 13, 17, 19, 20, 21, 26, 27, 28, 32, 34, 35, 36, 44, 45, 46
HM: 4

Name	Level	Type	Power	Name	Level	Type	Power	Name	Level	Type	Power	Name	Level	Type	Power
Wrap	0	Normal	15	Bite	15	Dark	60	Acid	37	Poison	40				
Leer	0	Normal	-	Glare	23	Normal	-	Haze	43	Ice	-				
Poison Sting	9	Poison	15	Screech	29	Normal	-								

#24 ARBOK

TYPE: Poison

STATS	HP	Attack	Defense	Speed	SpAttack	SpDefense
	60	85	69	80	65	79

BREEDABLE MOVES: Spite | Slam | Pursuit | Beat Up

ABLE TO LEARN: TM: 2, 3, 6, 10, 11, 13, 15, 17, 19, 20, 21, 26, 27, 28, 32, 34, 35, 36, 44, 45, 46
HM: 4

Name	Level	Type	Power	Name	Level	Type	Power	Name	Level	Type	Power	Name	Level	Type	Power
Glare	25	Normal	-	Haze	51	Ice	-								
Screech	33	Normal	-												
Acid	43	Poison	40												

#25 PIKACHU

TYPE: Electric

STATS	HP	Attack	Defense	Speed	SpAttack	SpDefense
	35	55	30	90	50	40

BREEDABLE MOVES: Encore | Bide | Present | Double Slap | Reversal

ABLE TO LEARN: TM: 1, 2, 3, 4, 6, 7, 10, 13, 17, 18, 20, 21, 23, 25, 27, 31, 32, 34, 35, 39, 40, 41, 43, 44, 45
HM: 4, 5

Name	Level	Type	Power	Name	Level	Type	Power	Name	Level	Type	Power	Name	Level	Type	Power
Thundershock	0	Electric	40	Thunder Wave	8	Electric	-	Slam	20	Normal	80	Thunder	41	Electric	120
Growl	0	Normal	-	Quick Attack	11	Normal	40	Thunderbolt	26	Electric	95	Light Screen	50	Psychic	-
Tail Whip	6	Normal	-	Double Team	15	Normal	-	Agility	33	Psychic	-				

#26 RAICHU

TYPE: Electric

STATS	HP	Attack	Defense	Speed	SpAttack	SpDefense
	60	90	55	100	90	80

BREEDABLE MOVES: Encore | Bide | Present | Doubleslap | Reversal

ABLE TO LEARN: TM: 1, 2, 3, 4, 6, 7, 10, 13, 17, 18, 20, 21, 23, 25, 27, 31, 32, 34, 35, 39, 40, 41, 43, 44, 45, 46
HM: 4, 5

Name	Level	Type	Power	Name	Level	Type	Power	Name	Level	Type	Power	Name	Level	Type	Power
None															

#27 SANDSHREW

TYPE: Ground

STATS	HP	Attack	Defense	Speed	SpAttack	SpDefense
	50	75	85	40	20	30

BREEDABLE MOVES: Counter | Flail | Rapid Spin | Safeguard

ABLE TO LEARN: TM: 1, 2, 3, 4, 6, 8, 10, 11, 13, 17, 20, 21, 23, 26, 27, 28, 31, 32, 34, 35, 37, 39, 40, 43, 44, 45, 46, 49
HM: 1, 4

Name	Level	Type	Power	Name	Level	Type	Power	Name	Level	Type	Power	Name	Level	Type	Power
Scratch	0	Normal	40	Poison Sting	17	Poison	15	Fury Swipes	37	Normal	18				
Defense Curl	6	Normal	-	Slash	23	Normal	70	Sandstorm	45	Rock	-				
Sand-Attack	11	Ground	-	Swift	30	Normal	60								

#28 SANDSLASH

STATS	HP	Attack	Defense	Speed	SpAttack	SpDefense
	75	100	110	65	45	55

TYPE: Ground

BREEDABLE MOVES

Counter	Flail
Rapid Spin	Safeguard

ABLE TO LEARN
TM: 1, 2, 3, 4, 6, 8, 10, 11, 13, 15, 17, 20, 21, 23, 26, 27, 28, 31, 32, 34, 35, 37, 39, 40, 43, 44, 45, 46, 49
HM: 1, 4

TECHNIQUES

Name	Level	Type	Power	Name	Level	Type	Power
Slash	24	Normal	70	Sandstorm	52	Rock	-
Swift	33	Normal	60				
Fury Swipes	42	Normal	18				

#29 NIDORAN♀

STATS	HP	Attack	Defense	Speed	SpAttack	SpDefense
	55	47	52	41	40	40

TYPE: Poison

BREEDABLE MOVES

Charm	Disable	Supersonic	Beat Up
Counter	Focus Energy	Take Down	

ABLE TO LEARN
TM: 2, 3, 6, 10, 11, 13, 14, 17, 18, 20, 21, 23, 25, 27, 31, 32, 34, 35, 40, 43, 44, 45, 46
HM: None

TECHNIQUES

Name	Level	Type	Power	Name	Level	Type	Power	Name	Level	Type	Power
Growl	0	Normal	-	Double Kick	12	Fighting	30	Bite	30	Dark	60
Tackle	0	Normal	35	Poison Sting	17	Poison	15	Fury Swipes	38	Normal	18
Scratch	8	Normal	40	Tail Whip	23	Normal	-				

#30 NIDORINA

STATS	HP	Attack	Defense	Speed	SpAttack	SpDefense
	70	62	67	56	55	55

TYPE: Poison

BREEDABLE MOVES

Charm	Disable	Supersonic	Beat Up
Counter	Focus Energy	Take Down	

ABLE TO LEARN
TM: 2, 3, 6, 8, 10, 11, 13, 14, 17, 18, 20, 21, 23, 25, 27, 31, 32, 34, 35, 40, 43, 44, 45, 46
HM: 4

TECHNIQUES

Name	Level	Type	Power	Name	Level	Type	Power
Poison Sting	19	Poison	15	Fury Swipes	46	Normal	18
Tail Whip	27	Normal	-				
Bite	36	Dark	60				

#31 NIDOQUEEN

STATS	HP	Attack	Defense	Speed	SpAttack	SpDefense
	90	82	87	76	75	85

TYPE: Poison/Ground

BREEDABLE MOVES

Charm	Disable	Supersonic	Beat Up
Counter	Focus Energy	Take Down	

ABLE TO LEARN
TM: 1, 2, 3, 5, 6, 8, 10, 11, 13, 14, 15, 16, 17, 18, 20, 21, 23, 25, 26, 27, 30, 31, 32, 33, 34, 35, 37, 38, 40, 41, 43, 44, 45, 46, 48, 49
HM: 3, 4

TECHNIQUES

Name	Level	Type	Power
Body Slam	23	Normal	85

#32 NIDORAN♂

STATS	HP	Attack	Defense	Speed	SpAttack	SpDefense
	46	57	40	50	40	40

TYPE: Poison

BREEDABLE MOVES

Counter	Supersonic	Confusion	Take Down
Disable	Amnesia	Beat Up	

ABLE TO LEARN
TM: 2, 3, 6, 10, 11, 13, 14, 17, 18, 20, 21, 23, 25, 27, 31, 32, 34, 35, 40, 43, 44, 45, 46
HM: None

TECHNIQUES

Name	Level	Type	Power	Name	Level	Type	Power	Name	Level	Type	Power
Leer	0	Normal	-	Double Kick	12	Fighting	30	Fury Attack	30	Normal	15
Tackle	0	Normal	35	Poison Sting	17	Poison	15	Horn Drill	38	Normal	-
Horn Attack	8	Normal	65	Focus Energy	23	Normal	-				

#33 NIDORINO

STATS	HP	Attack	Defense	Speed	SpAttack	SpDefense
	61	72	57	65	55	55

TYPE: Poison

BREEDABLE MOVES

Counter	Supersonic	Confusion	Take Down
Disable	Amnesia	Beat Up	

ABLE TO LEARN
TM: 2, 3, 6, 8, 10, 11, 13, 14, 17, 18, 20, 21, 23, 25, 27, 31, 32, 34, 35, 40, 43, 44, 45, 46
HM: 4

TECHNIQUES

Name	Level	Type	Power	Name	Level	Type	Power
Poison Sting	19	Poison	15	Horn Drill	46	Normal	-
Focus Energy	27	Normal	-				
Fury Attack	36	Normal	15				

#34 NIDOKING

STATS	HP	Attack	Defense	Speed	SpAttack	SpDefense
	81	92	77	85	85	75

TYPE: Poison/Ground

BREEDABLE MOVES

Counter	Supersonic	Confusion	Take Down
Disable	Amnesia	Beat Up	

ABLE TO LEARN
TM: 1, 2, 3, 5, 6, 8, 10, 11, 13, 14, 15, 16, 17, 18, 20, 21, 23, 25, 26, 27, 30, 31, 32, 33, 34, 35, 37, 38, 40, 41, 43, 44, 45, 46, 48, 49
HM: 3, 4

TECHNIQUES

Name	Level	Type	Power
Thrash	23	Normal	90

#35 CLEFAIRY

STATS	HP	Attack	Defense	Speed	SpAttack	SpDefense
TYPE: Normal	70	45	48	35	60	65

BREEDABLE MOVES: Amnesia, Splash, Belly Drum, Present, Mimic, Metronome

ABLE TO LEARN TM: 1, 2, 3, 4, 6, 7, 9, 10, 11, 13, 14, 17, 18, 20, 21, 22, 23, 25, 27, 29, 30, 31, 32, 33, 34, 35, 38, 40, 41, 42, 43, 44, 45, 48, 50
HM: 4, 5

TECHNIQUES

Name	Level	Type	Power	Name	Level	Type	Power	Name	Level	Type	Power	Name	Level	Type	Power
Pound	0	Normal	40	Sing	8	Normal	-	Defense Curl	26	Normal	-	Light Screen	53	Psychic	-
Growl	0	Normal	-	Doubleslap	13	Normal	15	Metronome	34	Normal	-				
Encore	4	Normal	-	Minimize	19	Normal	-	Moonlight	43	Normal	-				

#36 CLEFABLE

STATS	HP	Attack	Defense	Speed	SpAttack	SpDefense
TYPE: Normal	95	70	73	60	85	90

BREEDABLE MOVES: Amnesia, Splash, Belly Drum, Present, Mimic, Metronome

ABLE TO LEARN TM: 1, 2, 3, 4, 6, 7, 9, 10, 11, 13, 14, 15, 17, 18, 20, 21, 22, 23, 25, 27, 29, 30, 31, 32, 33, 34, 35, 38, 40, 41, 42, 43, 44, 45, 48, 50
HM: 4, 5

TECHNIQUES

Name	Level	Type	Power	Name	Level	Type	Power	Name	Level	Type	Power	Name	Level	Type	Power
None															

#37 VULPIX

STATS	HP	Attack	Defense	Speed	SpAttack	SpDefense
TYPE: Fire	38	41	40	65	50	65

BREEDABLE MOVES: Spite, Disable, Hypnosis, Flail, Faint Attack

ABLE TO LEARN TM: 2, 3, 6, 10, 11, 13, 17, 20, 21, 23, 27, 28, 32, 34, 35, 38, 39, 44, 45
HM: None

TECHNIQUES

Name	Level	Type	Power	Name	Level	Type	Power	Name	Level	Type	Power	Name	Level	Type	Power
Ember	0	Fire	40	Confuse Ray	13	Ghost	-	Flamethrower	31	Fire	95				
Tail Whip	0	Normal	-	Safeguard	19	Normal	-	Fire Spin	35	Fire	15				
Quick Attack	7	Normal	40	Roar	25	Normal	-								

#38 NINETALES

STATS	HP	Attack	Defense	Speed	SpAttack	SpDefense
TYPE: Fire	73	76	75	100	81	100

BREEDABLE MOVES: Spite, Disable, Hypnosis, Flail, Faint Attack

ABLE TO LEARN TM: 2, 3, 5, 6, 10, 11, 13, 15, 17, 20, 21, 23, 27, 28, 32, 34, 35, 38, 39, 44, 45
HM: None

TECHNIQUES

Name	Level	Type	Power	Name	Level	Type	Power	Name	Level	Type	Power	Name	Level	Type	Power
Fire Spin	43	Fire	15												

#39 JIGGLYPUFF

STATS	HP	Attack	Defense	Speed	SpAttack	SpDefense
TYPE: Normal	115	45	20	20	45	25

BREEDABLE MOVES: Faint Attack, Present, Perish Song

ABLE TO LEARN TM: 1, 2, 3, 4, 6, 7, 9, 10, 11, 13, 14, 17, 18, 20, 21, 22, 25, 27, 29, 30, 31, 32, 33, 34, 35, 38, 40, 41, 42, 43, 44, 45, 48, 50
HM: 4, 5

TECHNIQUES

Name	Level	Type	Power	Name	Level	Type	Power	Name	Level	Type	Power	Name	Level	Type	Power
Sing	0	Normal	-	Disable	14	Normal	-	Rest	29	Psychic	-				
Defense Curl	4	Normal	-	Rollout	19	Rock	30	Body Slam	34	Normal	85				
Pound	9	Normal	40	Doubleslap	24	Normal	15	Double-Edge	39	Normal	120				

#40 WIGGLYTUFF

STATS	HP	Attack	Defense	Speed	SpAttack	SpDefense
TYPE: Normal	140	70	45	45	75	50

BREEDABLE MOVES: Faint Attack, Present, Perish Song

ABLE TO LEARN TM: 1, 2, 3, 4, 6, 7, 9, 10, 11, 13, 14, 15, 17, 18, 20, 21, 22, 25, 27, 29, 30, 31, 32, 33, 34, 35, 38, 40, 41, 42, 43, 44, 45, 48, 50
HM: 4, 5

TECHNIQUES

Name	Level	Type	Power	Name	Level	Type	Power	Name	Level	Type	Power	Name	Level	Type	Power
None															

#41 ZUBAT

STATS	HP	Attack	Defense	Speed	SpAttack	SpDefense
TYPE: Poison/Flying	40	45	35	55	30	40

BREEDABLE MOVES: Pursuit, Gust, Faint Attack, Quick Attack, Whirlwind

ABLE TO LEARN TM: 3, 6, 10, 11, 13, 17, 19, 20, 21, 27, 32, 34, 35, 39, 43, 44, 45, 46, 47
HM: None

TECHNIQUES

Name	Level	Type	Power	Name	Level	Type	Power	Name	Level	Type	Power	Name	Level	Type	Power
Leech Life	0	Bug	20	Confuse Ray	19	Ghost	-	Haze	46	Ice	-				
Supersonic	6	Normal	-	Wing Attack	27	Flying	60								
Bite	12	Dark	60	Mean Look	36	Normal	-								

POKéMON STADIUM 2

#42 GOLBAT

TYPE: Poison/Flying

STATS	HP	Attack	Defense	Speed	SpAttack	SpDefense
	75	80	70	90	65	75

BREEDABLE MOVES: Pursuit, Gust, Faint Attack, Quick Attack, Whirlwind

ABLE TO LEARN: TM: 3, 6, 10, 11, 13, 15, 17, 19, 20, 21, 27, 32, 34, 35, 39, 43, 44, 45, 46, 47
HM: None

Name	Level	Type	Power
Wing Attack	30	Flying	60
Mean Look	42	Normal	-
Haze	55	Ice	-

#43 ODDISH

TYPE: Grass/Poison

STATS	HP	Attack	Defense	Speed	SpAttack	SpDefense
	45	50	55	30	75	65

BREEDABLE MOVES: Synthesis, Flail, Razor Leaf, Swords Dance

ABLE TO LEARN: TM: 3, 6, 10, 11, 12, 13, 17, 19, 20, 21, 22, 27, 32, 34, 35, 36, 44, 45
HM: 1, 5

Name	Level	Type	Power	Name	Level	Type	Power	Name	Level	Type	Power
Absorb	0	Grass	20	Stun Spore	16	Grass	-	Moonlight	32	Normal	-
Sweet Scent	7	Normal	-	Sleep Powder	18	Grass	-	Petal Dance	39	Grass	70
Poisonpowder	14	Poison	-	Acid	23	Poison	40				

#44 GLOOM

TYPE: Grass/Poison

STATS	HP	Attack	Defense	Speed	SpAttack	SpDefense
	60	65	70	40	85	75

BREEDABLE MOVES: Synthesis, Flail, Razor Leaf, Swords Dance

ABLE TO LEARN: TM: 3, 6, 10, 11, 12, 13, 17, 19, 20, 21, 22, 27, 32, 34, 35, 36, 44, 45
HM: 1, 5

Name	Level	Type	Power
Acid	24	Poison	40
Moonlight	35	Normal	-
Petal Dance	44	Grass	70

#45 VILEPLUME

TYPE: Grass/Poison

STATS	HP	Attack	Defense	Speed	SpAttack	SpDefense
	75	80	85	50	100	90

BREEDABLE MOVES: Synthesis, Flail, Razor Leaf, Swords Dance

ABLE TO LEARN: TM: 3, 6, 10, 11, 12, 13, 15, 17, 19, 20, 21, 22, 27, 32, 34, 35 ,36, 44, 45
HM: 1, 5

Name	Level	Type	Power
None			

#46 PARAS

TYPE: Bug/Grass

STATS	HP	Attack	Defense	Speed	SpAttack	SpDefense
	35	70	55	25	45	55

BREEDABLE MOVES: Screech, Pursuit, Counter, Psybeam, Flail, Light Screen, False Swipe

ABLE TO LEARN: TM: 3, 6, 8, 10, 11, 12, 13, 17, 19, 20, 21, 22, 27, 28, 32, 34, 35, 36, 44, 45, 46, 49
HM: 1, 5

Name	Level	Type	Power	Name	Level	Type	Power	Name	Level	Type	Power
Scratch	0	Normal	40	Leech Life	19	Bug	20	Growth	37	Normal	-
Stun Spore	7	Grass	-	Spore	25	Grass	-	Giga Drain	43	Grass	60
Poisonpowder	13	Poison	-	Slash	31	Normal	70				

#47 PARASECT

TYPE: Bug/Grass

STATS	HP	Attack	Defense	Speed	SpAttack	SpDefense
	60	95	80	30	60	80

BREEDABLE MOVES: Screech, Pursuit, Counter, Psybeam, Flail, Light Screen, False Swipe

ABLE TO LEARN: TM: 3, 6, 8, 10, 11, 12, 13, 15, 17, 19, 20, 21, 22, 27, 28, 32, 34, 35, 36, 44, 45, 46, 49
HM: 1, 5

Name	Level	Type	Power	Name	Level	Type	Power
Spore	28	Grass	-	Giga Drain	55	Grass	60
Slash	37	Normal	70				
Growth	46	Normal	-				

#48 VENONAT

TYPE: Bug/Poison

STATS	HP	Attack	Defense	Speed	SpAttack	SpDefense
	60	55	50	45	40	55

BREEDABLE MOVES: Screech, Baton Pass

ABLE TO LEARN: TM: 3, 6, 10, 11, 12, 13, 17, 19, 20, 21, 22, 27, 29, 32, 34, 35, 36, 39, 44, 45, 46
HM: None

Name	Level	Type	Power	Name	Level	Type	Power	Name	Level	Type	Power	Name	Level	Type	Power
Tackle	0	Normal	35	Supersonic	9	Normal	-	Leech Life	25	Bug	20	Sleep Powder	36	Grass	-
Disable	0	Normal	-	Confusion	17	Psychic	50	Stun Spore	28	Grass	-	Psychic	41	Psychic	90
Foresight	0	Normal	-	Poisonpowder	20	Poison	-	Psybeam	33	Psychic	65				

#49 VENOMOTH

TYPE: Bug/Poison

STATS	HP	Attack	Defense	Speed	SpAttack	SpDefense
	70	65	60	90	90	75

BREEDABLE MOVES: Screech, Baton Pass

ABLE TO LEARN: TM: 3, 6, 10, 11, 12, 13, 15, 17, 19, 20, 21, 22, 27, 29, 32, 34, 35, 36, 39, 44, 45, 46 HM: 5

TECHNIQUES

Name	Level	Type	Power	Name	Level	Type	Power
Gust	31	Flying	40	Psychic	52	Psychic	90
Psybeam	36	Psychic	65				
Sleep Powder	42	Grass	-				

#50 DIGLETT

TYPE: Ground

STATS	HP	Attack	Defense	Speed	SpAttack	SpDefense
	10	55	25	95	35	45

BREEDABLE MOVES: Screech, Pursuit, Ancientpower, Faint Attack, Beat Up

ABLE TO LEARN: TM: 3, 6, 8, 10, 11, 13, 17, 20, 21, 26, 27, 28, 31, 32, 34, 35, 36, 44, 45, 46 HM: 1

TECHNIQUES

Name	Level	Type	Power	Name	Level	Type	Power	Name	Level	Type	Power
Scratch	0	Normal	40	Dig	17	Ground	60	Earthquake	41	Ground	100
Growl	5	Normal	-	Sand-Attack	25	Ground	-	Fissure	49	Ground	-
Magnitude	9	Ground	-	Slash	33	Normal	70				

#51 DUGTRIO

TYPE: Ground

STATS	HP	Attack	Defense	Speed	SpAttack	SpDefense
	35	80	50	120	50	70

BREEDABLE MOVES: Screech, Pursuit, Ancientpower, Faint Attack, Beat Up

ABLE TO LEARN: TM: 3, 6, 8, 10, 11, 13, 15, 17, 20, 21, 26, 27, 28, 31, 32, 34, 35, 36, 44, 45, 46 HM: 1

TECHNIQUES

Name	Level	Type	Power
Slash	37	Normal	70
Earthquake	49	Ground	100
Fissure	61	Ground	-

#52 MEOWTH

TYPE: Normal

STATS	HP	Attack	Defense	Speed	SpAttack	SpDefense
	40	45	35	90	40	40

BREEDABLE MOVES: Charm, Spite, Hypnosis, Amnesia

ABLE TO LEARN: TM: 2, 3, 6, 7, 9, 10, 11, 13, 16, 17, 20, 21, 23, 25, 27, 30, 31, 32, 34, 35, 39, 40, 42, 43, 44, 45, 46, 50 HM: None

TECHNIQUES

Name	Level	Type	Power	Name	Level	Type	Power	Name	Level	Type	Power
Scratch	0	Normal	40	Pay Day	20	Normal	40	Fury Swipes	41	Normal	18
Growl	0	Normal	-	Faint Attack	28	Dark	60	Slash	46	Normal	70
Bite	11	Dark	60	Screech	35	Normal	-				

#53 PERSIAN

TYPE: Normal

STATS	HP	Attack	Defense	Speed	SpAttack	SpDefense
	65	70	60	115	65	65

BREEDABLE MOVES: Charm, Spite, Hypnosis, Amnesia

ABLE TO LEARN: TM: 2, 3, 5, 6, 7, 9, 10, 11, 13, 15, 16, 17, 20, 21, 23, 25, 27, 30, 31, 32, 34, 35, 39, 40, 42, 43, 44, 45, 46, 50 HM: None

TECHNIQUES

Name	Level	Type	Power	Name	Level	Type	Power
Faint Attack	29	Dark	60	Slash	53	Normal	-
Screech	38	Normal	-				
Fury Swipes	46	Normal	15				

#54 PSYDUCK

TYPE: Water

STATS	HP	Attack	Defense	Speed	SpAttack	SpDefense
	50	52	48	55	65	50

BREEDABLE MOVES: Psybeam, Psychic, Hypnosis, Light Screen, Foresight, Future Sight, Ice Beam

ABLE TO LEARN: TM: 1, 2, 3, 6, 8, 9, 10, 13, 14, 16, 17, 18, 20, 21, 23, 27, 28, 31, 32, 33, 34, 35, 39, 44, 45 HM: 3, 4, 5, 6, 7

TECHNIQUES

Name	Level	Type	Power	Name	Level	Type	Power	Name	Level	Type	Power
Scratch	0	Normal	40	Confusion	16	Psychic	50	Fury Swipes	40	Normal	18
Tail Whip	5	Normal	-	Screech	23	Normal	-	Hydro Pump	50	Water	120
Disable	10	Normal	-	Psych Up	31	Normal	-				

#55 GOLDUCK

TYPE: Water

STATS	HP	Attack	Defense	Speed	SpAttack	SpDefense
	80	82	78	85	95	80

BREEDABLE MOVES: Psybeam, Psychic, Hypnosis, Light Screen, Foresight, Future Sight, Ice Beam

ABLE TO LEARN: TM: 1, 2, 3, 6, 8, 9, 10, 13, 14, 15, 16, 17, 18, 20, 21, 23, 27, 28, 31, 32, 33, 34, 35, 39, 44, 45, 49 HM: 3, 4, 5, 6, 7

TECHNIQUES

Name	Level	Type	Power
Fury Swipes	44	Normal	18
Hydro Pump	58	Water	120

#56 MANKEY

TYPE: Fighting

STATS	HP	Attack	Defense	Speed	SpAttack	SpDefense
	40	80	35	70	35	45

BREEDABLE MOVES

Reversal	Foresight	Rock Slide	
Beat Up	Meditate	Counter	

ABLE TO LEARN
TM: 1, 2, 3, 6, 8, 9, 10, 11, 13, 17, 20, 21, 23, 25, 27, 28, 31, 32, 33, 34, 35, 39, 40, 41, 43, 44, 45, 46, 48
HM: 4

TECHNIQUES

Name	Level	Type	Power	Name	Level	Type	Power	Name	Level	Type	Power	Name	Level	Type	Power
Scratch	0	Normal	40	Karate Chop	15	Fighting	50	Seismic Toss	33	Fighting	-	Thrash	51	Normal	90
Leer	0	Normal	-	Fury Swipes	21	Normal	18	Cross Chop	39	Fighting	100				
Low Kick	9	Fighting	50	Focus Energy	27	Normal	-	Screech	45	Normal	-				

#57 PRIMEAPE

TYPE: Fighting

STATS	HP	Attack	Defense	Speed	SpAttack	SpDefense
	65	105	60	95	60	70

BREEDABLE MOVES

Reversal	Foresight	Rock Slide	
Beat Up	Meditate	Counter	

ABLE TO LEARN
TM: 1, 2, 3, 6, 8, 9, 10, 11, 13, 15, 17, 20, 21, 23, 25, 27, 28, 31, 32, 33, 34, 35, 39, 40, 41, 43, 44, 45, 46, 48
HM: 4

TECHNIQUES

Name	Level	Type	Power	Name	Level	Type	Power
Rage	28	Normal	20	Screech	54	Normal	-
Seismic Toss	36	Fighting	-	Thrash	63	Normal	90
Cross Chop	45	Fighting	100				

#58 GROWLITHE

TYPE: Fire

STATS	HP	Attack	Defense	Speed	SpAttack	SpDefense
	55	70	45	60	70	50

BREEDABLE MOVES

Thrash	Safeguard	Body Slam
Crunch	Fire Spin	

ABLE TO LEARN
TM: 2, 3, 5, 6, 8, 10, 11, 13, 17, 20, 21, 23, 24, 27, 28, 32, 34, 35, 38, 39, 44, 45
HM: None

TECHNIQUES

Name	Level	Type	Power	Name	Level	Type	Power	Name	Level	Type	Power
Bite	0	Dark	60	Leer	18	Normal	-	Agility	42	Psychic	-
Roar	0	Normal	-	Take Down	26	Normal	90	Flamethrower	50	Fire	95
Ember	9	Fire	40	Flame Wheel	34	Fire	60				

#59 ARCANINE

TYPE: Fire

STATS	HP	Attack	Defense	Speed	SpAttack	SpDefense
	90	110	80	95	100	80

BREEDABLE MOVES

Thrash	Safeguard	Body Slam
Crunch	Fire Spin	

ABLE TO LEARN
TM: 2, 3, 5, 6, 8, 10, 11, 13, 15, 17, 20, 21, 23, 24, 27, 28, 32, 34, 35, 38, 39, 44, 45
HM: None

TECHNIQUES

Name	Level	Type	Power
Extremespeed	50	Normal	80

#60 POLIWAG

TYPE: Water

STATS	HP	Attack	Defense	Speed	SpAttack	SpDefense
	40	50	40	90	40	40

BREEDABLE MOVES

Haze	Mist	Bubblebeam
Mind Reader	Splash	

ABLE TO LEARN
TM: 2, 3, 6, 10, 13, 14, 16, 17, 18, 20, 21, 27, 29, 32, 34, 35, 40, 44, 45, 46
HM: 3, 6, 7

TECHNIQUES

Name	Level	Type	Power	Name	Level	Type	Power	Name	Level	Type	Power
Bubble	0	Water	20	Doubleslap	19	Normal	15	Belly Drum	37	Normal	-
Hypnosis	7	Psychic	-	Rain Dance	25	Water	-	Hydro Pump	43	Water	120
Water Gun	13	Water	40	Body Slam	31	Normal	85				

#61 POLIWHIRL

TYPE: Water

STATS	HP	Attack	Defense	Speed	SpAttack	SpDefense
	65	65	65	90	50	50

BREEDABLE MOVES

Haze	Mist	Bubblebeam
Mind Reader	Splash	

ABLE TO LEARN
TM: 2, 3, 6, 8, 10, 13, 14, 16, 17, 18, 20, 21, 26, 27, 29, 31, 32, 33, 34, 35, 40, 43, 44, 45, 46
HM: 3, 4, 6, 7

TECHNIQUES

Name	Level	Type	Power	Name	Level	Type	Power
Rain Dance	27	Water	-	Hydro Pump	51	Water	120
Body Slam	35	Normal	85				
Belly Drum	43	Normal	-				

#62 POLIWRATH

TYPE: Water/Fighting

STATS	HP	Attack	Defense	Speed	SpAttack	SpDefense
	90	85	95	70	70	90

BREEDABLE MOVES

Haze	Mist	Bubblebeam
Mind Reader	Splash	

ABLE TO LEARN
TM: 1, 2, 3, 6, 8, 10, 13, 14, 15, 16, 17, 18, 20, 21, 26, 27, 29, 31, 32, 33, 34, 35, 40, 43, 44, 45, 46
HM: 3, 4, 6, 7

TECHNIQUES

Name	Level	Type	Power
Submission	35	Fighting	80
Mind Reader	51	Normal	-

#63 ABRA

TYPE: Psychic

STATS	HP	Attack	Defense	Speed	SpAttack	SpDefense
	25	20	15	90	105	55

ABLE TO LEARN: TM: 1, 2, 3, 6, 7, 9, 10, 11, 13, 17, 18, 20, 21, 27, 29, 30, 32, 33, 34, 35, 41, 42, 44, 45, 46, 48, 50
HM: 5

BREEDABLE MOVES: Encore, Barrier, Light Screen

TECHNIQUES

Name	Level	Type	Power
Teleport	0	Psychic	-

#64 KADABRA

TYPE: Psychic

STATS	HP	Attack	Defense	Speed	SpAttack	SpDefense
	40	35	30	105	120	70

ABLE TO LEARN: TM: 1, 2, 3, 6, 7, 9, 10, 11, 13, 17, 18, 20, 21, 27, 28, 29, 30, 32, 33, 34, 35, 41, 42, 44, 45, 46, 48, 50
HM: 5

BREEDABLE MOVES: Encore, Barrier, Light Screen

TECHNIQUES

Name	Level	Type	Power	Name	Level	Type	Power	Name	Level	Type	Power
Confusion	16	Psychic	50	Recover	26	Normal	-	Reflect	45	Psychic	-
Disable	18	Normal	-	Future Sight	31	Psychic	80				
Psybeam	21	Psychic	65	Psychic	38	Psychic	90				

#65 ALAKAZAM

TYPE: Psychic

STATS	HP	Attack	Defense	Speed	SpAttack	SpDefense
	55	50	45	120	135	85

ABLE TO LEARN: TM: 1, 2, 3, 6, 7, 9, 10, 11, 13, 15, 17, 18, 20, 21, 27, 28, 29, 30, 32, 33, 34, 35, 41, 42, 44, 45, 46, 48, 50
HM: 5

BREEDABLE MOVES: Encore, Barrier, Light Screen

TECHNIQUES

Name	Level	Type	Power	Name	Level	Type	Power	Name	Level	Type	Power
Confusion	16	Psychic	50	Recover	26	Normal	-	Reflect	45	Psychic	-
Disable	18	Normal	-	Future Sight	31	Psychic	80				
Psybeam	21	Psychic	65	Psychic	38	Psychic	90				

#66 MACHOP

TYPE: Fighting

STATS	HP	Attack	Defense	Speed	SpAttack	SpDefense
	70	80	50	35	35	35

ABLE TO LEARN: TM: 1, 2, 3, 6, 8, 10, 11, 13, 17, 20, 21, 26, 27, 28, 31, 32, 33, 34, 35, 38, 41, 43, 44, 45, 46, 48
HM: 4

BREEDABLE MOVES: Encore, Light Screen, Rolling Kick, Meditate

TECHNIQUES

Name	Level	Type	Power	Name	Level	Type	Power	Name	Level	Type	Power	Name	Level	Type	Power
Low Kick	0	Fighting	50	Karate Chop	13	Fighting	50	Vital Throw	31	Fighting	70	Submission	49	Fighting	80
Leer	0	Normal	-	Seismic Toss	19	Fighting	-	Cross Chop	37	Fighting	100				
Focus Energy	7	Normal	-	Foresight	25	Normal	-	Scary Face	43	Normal	-				

#67 MACHOKE

TYPE: Fighting

STATS	HP	Attack	Defense	Speed	SpAttack	SpDefense
	80	100	70	45	50	50

ABLE TO LEARN: TM: 1, 2, 3, 6, 8, 10, 11, 13, 17, 20, 21, 26, 27, 28, 31, 32, 33, 34, 35, 38, 41, 43, 44, 45, 46, 48
HM: 4

BREEDABLE MOVES: Encore, Light Screen, Rolling Kick, Meditate

TECHNIQUES

Name	Level	Type	Power	Name	Level	Type	Power
Vital Throw	34	Fighting	70	Submission	61	Fighting	80
Cross Chop	43	Fighting	100				
Scary Face	52	Normal	-				

#68 MACHAMP

TYPE: Fighting

STATS	HP	Attack	Defense	Speed	SpAttack	SpDefense
	90	130	80	55	65	85

ABLE TO LEARN: TM: 1, 2, 3, 6, 8, 10, 11, 13, 15, 17, 20, 21, 26, 27, 28, 31, 32, 33, 34, 35, 38, 41, 43, 44, 45, 46, 48
HM: 4

BREEDABLE MOVES: Encore, Light Screen, Rolling Kick, Meditate

TECHNIQUES

Name	Level	Type	Power	Name	Level	Type	Power
Vital Throw	34	Fighting	70	Submission	61	Fighting	80
Cross Chop	43	Fighting	100				
Scary Face	52	Normal	-				

#69 BELLSPROUT

TYPE: Grass/Poison

STATS	HP	Attack	Defense	Speed	SpAttack	SpDefense
	50	75	35	40	70	30

ABLE TO LEARN: TM: 3, 6, 10, 11, 12, 13, 17, 19, 20, 21, 22, 27, 32, 34, 35, 36, 44, 45
HM: 1, 5

BREEDABLE MOVES: Encore, Leech Life, Synthesis, Reflect, Swords Dance

TECHNIQUES

Name	Level	Type	Power	Name	Level	Type	Power	Name	Level	Type	Power	Name	Level	Type	Power
Vine Whip	0	Grass	35	Sleep Powder	15	Grass	-	Acid	23	Poison	40	Slam	45	Normal	80
Growth	6	Normal	-	Poisonpowder	17	Poison	-	Sweet Scent	30	Normal	-				
Wrap	11	Normal	15	Stun Spore	19	Grass	-	Razor Leaf	37	Grass	55				

#70 WEEPINBELL

TYPE: Grass/Poison

STATS	HP	Attack	Defense	Speed	SpAttack	SpDefense
	65	90	50	55	85	45

BREEDABLE MOVES: Encore, Leech Life, Synthesis, Reflect, Swords Dance

ABLE TO LEARN TM: 3, 6, 10, 11, 12, 13, 17, 19, 20, 21, 22, 27, 32, 34, 35, 36, 44, 45
HM: 1, 5

Name	Level	Type	Power	Name	Level	Type	Power
Acid	24	Poison	40	Slam	54	Normal	80
Sweet Scent	33	Normal	-				
Razor Leaf	42	Grass	55				

#71 VICTREEBEL

TYPE: Grass/Poison

STATS	HP	Attack	Defense	Speed	SpAttack	SpDefense
	80	105	65	70	100	60

BREEDABLE MOVES: Encore, Leech Life, Synthesis, Reflect, Swords Dance

ABLE TO LEARN TM: 3, 6, 10, 11, 12, 13, 15, 17, 19, 20, 21, 22, 27, 32, 34, 35, 36, 44, 45
HM: 1, 5

Name	Level	Type	Power
None			

#72 TENTACOOL

TYPE: Water/Poison

STATS	HP	Attack	Defense	Speed	SpAttack	SpDefense
	40	40	35	70	50	100

BREEDABLE MOVES: Aurora Beam, Haze, Rapid Spin, Safeguard, Mirror Coat

ABLE TO LEARN TM: 3, 6, 10, 13, 14, 16, 17, 18, 19, 20, 21, 27, 32, 34, 35, 36, 44, 45
HM: 1, 3, 6

Name	Level	Type	Power	Name	Level	Type	Power	Name	Level	Type	Power
Poison Sting	0	Poison	15	Acid	19	Poison	40	Barrier	36	Psychic	-
Supersonic	6	Normal	-	Bubblebeam	25	Water	65	Screech	43	Normal	-
Constrict	12	Normal	10	Wrap	30	Normal	15	Hydro Pump	49	Water	120

#73 TENTACRUEL

TYPE: Water/Poison

STATS	HP	Attack	Defense	Speed	SpAttack	SpDefense
	80	70	65	100	80	120

BREEDABLE MOVES: Aurora Beam, Haze, Rapid Spin, Safeguard, Mirror Coat

ABLE TO LEARN TM: 3, 6, 10, 13, 14, 15, 16, 17, 18, 19, 20, 21, 27, 32, 34, 35, 36, 44, 45
HM: 1, 3, 6

Name	Level	Type	Power
Barrier	38	Psychic	-
Screech	47	Normal	-
Hydro Pump	55	Water	120

#74 GEODUDE

TYPE: Rock/Ground

STATS	HP	Attack	Defense	Speed	SpAttack	SpDefense
	40	80	100	20	30	30

BREEDABLE MOVES: Mega Punch, Rock Slide

ABLE TO LEARN TM: 1, 2, 3, 4, 6, 8, 10, 11, 13, 17, 20, 21, 26, 27, 28, 31, 32, 34, 35, 37, 38, 40, 44, 45, 48
HM: 4

Name	Level	Type	Power	Name	Level	Type	Power	Name	Level	Type	Power
Tackle	0	Normal	35	Magnitude	16	Ground	-	Rollout	31	Rock	30
Defense Curl	6	Normal	-	Selfdestruct	21	Normal	200	Earthquake	36	Ground	100
Rock Throw	11	Rock	50	Harden	26	Normal	-	Explosion	41	Normal	250

#75 GRAVELER

TYPE: Rock/Ground

STATS	HP	Attack	Defense	Speed	SpAttack	SpDefense
	55	95	115	35	45	45

BREEDABLE MOVES: Mega Punch, Rock Slide

ABLE TO LEARN TM: 1, 2, 3, 4, 6, 8, 10, 11, 13, 17, 20, 21, 26, 27, 28, 31, 32, 34, 35, 37, 38, 40, 44, 45, 48
HM: 4

Name	Level	Type	Power	Name	Level	Type	Power
Harden	27	Normal	-	Explosion	48	Normal	250
Rollout	34	Rock	30				
Earthquake	41	Ground	100				

#76 GOLEM

TYPE: Rock/Ground

STATS	HP	Attack	Defense	Speed	SpAttack	SpDefense
	80	110	130	45	55	65

BREEDABLE MOVES: Mega Punch, Rock Slide

ABLE TO LEARN TM: 1, 2, 3, 4, 5, 6, 8, 10, 11, 13, 17, 20, 21, 26, 27, 28, 31, 32, 34, 35, 37, 38, 40, 44, 45, 48, 49
HM: 4

Name	Level	Type	Power	Name	Level	Type	Power
Harden	27	Normal	-	Explosion	48	Normal	250
Rollout	34	Rock	30				
Earthquake	41	Ground	100				

#77 PONYTA

TYPE: Fire

STATS	HP	Attack	Defense	Speed	SpAttack	SpDefense
	50	85	55	90	65	65

BREEDABLE MOVES: Thrash, Charm, Flame Wheel, Hypnosis, Quick Attack, Double Kick

ABLE TO LEARN TM: 2, 3, 6, 10, 11, 13, 17, 20, 21, 23, 27, 32, 34, 35, 38, 39, 44, 45
HM: None

TECHNIQUES

Name	Level	Type	Power	Name	Level	Type	Power	Name	Level	Type	Power
Tackle	0	Normal	35	Ember	13	Fire	40	Take Down	34	Normal	90
Growl	4	Normal	-	Stomp	19	Normal	65	Agility	43	Psychic	-
Tail Whip	8	Normal	-	Fire Spin	26	Fire	15	Fire Blast	53	Fire	120

#78 RAPIDASH

TYPE: Fire

STATS	HP	Attack	Defense	Speed	SpAttack	SpDefense
	65	100	70	105	80	80

BREEDABLE MOVES: Thrash, Charm, Flame Wheel, Hypnosis, Quick Attack, Double Kick

ABLE TO LEARN TM: 2, 3, 6, 10, 11, 13, 15, 17, 20, 21, 23, 27, 32, 34, 35, 38, 39, 44, 45
HM: None

TECHNIQUES

Name	Level	Type	Power
Fury Attack	40	Normal	15
Agility	47	Psychic	-
Fire Blast	61	Fire	120

#79 SLOWPOKE

TYPE: Water/Psychic

STATS	HP	Attack	Defense	Speed	SpAttack	SpDefense
	90	65	65	15	40	40

BREEDABLE MOVES: Safeguard, Belly Drum, Stomp, Future Sight

ABLE TO LEARN TM: 2, 3, 6, 7, 9, 10, 11, 13, 14, 16, 17, 18, 20, 21, 23, 26, 27, 28, 29, 30, 31, 32, 34, 35, 38, 39, 42, 44, 45, 50
HM: 3, 4, 5

TECHNIQUES

Name	Level	Type	Power	Name	Level	Type	Power	Name	Level	Type	Power
Tackle	0	Normal	35	Water Gun	15	Water	40	Headbutt	34	Normal	70
Curse	0	???	-	Confusion	20	Psychic	50	Amnesia	43	Psychic	-
Growl	6	Normal	-	Disable	29	Normal	-	Psychic	48	Psychic	90

#80 SLOWBRO

TYPE: Water/Psychic

STATS	HP	Attack	Defense	Speed	SpAttack	SpDefense
	95	75	110	30	100	80

BREEDABLE MOVES: Safeguard, Belly Drum, Stomp, Future Sight

ABLE TO LEARN TM: 1, 2, 3, 6, 7, 9, 10, 11, 13, 14, 16, 17, 18, 20, 21, 23, 26, 27, 28, 29, 30, 31, 32, 33, 34, 35, 38, 39, 42, 44, 45, 49, 50
HM: 3, 4, 5

TECHNIQUES

Name	Level	Type	Power
Withdraw	37	Water	-
Amnesia	46	Psychic	-
Psychic	54	Psychic	90

#81 MAGNEMITE

TYPE: Electric/Steel

STATS	HP	Attack	Defense	Speed	SpAttack	SpDefense
	25	35	70	45	95	55

BREEDABLE MOVES: None

ABLE TO LEARN TM: 3, 4, 6, 7, 10, 13, 17, 18, 20, 21, 25, 27, 32, 34, 35, 39, 44
HM: 5

TECHNIQUES

Name	Level	Type	Power	Name	Level	Type	Power	Name	Level	Type	Power
Tackle	0	Normal	35	Sonicboom	16	Normal	20	Swift	33	Normal	60
Thundershock	6	Electric	40	Thunder Wave	21	Electric	-	Screech	39	Normal	-
Supersonic	11	Normal	-	Lock-On	27	Normal	-	Zap Cannon	45	Electric	100

#82 MAGNETON

TYPE: Electric/Steel

STATS	HP	Attack	Defense	Speed	SpAttack	SpDefense
	50	60	95	70	120	70

BREEDABLE MOVES: None

ABLE TO LEARN TM: 3, 4, 6, 7, 10, 13, 15, 17, 18, 20, 21, 25, 27, 32, 34, 35, 39, 44
HM: 5

TECHNIQUES

Name	Level	Type	Power
Swift	35	Normal	60
Screech	43	Normal	-
Zap Cannon	53	Electric	100

#83 FARFETCH'D

TYPE: Normal/Flying

STATS	HP	Attack	Defense	Speed	SpAttack	SpDefense
	52	65	55	60	58	62

BREEDABLE MOVES: Mirror Move, Gust, Flail, Quick Attack, Foresight

ABLE TO LEARN TM: 2, 3, 6, 9, 10, 11, 13, 17, 20, 21, 23, 27, 31, 32, 34, 35, 39, 43, 44, 45, 46, 47
HM: 1, 2

TECHNIQUES

Name	Level	Type	Power	Name	Level	Type	Power	Name	Level	Type	Power
Peck	0	Flying	35	Fury Attack	19	Normal	15	Slash	37	Normal	70
Sand-Attack	7	Ground	-	Swords Dance	25	Normal	-	False Swipe	44	Normal	40
Leer	13	Normal	-	Agility	31	Psychic	-				

Pokémon STADIUM 2

#84 DODUO

TYPE: Normal/Flying

STATS	HP	Attack	Defense	Speed	SpAttack	SpDefense
	35	85	45	75	35	35

BREEDABLE MOVES: Haze, Flail, Supersonic, Quick Attack, Faint Attack

ABLE TO LEARN: TM: 3, 6, 10, 11, 13, 17, 20 , 21, 27, 31, 32, 34, 35, 39, 44, 45, 46, 47 / HM: 2

Name	Level	Type	Power	Name	Level	Type	Power	Name	Level	Type	Power	Name	Level	Type	Power
Peck	0	Flying	35	Fury Attack	13	Normal	15	Drill Peck	33	Flying	80				
Growl	0	Normal	-	Tri Attack	21	Normal	80	Agility	37	Psychic	-				
Pursuit	9	Dark	40	Rage	25	Normal	20								

#85 DODRIO

TYPE: Normal/Flying

STATS	HP	Attack	Defense	Speed	SpAttack	SpDefense
	60	110	70	100	60	60

BREEDABLE MOVES: Haze, Flail, Supersonic, Quick Attack, Faint Attack

ABLE TO LEARN: TM: 3, 6, 10, 11, 13, 15, 17, 20, 21, 27, 31, 32, 34, 35, 39, 44, 45, 46, 47 / HM: 2

Name	Level	Type	Power	Name	Level	Type	Power	Name	Level	Type	Power	Name	Level	Type	Power
Drill Peck	38	Flying	80												
Agility	47	Psychic	-												

#86 SEEL

TYPE: Water

STATS	HP	Attack	Defense	Speed	SpAttack	SpDefense
	65	45	55	45	45	70

BREEDABLE MOVES: Encore, Disable, Lick, Slam, Perish Song, Peck

ABLE TO LEARN: TM: 2, 3, 6, 10, 13, 14, 16, 17, 18, 20, 21, 27, 32, 34, 35, 44, 45 / HM: 3, 6, 7

Name	Level	Type	Power	Name	Level	Type	Power	Name	Level	Type	Power	Name	Level	Type	Power
Headbutt	0	Normal	70	Rest	21	Psychic	-	Safeguard	48	Normal	-				
Growl	5	Normal	-	Take Down	32	Normal	90								
Aurora Beam	16	Ice	65	Ice Beam	37	Ice	95								

#87 DEWGONG

TYPE: Water/Ice

STATS	HP	Attack	Defense	Speed	SpAttack	SpDefense
	90	70	80	70	70	70

BREEDABLE MOVES: Encore, Disable, Lick, Slam, Perish Song, Peck

ABLE TO LEARN: TM: 2, 3, 6, 10, 13, 14, 15, 16, 17, 18, 20, 21, 27, 32, 34, 35, 44, 45 / HM: 3, 6, 7

Name	Level	Type	Power	Name	Level	Type	Power	Name	Level	Type	Power	Name	Level	Type	Power
Ice Beam	43	Ice	95												
Safeguard	60	Normal	-												

#88 GRIMER

TYPE: Poison

STATS	HP	Attack	Defense	Speed	SpAttack	SpDefense
	80	80	50	25	40	50

BREEDABLE MOVES: Mean Look, Haze, Lick

ABLE TO LEARN: TM: 1, 3, 6, 7, 10, 11, 13, 17, 19, 20, 21, 25, 27, 31, 32, 33, 34, 35, 36, 38, 41, 44, 45, 46, 48 / HM: None

Name	Level	Type	Power	Name	Level	Type	Power	Name	Level	Type	Power	Name	Level	Type	Power
Pound	0	Normal	40	Disable	10	Normal	-	Screech	31	Normal	-				
Poison Gas	0	Poison	-	Sludge	16	Poison	65	Acid Armor	40	Poison	-				
Harden	5	Normal	-	Minimize	23	Normal	-	Sludge Bomb	50	Poison	90				

#89 MUK

TYPE: Poison

STATS	HP	Attack	Defense	Speed	SpAttack	SpDefense
	105	105	75	50	65	100

BREEDABLE MOVES: Mean Look, Haze, Lick

ABLE TO LEARN: TM: 1, 3, 6, 7, 10, 11, 13, 15, 17, 19, 20, 21, 25, 27, 31, 32, 33, 34, 35, 36, 38, 41, 44, 45, 46, 48 / HM: None

Name	Level	Type	Power	Name	Level	Type	Power	Name	Level	Type	Power	Name	Level	Type	Power
Acid Armor	45	Poison	-												
Sludge	45	Poison	65												
Sludge Bomb	60	Poison	90												

#90 SHELLDER

TYPE: Water

STATS	HP	Attack	Defense	Speed	SpAttack	SpDefense
	30	65	100	40	45	25

BREEDABLE MOVES: Screech, Rapid Spin, Barrier, Bubblebeam, Take Down

ABLE TO LEARN: TM: 3, 6, 10, 13, 14, 16, 17, 18, 20, 21, 27, 32, 34, 35, 39, 44, 45 / HM: 3, 6

Name	Level	Type	Power	Name	Level	Type	Power	Name	Level	Type	Power	Name	Level	Type	Power
Tackle	0	Normal	35	Aurora Beam	17	Ice	65	Clamp	41	Water	35				
Withdraw	0	Water	-	Protect	25	Normal	-	Ice Beam	49	Ice	95				
Supersonic	9	Normal	-	Leer	33	Normal	-								

#91 CLOYSTER

TYPE: Water/Ice

STATS	HP	Attack	Defense	Speed	SpAttack	SpDefense
	50	95	180	70	85	45

BREEDABLE MOVES

Screech	Barrier	Take Down
Rapid Spin	Bubblebeam	

ABLE TO LEARN
TM: 3, 6, 10, 13, 14, 15, 16, 17, 18, 20, 21, 27, 32, 34, 35, 39, 44, 45
HM: 3, 6

TECHNIQUES

Name	Level	Type	Power	Name	Level	Type	Power	Name	Level	Type	Power	Name	Level	Type	Power
Spike Cannon	41	Normal	20												

#92 GASTLY

TYPE: Ghost/Poison

STATS	HP	Attack	Defense	Speed	SpAttack	SpDefense
	30	35	30	80	100	35

BREEDABLE MOVES

Haze	Perish Song
Psywave	

ABLE TO LEARN
TM: 3, 6, 7, 9, 10, 11, 13, 17, 18, 19, 20, 21, 25, 27, 29, 30, 32, 34, 35, 42, 44, 45, 46, 50
HM: None

TECHNIQUES

Name	Level	Type	Power	Name	Level	Type	Power	Name	Level	Type	Power	Name	Level	Type	Power
Lick	0	Ghost	20	Mean Look	13	Normal	-	Confuse Ray	28	Ghost	-				
Hypnosis	0	Psychic	-	Curse	16	???	-	Dream Eater	33	Psychic	100				
Spite	8	Ghost	-	Night Shade	21	Ghost	-	Destiny Bond	36	Ghost	-				

#93 HAUNTER

TYPE: Ghost/Poison

STATS	HP	Attack	Defense	Speed	SpAttack	SpDefense
	45	50	45	95	115	55

BREEDABLE MOVES

Haze	Perish Song
Psywave	

ABLE TO LEARN
TM: 3, 6, 7, 9, 10, 11, 13, 17, 18, 19, 20, 21, 25, 27, 29, 30, 32, 34, 35, 42, 44, 45, 46, 50
HM: None

TECHNIQUES

Name	Level	Type	Power	Name	Level	Type	Power	Name	Level	Type	Power	Name	Level	Type	Power
Confuse Ray	31	Ghost	-												
Dream Eater	39	Psychic	100												
Destiny Bond	48	Ghost	-												

#94 GENGAR

TYPE: Ghost/Poison

STATS	HP	Attack	Defense	Speed	SpAttack	SpDefense
	60	65	60	110	130	75

BREEDABLE MOVES

Haze	Perish Song
Psywave	

ABLE TO LEARN
TM: 1, 2, 3, 6, 7, 8, 9, 10, 11, 13, 15, 17, 18, 19, 20, 21, 25, 27, 29, 30, 32, 33, 34, 35, 41, 42, 44, 45, 46, 48, 50
HM: 4

TECHNIQUES

Name	Level	Type	Power	Name	Level	Type	Power	Name	Level	Type	Power	Name	Level	Type	Power
Confuse Ray	31	Ghost	-												
Dream Eater	39	Psychic	100												
Destiny Bond	48	Ghost	-												

#95 ONIX

TYPE: Rock/Ground

STATS	HP	Attack	Defense	Speed	SpAttack	SpDefense
	35	45	160	70	30	45

BREEDABLE MOVES

Flail
Rock Slide

ABLE TO LEARN
TM: 2, 3, 4, 5, 6, 8, 10, 11, 13, 17, 20, 21, 23, 26, 27, 28, 31, 32, 34, 35, 37, 40, 44, 45
HM: 4

TECHNIQUES

Name	Level	Type	Power	Name	Level	Type	Power	Name	Level	Type	Power	Name	Level	Type	Power
Tackle	0	Normal	35	Rock Throw	14	Rock	50	Sandstorm	36	Rock	-				
Screech	0	Normal	-	Harden	23	Normal	-	Slam	40	Normal	80				
Bind	10	Normal	15	Rage	27	Normal	20								

#96 DROWZEE

TYPE: Psychic

STATS	HP	Attack	Defense	Speed	SpAttack	SpDefense
	60	48	45	42	43	90

BREEDABLE MOVES

Barrier
Light Screen

ABLE TO LEARN
TM: 1, 2, 3, 6, 7, 9, 10, 11, 13, 17, 18, 20, 21, 27, 29, 30, 32, 33, 34, 35, 41, 42, 44, 45, 48, 50
HM: 5

TECHNIQUES

Name	Level	Type	Power	Name	Level	Type	Power	Name	Level	Type	Power	Name	Level	Type	Power
Pound	0	Normal	40	Confusion	18	Psychic	50	Meditate	36	Psychic	-	Future Sight	45	Psychic	80
Hypnosis	0	Psychic	-	Headbutt	25	Normal	70	Psychic	40	Psychic	90				
Disable	10	Normal	-	Poison Gas	31	Poison	-	Psych Up	43	Normal	-				

#97 HYPNO

TYPE: Psychic

STATS	HP	Attack	Defense	Speed	SpAttack	SpDefense
	85	73	70	67	73	115

BREEDABLE MOVES

Barrier
Light Screen

ABLE TO LEARN
TM: 1, 2, 3, 6, 7, 9, 10, 11, 13, 15, 17, 18, 20, 21, 27, 29, 30, 32, 33, 34, 35, 41, 42, 44, 45, 48, 50
HM: 5

TECHNIQUES

Name	Level	Type	Power	Name	Level	Type	Power	Name	Level	Type	Power	Name	Level	Type	Power
Poison Gas	33	Poison	-	Psych Up	55	Normal	-								
Meditate	40	Psychic	-	Future Sight	60	Psychic	80								
Psychic	49	Psychic	90												

Pokémon STADIUM

#98 KRABBY

TYPE: Water

STATS	HP	Attack	Defense	Speed	SpAttack	SpDefense
	30	105	90	50	25	25

BREEDABLE MOVES: Dig, Flail, Amnesia, Haze, Slam

ABLE TO LEARN: TM: 3, 6, 8, 10, 13, 14, 16, 17, 18, 20, 21, 27, 31, 32, 34, 35, 44, 45, 46, 49
HM: 1, 3, 4, 6

TECHNIQUES

Name	Level	Type	Power	Name	Level	Type	Power	Name	Level	Type	Power
Bubble	0	Water	20	Harden	16	Normal	-	Protect	34	Normal	-
Leer	5	Normal	-	Stomp	23	Normal	65	Crabhammer	41	Water	90
Vicegrip	12	Normal	55	Guillotine	27	Normal	-				

#99 KINGLER

TYPE: Water

STATS	HP	Attack	Defense	Speed	SpAttack	SpDefense
	55	130	115	75	50	50

BREEDABLE MOVES: Dig, Flail, Amnesia, Haze, Slam

ABLE TO LEARN: TM: 3, 6, 8, 10, 13, 14, 15, 16, 17, 18, 20, 21, 27, 31, 32, 34, 35, 44, 45, 46, 49
HM: 1, 3, 4, 6

TECHNIQUES

Name	Level	Type	Power	Name	Level	Type	Power
Protect	38	Normal	-				
Crabhammer	49	Water	90				

#100 VOLTORB

TYPE: Electric

STATS	HP	Attack	Defense	Speed	SpAttack	SpDefense
	40	30	50	100	55	55

BREEDABLE MOVES: None

ABLE TO LEARN: TM: 2, 3, 4, 6, 7, 10, 13, 17, 18, 20, 21, 25, 27, 32, 34, 35, 39, 44
HM: 5

TECHNIQUES

Name	Level	Type	Power	Name	Level	Type	Power	Name	Level	Type	Power
Tackle	0	Normal	35	Selfdestruct	23	Normal	200	Swift	37	Normal	60
Screech	9	Normal	-	Rollout	29	Rock	30	Explosion	39	Normal	250
Sonicboom	17	Normal	20	Light Screen	33	Psychic	-	Mirror Coat	41	Psychic	-

#101 ELECTRODE

TYPE: Electric

STATS	HP	Attack	Defense	Speed	SpAttack	SpDefense
	60	50	70	140	80	80

BREEDABLE MOVES: None

ABLE TO LEARN: TM: 2, 3, 4, 6, 7, 10, 13, 15, 17, 18, 20, 21, 25, 27, 32, 34, 35, 39, 44
HM: 5

TECHNIQUES

Name	Level	Type	Power	Name	Level	Type	Power
Light Screen	34	Psychic	-	Mirror Coat	48	Psychic	-
Swift	40	Normal	60				
Explosion	44	Normal	250				

#102 EXEGGCUTE

TYPE: Grass/Psychic

STATS	HP	Attack	Defense	Speed	SpAttack	SpDefense
	60	40	80	40	60	45

BREEDABLE MOVES: Ancientpower, Moonlight, Reflect, Synthesis, Mega Drain

ABLE TO LEARN: TM: 3, 4, 6, 9, 10, 11, 13, 17, 19, 20, 21, 22, 27, 29, 32, 34, 35, 36, 42, 44, 45, 46, 50
HM: 4, 5

TECHNIQUES

Name	Level	Type	Power	Name	Level	Type	Power	Name	Level	Type	Power
Barrage	0	Normal	15	Leech Seed	13	Grass	-	Poisonpowder	31	Poison	-
Hypnosis	0	Psychic	-	Confusion	19	Psychic	50	Sleep Powder	37	Grass	-
Reflect	7	Psychic	-	Stun Spore	25	Grass	-	Solarbeam	43	Grass	120

#103 EXEGGUTOR

TYPE: Grass/Psychic

STATS	HP	Attack	Defense	Speed	SpAttack	SpDefense
	95	95	85	55	125	65

BREEDABLE MOVES: Ancientpower, Moonlight, Reflect, Synthesis, Mega Drain

ABLE TO LEARN: TM: 2, 3, 4, 6, 9, 10, 11, 13, 15, 17, 19, 20, 21, 22, 27, 29, 32, 34, 35, 36, 42, 44, 45, 46, 50
HM: 4, 5

TECHNIQUES

Name	Level	Type	Power	Name	Level	Type	Power
Stomp	19	Normal	65				
Egg Bomb	31	Normal	100				

#104 CUBONE

TYPE: Ground

STATS	HP	Attack	Defense	Speed	SpAttack	SpDefense
	50	50	95	35	40	50

BREEDABLE MOVES: Screech, Ancientpower, Perish Song, Rock Slide, Belly Drum, Skull Bash

ABLE TO LEARN: TM: 1, 2, 3, 6, 8, 10, 11, 13, 14, 16, 17, 20, 21, 23, 26, 27, 28, 31, 32, 34, 35, 37, 38, 41, 43, 44, 45, 46, 48
HM: 4

TECHNIQUES

Name	Level	Type	Power	Name	Level	Type	Power	Name	Level	Type	Power	Name	Level	Type	Power
Growl	0	Normal	-	Headbutt	13	Normal	70	Bonemerang	25	Ground	50	Thrash	37	Normal	90
Tail Whip	5	Normal	-	Leer	17	Normal	-	Rage	29	Normal	20	Bone Rush	41	Ground	25
Bone Club	9	Ground	65	Focus Energy	21	Normal	-	False Swipe	33	Normal	40				

#105 MAROWAK

TYPE: Ground

STATS	HP	Attack	Defense	Speed	SpAttack	SpDefense
	60	80	110	45	50	80

BREEDABLE MOVES: Screech / Rock Slide | Ancientpower / Belly Drum | Perish Song / Skull Bash

ABLE TO LEARN: TM: 1, 2, 3, 6, 8, 10, 11, 13, 14, 15, 16, 17, 20, 21, 23, 26, 27, 28, 31, 32, 34, 35, 37, 38, 41, 43, 44, 45, 46, 48
HM: 4

TECHNIQUES

Name	Level	Type	Power	Name	Level	Type	Power
Rage	32	Normal	20	Bone Rush	53	Ground	25
False Swipe	39	Normal	40				
Thrash	46	Normal	90				

#106 HITMONLEE

TYPE: Fighting

STATS	HP	Attack	Defense	Speed	SpAttack	SpDefense
	50	120	53	87	35	110

BREEDABLE MOVES: Rapid Spin / Mind Reader | Hi Jump Kick / Mach Punch

ABLE TO LEARN: TM: 1, 2, 3, 6, 8, 10, 11, 13, 17, 20, 21, 27, 31, 32, 34, 35, 37, 39, 43, 44, 45, 46
HM: 4

TECHNIQUES

Name	Level	Type	Power	Name	Level	Type	Power	Name	Level	Type	Power	Name	Level	Type	Power
Double Kick	0	Fighting	30	Jump Kick	16	Fighting	70	Mind Reader	31	Normal	-	Mega Kick	46	Normal	120
Meditate	6	Psychic	-	Focus Energy	21	Normal	-	Foresight	36	Normal	-	Reversal	51	Fighting	-
Rolling Kick	11	Fighting	60	Hi Jump Kick	26	Fighting	85	Endure	41	Normal	-				

#107 HITMONCHAN

TYPE: Fighting

STATS	HP	Attack	Defense	Speed	SpAttack	SpDefense
	50	105	79	76	35	110

BREEDABLE MOVES: Rapid Spin / Mind Reader | Hi Jump Kick / Mach Punch

ABLE TO LEARN: TM: 1, 2, 3, 6, 8, 10, 11, 13, 17, 20, 21, 27, 31, 32, 33, 34, 35, 39, 41, 43, 44, 45, 46, 48
HM: 4

TECHNIQUES

Name	Level	Type	Power	Name	Level	Type	Power	Name	Level	Type	Power	Name	Level	Type	Power
Comet Punch	0	Normal	18	Fire Punch	26	Fire	75	Mach Punch	32	Fighting	40	Counter	50	Fighting	-
Agility	7	Psychic	-	Ice Punch	26	Ice	75	Mega Punch	38	Normal	80				
Pursuit	13	Dark	40	Thunderpunch	26	Electric	75	Detect	44	Fighting	-				

#108 LICKITUNG

TYPE: Normal

STATS	HP	Attack	Defense	Speed	SpAttack	SpDefense
	90	55	75	30	60	75

BREEDABLE MOVES: Belly Drum / Magnitude | Body Slam

ABLE TO LEARN: TM: 1, 2, 3, 4, 6, 8, 9, 10, 11, 13, 14, 15, 16, 17, 18, 20, 21, 23, 25, 26, 27, 30, 31, 32, 33, 34, 35, 37, 38, 40, 41, 42, 44, 45, 46, 48, 50
HM: 1, 3, 4

TECHNIQUES

Name	Level	Type	Power	Name	Level	Type	Power	Name	Level	Type	Power
Lick	0	Ghost	20	Stomp	19	Normal	65	Slam	37	Normal	80
Supersonic	7	Normal	-	Wrap	25	Normal	15	Screech	43	Normal	-
Defense Curl	13	Normal	-	Disable	31	Normal	-				

#109 KOFFING

TYPE: Poison

STATS	HP	Attack	Defense	Speed	SpAttack	SpDefense
	40	65	95	35	60	45

BREEDABLE MOVES: Pain Split / Screech | Psybeam / Psywave | Destiny Bond

ABLE TO LEARN: TM: 3, 4, 6, 7, 10, 11, 13, 17, 20, 21, 25, 27, 32, 34, 35, 36, 38, 44, 45, 46
HM: None

TECHNIQUES

Name	Level	Type	Power	Name	Level	Type	Power	Name	Level	Type	Power
Poison Gas	0	Poison	-	Selfdestruct	17	Normal	200	Haze	33	Ice	-
Tackle	0	Normal	35	Sludge	21	Poison	65	Explosion	41	Normal	250
Smog	9	Poison	20	Smokescreen	25	Normal	-	Destiny Bond	45	Ghost	-

#110 WEEZING

TYPE: Poison

STATS	HP	Attack	Defense	Speed	SpAttack	SpDefense
	65	90	120	60	85	70

BREEDABLE MOVES: Pain Split / Screech | Psybeam / Psywave | Destiny Bond

ABLE TO LEARN: TM: 3, 4, 6, 7, 10, 11, 13, 15, 17, 20, 21, 25, 27, 32, 34, 35, 36, 38, 44, 45, 46
HM: None

TECHNIQUES

Name	Level	Type	Power
Explosion	44	Normal	-
Destiny Bond	51	Ghost	-

#111 RHYHORN

TYPE: Ground/Rock

STATS	HP	Attack	Defense	Speed	SpAttack	SpDefense
	80	85	95	25	30	30

BREEDABLE MOVES: Thrash / Pursuit | Counter / Crunch | Reversal / Magnitude | Rock Slide

ABLE TO LEARN: TM: 2, 3, 4, 5, 6, 7, 8, 10, 11, 13, 14, 16, 17, 20, 21, 23, 25, 26, 27, 28, 31, 32, 34, 35, 37, 38, 44, 45
HM: 4

TECHNIQUES

Name	Level	Type	Power	Name	Level	Type	Power	Name	Level	Type	Power
Horn Attack	0	Normal	65	Fury Attack	19	Normal	15	Take Down	49	Normal	90
Tail Whip	0	Normal	-	Scary Face	31	Normal	-	Earthquake	55	Ground	100
Stomp	13	Normal	65	Horn Drill	37	Normal	-				

#112 RHYDON

TYPE: Ground/Rock

STATS	HP	Attack	Defense	Speed	SpAttack	SpDefense
	105	130	120	40	45	45

BREEDABLE MOVES: Thrash, Pursuit, Counter, Crunch, Reversal, Magnitude, Rock Slide

ABLE TO LEARN — TM: 1, 2, 3, 4, 5, 6, 7, 8, 10, 11, 13, 14, 15, 16, 17, 20, 21, 23, 25, 26, 27, 28, 31, 32, 34, 35, 37, 38, 41, 44, 45, 48, 49 HM: 3, 4

TECHNIQUES

Name	Level	Type	Power
Take Down	54	Normal	90
Earthquake	65	Ground	100

#113 CHANSEY

TYPE: Normal

STATS	HP	Attack	Defense	Speed	SpAttack	SpDefense
	250	5	5	50	35	105

BREEDABLE MOVES: Heal Bell, Present, Metronome

ABLE TO LEARN — TM: 1, 2, 3, 4, 6, 7, 8, 9, 10, 11, 13, 14, 15, 16, 17, 18, 20, 21, 22, 23, 25, 27, 29, 30, 31, 32, 34, 35, 37, 38, 40, 42, 44, 45 HM: 4, 5

TECHNIQUES

Name	Level	Type	Power	Name	Level	Type	Power	Name	Level	Type	Power	Name	Level	Type	Power
Pound	0	Normal	40	Softboiled	13	Normal	-	Sing	29	Normal	-	Light Screen	49	Psychic	-
Growl	5	Normal	-	Doubleslap	17	Normal	15	Egg Bomb	35	Normal	100	Double-Edge	57	Normal	120
Tail Whip	9	Normal	-	Minimize	23	Normal	-	Defense Curl	41	Normal	-				

#114 TANGELA

TYPE: Grass

STATS	HP	Attack	Defense	Speed	SpAttack	SpDefense
	65	55	115	60	100	40

BREEDABLE MOVES: Flail, Amnesia, Confusion, Reflect, Mega Drain

ABLE TO LEARN — TM: 2, 3, 6, 9, 10, 11, 12, 13, 15, 17, 19, 20, 21, 22, 27, 32, 34, 35, 36, 44, 45, 46 HM: 1, 5

TECHNIQUES

Name	Level	Type	Power	Name	Level	Type	Power	Name	Level	Type	Power	Name	Level	Type	Power
Constrict	0	Normal	10	Poisonpowder	13	Poison	-	Mega Drain	31	Grass	40	Growth	46	Normal	-
Sleep Powder	4	Grass	-	Vine Whip	19	Grass	35	Stun Spore	34	Grass	-				
Absorb	10	Grass	20	Bind	25	Normal	15	Slam	40	Normal	80				

#115 KANGASKHAN

TYPE: Normal

STATS	HP	Attack	Defense	Speed	SpAttack	SpDefense
	105	95	80	90	40	80

BREEDABLE MOVES: Disable, Focus Energy, Safeguard, Stomp, Foresight

ABLE TO LEARN — TM: 1, 2, 3, 5, 6, 7, 8, 10, 11, 13, 14, 15, 16, 17, 18, 20, 21, 23, 25, 26, 27, 30, 31, 32, 33, 34, 35, 37, 38, 41, 44, 45, 48, 49 HM: 3, 4

TECHNIQUES

Name	Level	Type	Power	Name	Level	Type	Power	Name	Level	Type	Power	Name	Level	Type	Power
Comet Punch	0	Normal	18	Tail Whip	19	Normal	-	Endure	37	Normal	-				
Leer	7	Normal	-	Mega Punch	25	Normal	80	Dizzy Punch	43	Normal	70				
Bite	13	Dark	60	Rage	31	Normal	20	Reversal	49	Fighting	-				

#116 HORSEA

TYPE: Water

STATS	HP	Attack	Defense	Speed	SpAttack	SpDefense
	30	40	70	60	70	25

BREEDABLE MOVES: Aurora Beam, Octazooka, Disable, Flail, Splash, Dragon Rage

ABLE TO LEARN — TM: 2, 3, 6, 10, 13, 14, 16, 17, 18, 20, 21, 24, 27, 32, 34, 35, 39, 44, 45 HM: 3, 6, 7

TECHNIQUES

Name	Level	Type	Power	Name	Level	Type	Power	Name	Level	Type	Power
Bubble	0	Water	20	Water Gun	22	Water	40	Hydro Pump	43	Water	120
Smokescreen	8	Normal	-	Twister	29	Dragon	40				
Leer	15	Normal	-	Agility	36	Psychic	-				

#117 SEADRA

TYPE: Water

STATS	HP	Attack	Defense	Speed	SpAttack	SpDefense
	55	65	95	85	95	45

BREEDABLE MOVES: Aurora Beam, Octazooka, Disable, Flail, Splash, Dragon Rage

ABLE TO LEARN — TM: 2, 3, 6, 10, 13, 14, 15, 16, 17, 18, 20, 21, 24, 27, 32, 34, 35, 39, 44, 45 HM: 3, 6, 7

TECHNIQUES

Name	Level	Type	Power
Agility	40	Psychic	-
Hydro Pump	51	Water	120

#118 GOLDEEN

TYPE: Water

STATS	HP	Attack	Defense	Speed	SpAttack	SpDefense
	45	67	60	63	35	50

BREEDABLE MOVES: Haze, Psybeam, Hydro Pump

ABLE TO LEARN — TM: 3, 6, 10, 13, 14, 15, 16, 17, 18, 20, 21, 27, 32, 34, 35, 39, 44, 45 HM: 3, 7

TECHNIQUES

Name	Level	Type	Power	Name	Level	Type	Power	Name	Level	Type	Power
Peck	0	Flying	35	Horn Attack	15	Normal	65	Waterfall	38	Water	80
Tail Whip	0	Normal	-	Flail	24	Normal	-	Horn Drill	43	Normal	-
Supersonic	10	Normal	-	Fury Attack	29	Normal	15	Agility	52	Psychic	-

#119 SEAKING

TYPE: Water

STATS	HP	Attack	Defense	Speed	SpAttack	SpDefense
	80	92	65	68	65	80

BREEDABLE MOVES: Haze, Hydro Pump, Psybeam

ABLE TO LEARN TM: 3, 6, 10, 13, 14, 15, 16, 17, 18, 20, 21, 27, 32, 34, 35, 39, 44, 45
HM: 3, 7

Name	Level	Type	Power	Name	Level	Type	Power	Name	Level	Type	Power	Name	Level	Type	Power
Waterfall	41	Water	80												
Horn Drill	49	Normal	-												
Agility	61	Psychic	-												

#120 STARYU

TYPE: Water

STATS	HP	Attack	Defense	Speed	SpAttack	SpDefense
	30	45	55	85	70	55

BREEDABLE MOVES: None

ABLE TO LEARN TM: 3, 6, 7, 9, 10, 13, 14, 16, 17, 18, 20, 21, 25, 27, 29, 32, 34, 35, 39, 44, 45
HM: 3, 5, 6, 7

Name	Level	Type	Power	Name	Level	Type	Power	Name	Level	Type	Power	Name	Level	Type	Power
Tackle	0	Normal	35	Rapid Spin	13	Normal	20	Bubblebeam	31	Water	65	Hydro Pump	50	Water	120
Harden	0	Normal	-	Recover	19	Normal	-	Minimize	37	Normal	-				
Water Gun	7	Water	40	Swift	25	Normal	60	Light Screen	43	Psychic	-				

#121 STARMIE

TYPE: Water/Psychic

STATS	HP	Attack	Defense	Speed	SpAttack	SpDefense
	60	75	85	115	100	85

BREEDABLE MOVES: None

ABLE TO LEARN TM: 3, 6, 7, 9, 10, 13, 14, 15, 16, 17, 18, 20, 21, 25, 27, 29, 32, 34, 35, 39, 42, 44, 45, 50
HM: 3, 5, 6, 7

Name	Level	Type	Power	Name	Level	Type	Power	Name	Level	Type	Power	Name	Level	Type	Power
Confuse Ray	37	Ghost	-												

#122 MR. MIME

TYPE: Psychic

STATS	HP	Attack	Defense	Speed	SpAttack	SpDefense
	40	45	65	90	100	120

BREEDABLE MOVES: Hypnosis, Mimic, Future Sight

ABLE TO LEARN TM: 1, 2, 3, 6, 7, 9, 10, 11, 13, 15, 17, 20, 21, 22, 25, 27, 29, 30, 31, 32, 33, 34, 35, 41, 42, 44, 45, 46, 48, 50
HM: 5

Name	Level	Type	Power	Name	Level	Type	Power	Name	Level	Type	Power	Name	Level	Type	Power
Barrier	0	Psychic	-	Meditate	16	Psychic	-	Reflect	26	Psychic	-	Baton Pass	41	Normal	-
Confusion	6	Psychic	50	Doubleslap	21	Normal	15	Encore	31	Normal	-	Safeguard	46	Normal	-
Substitute	11	Normal	-	Light Screen	26	Psychic	-	Psybeam	36	Psychic	65				

#123 SCYTHER

TYPE: Bug/Flying

STATS	HP	Attack	Defense	Speed	SpAttack	SpDefense
	70	110	80	105	55	80

BREEDABLE MOVES: Counter, Reversal, Baton Pass, Razor Wind, Safeguard, Light Screen

ABLE TO LEARN TM: 2, 3, 6, 8, 10, 11, 13, 15, 17, 20, 21, 27, 32, 34, 35, 39, 43, 44, 45, 46, 47, 49
HM: 1

Name	Level	Type	Power	Name	Level	Type	Power	Name	Level	Type	Power	Name	Level	Type	Power
Quick Attack	0	Normal	40	Pursuit	12	Dark	40	Wing Attack	30	Flying	60	Double Team	48	Normal	-
Leer	0	Normal	-	False Swipe	18	Normal	40	Slash	36	Normal	70				
Focus Energy	6	Normal	-	Agility	24	Psychic	-	Swords Dance	42	Normal	-				

#124 JYNX

TYPE: Ice/Psychic

STATS	HP	Attack	Defense	Speed	SpAttack	SpDefense
	65	50	35	95	115	95

BREEDABLE MOVES: Meditate

ABLE TO LEARN TM: 1, 2, 3, 6, 9, 10, 12, 13, 14, 15, 16, 17, 18, 20, 21, 27, 29, 30, 31, 32, 33, 34, 35, 42, 44, 45, 46, 50
HM: None

Name	Level	Type	Power	Name	Level	Type	Power	Name	Level	Type	Power	Name	Level	Type	Power
Pound	0	Normal	40	Powder Snow	13	Ice	40	Mean Look	35	Normal	-	Blizzard	57	Ice	120
Lick	0	Ghost	20	Doubleslap	21	Normal	15	Body Slam	41	Normal	85				
Lovely Kiss	9	Normal	-	Ice Punch	25	Ice	75	Perish Song	51	Normal	-				

#125 ELECTABUZZ

TYPE: Electric

STATS	HP	Attack	Defense	Speed	SpAttack	SpDefense
	65	83	57	105	95	85

BREEDABLE MOVES: Karate Chop, Rolling Kick, Barrier, Meditate

ABLE TO LEARN TM: 1, 2, 3, 6, 7, 8, 10, 13, 15, 17, 18, 20, 21, 23, 25, 27, 29, 31, 32, 33, 34, 35, 39, 41, 43, 44, 45, 46, 48
HM: 4, 5

Name	Level	Type	Power	Name	Level	Type	Power	Name	Level	Type	Power	Name	Level	Type	Power
Quick Attack	0	Normal	40	Light Screen	17	Psychic	-	Thunderbolt	47	Electric	95				
Leer	0	Normal	-	Swift	25	Normal	60	Thunder	58	Electric	120				
Thunderpunch	9	Electric	75	Screech	36	Normal	-								

#126 MAGMAR

TYPE: Fire

STATS	HP	Attack	Defense	Speed	SpAttack	SpDefense
	65	95	57	93	100	85

BREEDABLE MOVES: Screech, Barrier, Karate Chop, Mega Punch

ABLE TO LEARN
TM: 1, 2, 3, 6, 8, 10, 11, 13, 15, 17, 20, 21, 23, 27, 29, 31, 32, 34, 35, 38, 41, 43, 44, 45, 46, 48
HM: 4

Name	Level	Type	Power	Name	Level	Type	Power	Name	Level	Type	Power	Name	Level	Type	Power
Ember	0	Fire	40	Smog	13	Poison	20	Flamethrower	41	Fire	95				
Leer	7	Normal	-	Smokescreen	25	Normal	-	Confuse Ray	49	Ghost	-				
Fire Punch	19	Fire	75	Sunny Day	33	Fire	-	Fire Blast	57	Fire	120				

#127 PINSIR

TYPE: Bug

STATS	HP	Attack	Defense	Speed	SpAttack	SpDefense
	65	125	100	85	55	70

BREEDABLE MOVES: Flail, Fury Attack

ABLE TO LEARN
TM: 2, 3, 6, 8, 10, 11, 13, 15, 17, 20, 21, 27, 32, 34, 35, 44, 45, 46, 49
HM: 1, 4

Name	Level	Type	Power	Name	Level	Type	Power	Name	Level	Type	Power	Name	Level	Type	Power
Vicegrip	0	Normal	55	Seismic Toss	19	Fighting	-	Submission	37	Fighting	80				
Focus Energy	7	Normal	-	Harden	25	Normal	-	Swords Dance	43	Normal	-				
Bind	13	Normal	15	Guillotine	31	Normal	-								

#128 TAUROS

TYPE: Normal

STATS	HP	Attack	Defense	Speed	SpAttack	SpDefense
	75	100	95	110	40	70

BREEDABLE MOVES: None

ABLE TO LEARN
TM: 2, 3, 6, 7, 8, 10, 11, 13, 14, 15, 16, 17, 20, 21, 23, 25, 26, 27, 32, 34, 35, 38, 44, 45
HM: 3, 4

Name	Level	Type	Power	Name	Level	Type	Power	Name	Level	Type	Power	Name	Level	Type	Power
Tackle	0	Normal	35	Horn Attack	13	Normal	65	Rest	34	Psychic	-				
Tail Whip	4	Normal	-	Scary Face	19	Normal	-	Thrash	43	Normal	90				
Rage	8	Normal	20	Pursuit	26	Dark	40	Take Down	53	Normal	90				

#129 MAGIKARP

TYPE: Water

STATS	HP	Attack	Defense	Speed	SpAttack	SpDefense
	20	10	55	80	15	20

BREEDABLE MOVES: None

ABLE TO LEARN
TM: None
HM: None

Name	Level	Type	Power	Name	Level	Type	Power	Name	Level	Type	Power	Name	Level	Type	Power
Splash	0	Normal	-												
Tackle	15	Normal	35												
Flail	30	Normal	-												

#130 GYARADOS

TYPE: Water/Flying

STATS	HP	Attack	Defense	Speed	SpAttack	SpDefense
	95	125	79	81	60	100

BREEDABLE MOVES: None

ABLE TO LEARN
TM: 2, 3, 5, 6, 7, 8, 10, 13, 14, 15, 16, 17, 18, 20, 21, 24, 25, 27, 32, 34, 35, 37, 38, 44, 45
HM: 3, 4, 6, 7

Name	Level	Type	Power	Name	Level	Type	Power	Name	Level	Type	Power	Name	Level	Type	Power
Bite	20	Dark	60	Twister	35	Dragon	40	Hyper Beam	50	Normal	150				
Dragon Rage	25	Dragon	40	Hydro Pump	40	Water	120								
Leer	30	Normal	-	Rain Dance	45	Water	-								

#131 LAPRAS

TYPE: Water/Ice

STATS	HP	Attack	Defense	Speed	SpAttack	SpDefense
	130	85	80	60	85	95

BREEDABLE MOVES: Aurora Beam, Foresight

ABLE TO LEARN
TM: 2, 3, 6, 7, 8, 10, 13, 14, 15, 16, 17, 18, 20, 21, 23, 24, 25, 27, 29, 32, 34, 35, 42, 44, 45, 50
HM: 3, 4, 6

Name	Level	Type	Power	Name	Level	Type	Power	Name	Level	Type	Power	Name	Level	Type	Power
Water Gun	0	Water	40	Mist	8	Ice	-	Perish Song	29	Normal	-	Safeguard	50	Normal	-
Growl	0	Normal	-	Body Slam	15	Normal	85	Ice Beam	36	Ice	95	Hydro Pump	57	Water	120
Sing	0	Normal	-	Confuse Ray	22	Ghost	-	Rain Dance	43	Water	-				

#132 DITTO

TYPE: Normal

STATS	HP	Attack	Defense	Speed	SpAttack	SpDefense
	48	48	48	48	48	48

BREEDABLE MOVES: None

ABLE TO LEARN
TM: None
HM: None

Name	Level	Type	Power	Name	Level	Type	Power	Name	Level	Type	Power	Name	Level	Type	Power
Transform	0	Normal	-												

#133 EEVEE

TYPE: Normal

STATS	HP	Attack	Defense	Speed	SpAttack	SpDefense
	55	55	50	55	45	65

BREEDABLE MOVES: Charm, Flail

ABLE TO LEARN TM: 2, 3, 6, 10, 11, 13, 17, 18, 20, 21, 23, 27, 30, 31, 32, 34, 35, 39, 43, 44, 45
HM: None

TECHNIQUES

Name	Level	Type	Power	Name	Level	Type	Power	Name	Level	Type	Power	Name	Level	Type	Power
Tackle	0	Normal	35	Growl	16	Normal	-	Focus Energy	36	Normal	-				
Tail Whip	0	Normal	-	Quick Attack	23	Normal	40	Take Down	42	Normal	90				
Sand-Attack	8	Ground	-	Bite	30	Dark	60								

#134 VAPOREON

TYPE: Water

STATS	HP	Attack	Defense	Speed	SpAttack	SpDefense
	130	65	60	65	110	95

BREEDABLE MOVES: Charm, Flail

ABLE TO LEARN TM: 2, 3, 5, 6, 10, 11, 13, 14, 15, 16, 17, 18, 20, 21, 23, 27, 30, 31, 32, 34, 35, 39, 43, 44, 45
HM: 3, 6, 7

TECHNIQUES

Name	Level	Type	Power	Name	Level	Type	Power	Name	Level	Type	Power	Name	Level	Type	Power
Sand-Attack	8	Ground	-	Quick Attack	23	Normal	40	Aurora Beam	36	Ice	65	Acid Armor	47	Poison	-
Water Gun	16	Water	40	Bite	30	Dark	60	Haze	742	Ice	-	Hydro Pump	52	Water	120

#135 JOLTEON

TYPE: Electric

STATS	HP	Attack	Defense	Speed	SpAttack	SpDefense
	65	65	60	130	110	95

BREEDABLE MOVES: Charm, Flail

ABLE TO LEARN TM: 2, 3, 5, 6, 7, 10, 11, 13, 15, 17, 18, 20, 21, 23, 25, 27, 30, 31, 32, 34, 35, 39, 43, 44, 45
HM: 5

TECHNIQUES

Name	Level	Type	Power	Name	Level	Type	Power	Name	Level	Type	Power	Name	Level	Type	Power
Sand-Attack	8	Ground	-	Double Kick	30	Fighting	30	Agility	47	Psychic	-				
Thundershock	16	Electric	40	Pin Missile	36	Bug	14	Thunder	52	Electric	120				
Quick Attack	23	Normal	40	Thunder Wave	42	Electric	-								

#136 FLAREON

TYPE: Fire

STATS	HP	Attack	Defense	Speed	SpAttack	SpDefense
	65	130	60	65	95	110

BREEDABLE MOVES: Charm, Flail

ABLE TO LEARN TM: 2, 3, 5, 6, 7, 10, 11, 13, 15, 17, 18, 20, 21, 23, 27, 30, 31, 32, 34, 35, 38, 39, 43, 44, 45
HM: None

TECHNIQUES

Name	Level	Type	Power	Name	Level	Type	Power	Name	Level	Type	Power	Name	Level	Type	Power
Sand-Attack	8	Ground	-	Bite	30	Dark	60	Leer	47	Normal	-				
Ember	16	Fire	40	Fire Spin	36	Fire	15	Flamethrower	52	Fire	95				
Quick Attack	23	Normal	40	Smog	42	Poison	20								

#137 PORYGON

TYPE: Normal

STATS	HP	Attack	Defense	Speed	SpAttack	SpDefense
	65	60	70	40	85	75

BREEDABLE MOVES: None

ABLE TO LEARN TM: 3, 6, 7, 9, 10, 11, 13, 14, 15, 16, 17, 18, 20, 21, 23, 25, 27, 29, 32, 34, 35, 39, 42, 44, 46, 50
HM: 5

TECHNIQUES

Name	Level	Type	Power	Name	Level	Type	Power	Name	Level	Type	Power	Name	Level	Type	Power
Tackle	0	Normal	35	Agility	9	Psychic	-	Sharpen	24	Normal	-	Zap Cannon	44	Electric	100
Conversion	0	Normal	-	Psybeam	12	Psychic	65	Lock-On	32	Normal	-				
Conversion2	0	Normal	-	Recover	20	Normal	-	Tri Attack	36	Normal	80				

#138 OMANYTE

TYPE: Rock/Water

STATS	HP	Attack	Defense	Speed	SpAttack	SpDefense
	35	40	100	35	90	55

BREEDABLE MOVES: Aurora Beam, Haze, Slam, Supersonic, Bubblebeam

ABLE TO LEARN TM: 2, 3, 4, 6, 8, 10, 13, 14, 16, 17, 18, 20, 21, 27, 32, 34, 35, 37, 44, 45, 46
HM: 3, 6

TECHNIQUES

Name	Level	Type	Power	Name	Level	Type	Power	Name	Level	Type	Power	Name	Level	Type	Power
Contrict	0	Normal	10	Water Gun	19	Water	40	Ancientpower	49	Rock	60				
Withdraw	0	Water	-	Leer	31	Normal	-	Hydro Pump	55	Water	120				
Bite	13	Dark	60	Protect	37	Normal	-								

#139 OMASTAR

TYPE: Rock/Water

STATS	HP	Attack	Defense	Speed	SpAttack	SpDefense
	70	60	125	55	115	70

BREEDABLE MOVES: Aurora Beam, Haze, Slam, Supersonic, Bubblebeam

ABLE TO LEARN TM: 2, 3, 4, 6, 8, 10, 13, 14, 15, 16, 17, 18, 20, 21, 27, 32, 34, 35, 37, 44, 45, 46
HM: 3, 6

TECHNIQUES

Name	Level	Type	Power	Name	Level	Type	Power	Name	Level	Type	Power	Name	Level	Type	Power
Spike Cannon	40	Normal	20												
Ancientpower	54	Rock	60												
Hydro Pump	65	Water	120												

#140 KABUTO

TYPE: Rock/Water

STATS	HP	Attack	Defense	Speed	SpAttack	SpDefense
	30	80	90	55	55	45

BREEDABLE MOVES: Dig, Aurora Beam, Rapid Spin, Flail, Bubblebeam

ABLE TO LEARN: TM: 3, 4, 6, 8, 10, 13, 14, 16, 17, 18, 19, 20, 21, 27, 32, 34, 35, 37, 44, 45, 46
HM: None

TECHNIQUES

Name	Level	Type	Power	Name	Level	Type	Power	Name	Level	Type	Power
Scratch	0	Normal	40	Leer	19	Normal	-	Mega Drain	46	Grass	40
Harden	0	Normal	-	Sand-Attack	28	Ground	-	Ancientpower	55	Rock	60
Absorb	10	Grass	20	Endure	37	Normal	-				

#141 KABUTOPS

TYPE: Rock/Water

STATS	HP	Attack	Defense	Speed	SpAttack	SpDefense
	60	115	105	80	65	70

BREEDABLE MOVES: Dig, Aurora Beam, Rapid Spin, Flail, Bubblebeam

ABLE TO LEARN: TM: 2, 3, 4, 6, 8, 10, 13, 14, 15, 16, 17, 18, 19, 20, 21, 27, 32, 34, 35, 37, 44, 45, 46, 49
HM: 1, 3, 6

TECHNIQUES

Name	Level	Type	Power
Slash	40	Normal	70
Mega Drain	51	Grass	40
Ancientpower	65	Rock	60

#142 AERODACTYL

TYPE: Rock/Flying

STATS	HP	Attack	Defense	Speed	SpAttack	SpDefense
	80	105	65	130	60	75

BREEDABLE MOVES: Pursuit, Foresight, Whirlwind

ABLE TO LEARN: TM: 2, 3, 5, 6, 8, 10, 13, 15, 17, 18, 20, 21, 23, 24, 26, 27, 32, 34, 35, 37, 38, 39, 43, 44, 45, 47
HM: 2

TECHNIQUES

Name	Level	Type	Power	Name	Level	Type	Power	Name	Level	Type	Power
Wing Attack	0	Flying	60	Supersonic	22	Normal	-	Take Down	43	Normal	90
Agility	8	Psychic	-	Ancientpower	29	Rock	60	Hyper Beam	50	Normal	150
Bite	15	Dark	60	Scary Face	36	Normal	-				

#143 SNORLAX

TYPE: Normal

STATS	HP	Attack	Defense	Speed	SpAttack	SpDefense
	160	110	65	30	65	110

BREEDABLE MOVES: Lick

ABLE TO LEARN: TM: 1, 2, 3, 4, 6, 7, 8, 9, 10, 11, 13, 14, 15, 16, 17, 18, 20, 21, 22, 25, 26, 27, 29, 30, 31, 32, 33, 34, 35, 37, 38, 40, 41, 44, 45, 48
HM: 3, 4

TECHNIQUES

Name	Level	Type	Power	Name	Level	Type	Power	Name	Level	Type	Power	Name	Level	Type	Power
Tackle	0	Normal	35	Belly Drum	22	Normal	-	Snore	36	Normal	40	Hyper Beam	57	Normal	150
Amnesia	8	Psychic	-	Headbutt	29	Normal	70	Body Slam	43	Normal	85				
Defense Curl	15	Normal	-	Rest	36	Psychic	-	Rollout	50	Rock	30				

#144 ARTICUNO

TYPE: Ice/Flying

STATS	HP	Attack	Defense	Speed	SpAttack	SpDefense
	90	85	100	85	95	125

BREEDABLE MOVES: None

ABLE TO LEARN: TM: 3, 5, 6, 8, 10, 11, 13, 14, 15, 16, 17, 18, 20, 21, 27, 31, 32, 34, 35, 37, 39, 43, 44, 47
HM: 2

TECHNIQUES

Name	Level	Type	Power	Name	Level	Type	Power	Name	Level	Type	Power
Gust	0	Flying	40	Agility	25	Psychic	-	Reflect	61	Psychic	-
Powder Snow	0	Ice	40	Mind Reader	37	Normal	-	Blizzard	73	Ice	120
Mist	13	Ice	-	Ice Beam	49	Ice	95				

#145 ZAPDOS

TYPE: Electric/Flying

STATS	HP	Attack	Defense	Speed	SpAttack	SpDefense
	90	90	85	100	125	90

BREEDABLE MOVES: None

ABLE TO LEARN: TM: 3, 5, 6, 7, 8, 10, 11, 13, 15, 17, 18, 20, 21, 25, 27, 31, 32, 34, 35, 37, 39, 43, 44, 47
HM: 2, 5

TECHNIQUES

Name	Level	Type	Power	Name	Level	Type	Power	Name	Level	Type	Power
Peck	0	Flying	35	Agility	25	Psychic	-	Light Screen	61	Psychic	-
Thundershock	0	Electric	40	Detect	37	Fighting	-	Thunder	73	Electric	120
Thunder Wave	13	Electric	-	Drill Peck	49	Flying	80				

#146 MOLTRES

TYPE: Fire/Flying

STATS	HP	Attack	Defense	Speed	SpAttack	SpDefense
	90	100	90	90	125	85

BREEDABLE MOVES: None

ABLE TO LEARN: TM: 3, 5, 6, 8, 10, 11, 13, 15, 17, 18, 20, 21, 27, 31, 32, 34, 35, 37, 38, 39, 43, 44, 47
HM: 2

TECHNIQUES

Name	Level	Type	Power	Name	Level	Type	Power	Name	Level	Type	Power
Wing Attack	0	Flying	60	Agility	25	Psychic	-	Safeguard	61	Normal	-
Ember	0	Fire	40	Endure	37	Normal	-	Sky Attack	73	Flying	140
Fire Spin	13	Fire	15	Flamethrower	49	Fire	95				

#147 DRATINI

TYPE: Dragon

STATS	HP	Attack	Defense	Speed	SpAttack	SpDefense
	41	64	45	50	50	50

BREEDABLE MOVES: Haze, Mist, Supersonic, Light Screen

ABLE TO LEARN: TM: 2, 3, 6, 7, 10, 13, 14, 16, 17, 18, 20, 21, 23, 24, 25, 27, 32, 34, 35, 38, 39, 43, 44, 45
HM: 3, 7

Name	Level	Type	Power	Name	Level	Type	Power	Name	Level	Type	Power	Name	Level	Type	Power
Wrap	0	Normal	15	Twister	15	Dragon	40	Agility	36	Psychic	-	Hyper Beam	57	Normal	150
Leer	0	Normal	-	Dragon Rage	22	Dragon	40	Safeguard	43	Normal	-				
Thunder Wave	8	Electric	-	Slam	29	Normal	80	Outrage	50	Dragon	90				

#148 DRAGONAIR

TYPE: Dragon

STATS	HP	Attack	Defense	Speed	SpAttack	SpDefense
	61	84	65	70	70	70

BREEDABLE MOVES: Haze, Mist, Supersonic, Light Screen

ABLE TO LEARN: TM: 2, 3, 6, 7, 10, 13, 14, 16, 17, 18, 20, 21, 23, 24, 25, 27, 32, 34, 35, 38, 39, 43, 44, 45
HM: 3, 7

Name	Level	Type	Power	Name	Level	Type	Power	Name	Level	Type	Power	Name	Level	Type	Power
Agility	38	Psychic	-	Hyper Beam	65	Normal	150								
Safeguard	47	Normal	-												
Outrage	56	Dragon	90												

#149 DRAGONITE

TYPE: Dragon/Flying

STATS	HP	Attack	Defense	Speed	SpAttack	SpDefense
	91	134	65	80	100	100

BREEDABLE MOVES: Haze, Mist, Supersonic, Light Screen

ABLE TO LEARN: TM: 1, 2, 3, 6, 7, 8, 10, 13, 14, 15, 16, 17, 18, 20, 21, 23, 24, 25, 27, 31, 32, 33, 34, 35, 37, 38, 39, 41, 43, 44, 45, 47, 48, 49
HM: 2, 3, 4, 6, 7

Name	Level	Type	Power	Name	Level	Type	Power	Name	Level	Type	Power	Name	Level	Type	Power
Wing Attack	55	Flying	60												
Outrage	61	Dragon	90												
Hyper Beam	75	Normal	150												

#150 MEWTWO

TYPE: Psychic

STATS	HP	Attack	Defense	Speed	SpAttack	SpDefense
	106	110	90	130	154	90

BREEDABLE MOVES: None

ABLE TO LEARN: TM: 1, 2, 3, 6, 7, 8, 9, 10, 11, 13, 14, 15, 16, 17, 18, 20, 21, 22, 23, 25, 27, 29, 30, 31, 32, 33, 34, 35, 38, 39, 41, 42, 43, 44, 48, 50
HM: 4, 5

Name	Level	Type	Power	Name	Level	Type	Power	Name	Level	Type	Power	Name	Level	Type	Power
Confusion	0	Psychic	50	Swift	22	Normal	60	Mist	55	Ice	-	Recover	88	Normal	-
Disable	0	Normal	-	Psych Up	33	Normal	-	Psychic	66	Psychic	90	Safeguard	99	Normal	-
Barrier	11	Psychic	-	Future Sight	44	Psychic	80	Amnesia	77	Psychic	-				

#151 MEW

TYPE: Psychic

STATS	HP	Attack	Defense	Speed	SpAttack	SpDefense
	100	100	100	100	100	100

BREEDABLE MOVES: None

ABLE TO LEARN: TM: All
HM: All

Name	Level	Type	Power	Name	Level	Type	Power	Name	Level	Type	Power	Name	Level	Type	Power
Pound	0	Normal	40	Metronome	30	Normal	-								
Transform	10	Normal	-	Psychic	40	Psychic	90								
Mega Punch	20	Normal	80	Ancientpower	50	Rock	60								

#152 CHIKORITA

TYPE: Grass

STATS	HP	Attack	Defense	Speed	SpAttack	SpDefense
	45	49	65	45	49	65

BREEDABLE MOVES: Counter, Ancientpower, Flail, Vine Whip, Leech Seed

ABLE TO LEARN: TM: 2, 3, 6, 10, 11, 12, 13, 17, 19, 20, 21, 22, 23, 27, 31, 32, 34, 35, 43, 44, 45
HM: 1, 5

Name	Level	Type	Power	Name	Level	Type	Power	Name	Level	Type	Power	Name	Level	Type	Power
Tackle	0	Normal	35	Reflect	12	Psychic	-	Body Slam	29	Normal	85	Solarbeam	50	Grass	120
Growl	0	Normal	-	Poisonpowder	15	Poison	-	Light Screen	36	Psychic	-				
Razor Leaf	8	Grass	55	Synthesis	22	Grass	-	Safeguard	43	Normal	-				

#153 BAYLEEF

TYPE: Grass

STATS	HP	Attack	Defense	Speed	SpAttack	SpDefense
	60	62	80	60	63	80

BREEDABLE MOVES: Counter, Ancientpower, Flail, Vine Whip, Leech Seed

ABLE TO LEARN: TM: 2, 3, 6, 8, 10, 11, 12, 13, 17, 19, 20, 21, 22, 23, 27, 31, 32, 34, 35, 43, 44, 45, 49
HM: 1, 4, 5

Name	Level	Type	Power	Name	Level	Type	Power	Name	Level	Type	Power	Name	Level	Type	Power
Synthesis	23	Grass	-	Safeguard	47	Normal	-								
Body Slam	31	Normal	85	Solarbeam	55	Grass	120								
Light Screen	39	Psychic	-												

#154 MEGANIUM

TYPE: Grass

STATS	HP	Attack	Defense	Speed	SpAttack	SpDefense
	80	82	100	80	83	100

BREEDABLE MOVES

Counter	Flail	Leech Seed
Ancientpower	Vine Whip	

ABLE TO LEARN
TM: 2, 3, 6, 8, 10, 11, 12, 13, 15, 17, 19, 20, 21, 22, 23, 26, 27, 31, 32, 34, 35, 43, 44, 45, 49
HM: 1, 4, 5

TECHNIQUES

Name	Level	Type	Power	Name	Level	Type	Power	Name	Level	Type	Power	Name	Level	Type	Power
Light Screen	41	Psychic	-												
Safeguard	51	Normal	-												
Solarbeam	61	Grass	120												

#155 CYNDAQUIL

TYPE: Fire

STATS	HP	Attack	Defense	Speed	SpAttack	SpDefense
	39	52	43	65	60	50

BREEDABLE MOVES

Thrash	Fury Swipes	Quick Attack
Reversal	Foresight	

ABLE TO LEARN
TM: 2, 3, 4, 6, 10, 11, 13, 17, 20, 21, 23, 27, 28, 31, 32, 34, 35, 38, 39, 40, 43, 44, 45
HM: 1

TECHNIQUES

Name	Level	Type	Power	Name	Level	Type	Power	Name	Level	Type	Power	Name	Level	Type	Power
Tackle	0	Normal	35	Ember	12	Fire	40	Swift	36	Normal	60				
Leer	0	Normal	-	Quick Attack	19	Normal	40	Flamethrower	46	Fire	95				
Smokescreen	6	Normal	-	Flame Wheel	27	Fire	60								

#156 QUILAVA

TYPE: Fire

STATS	HP	Attack	Defense	Speed	SpAttack	SpDefense
	58	64	58	80	80	65

BREEDABLE MOVES

Thrash	Fury Swipes	Quick Attack
Reversal	Foresight	

ABLE TO LEARN
TM: 2, 3, 4, 5, 6, 8, 10, 11, 13, 17, 20, 21, 23, 27, 28, 31, 32, 34, 35, 38, 39, 40, 43, 44, 45, 49
HM: 1, 4

TECHNIQUES

Name	Level	Type	Power	Name	Level	Type	Power	Name	Level	Type	Power	Name	Level	Type	Power
Quick Attack	21	Normal	40	Flamethrower	54	Fire	95								
Flame Wheel	31	Fire	60												
Swift	42	Normal	60												

#157 TYPHLOSION

TYPE: Fire

STATS	HP	Attack	Defense	Speed	SpAttack	SpDefense
	78	84	78	100	109	85

BREEDABLE MOVES

Thrash	Fury Swipes	Quick Attack
Reversal	Foresight	

ABLE TO LEARN
TM: 1, 2, 3, 4, 5, 6, 8, 10, 11, 13, 15, 17, 20, 21, 23, 26, 27, 28, 31, 32, 34, 35, 38, 39, 40, 41, 43, 44, 45, 48, 49
HM: 1, 4

TECHNIQUES

Name	Level	Type	Power	Name	Level	Type	Power	Name	Level	Type	Power	Name	Level	Type	Power
Swift	45	Normal	60												
Flamethrower	60	Fire	95												

#158 TOTODILE

TYPE: Water

STATS	HP	Attack	Defense	Speed	SpAttack	SpDefense
	50	65	64	43	44	48

BREEDABLE MOVES

Thrash	Razor Wind	Ancientpower
Rock Slide	Crunch	Hydro Pump

ABLE TO LEARN
TM: 1, 2, 3, 6, 10, 13, 14, 16, 17, 18, 20, 21, 23, 27, 28, 31, 32, 33, 34, 35, 43, 44, 45
HM: 1, 3, 6

TECHNIQUES

Name	Level	Type	Power	Name	Level	Type	Power	Name	Level	Type	Power	Name	Level	Type	Power
Scratch	0	Normal	40	Water Gun	13	Water	40	Slash	35	Normal	70				
Leer	0	Normal	-	Bite	20	Dark	60	Screech	43	Normal	-				
Rage	7	Normal	20	Scary Face	27	Normal	-	Hydro Pump	52	Water	120				

#159 CROCONAW

TYPE: Water

STATS	HP	Attack	Defense	Speed	SpAttack	SpDefense
	65	80	80	58	59	63

BREEDABLE MOVES

Thrash	Razor Wind	Ancientpower
Rock Slide	Crunch	Hydro Pump

ABLE TO LEARN
TM: 1, 2, 3, 5, 6, 8, 10, 13, 14, 16, 17, 18, 20, 21, 23, 27, 28, 31, 32, 33, 34, 35, 43, 44, 45, 49
HM: 1, 3, 4, 6

TECHNIQUES

Name	Level	Type	Power	Name	Level	Type	Power	Name	Level	Type	Power	Name	Level	Type	Power
Bite	21	Dark	60	Screech	45	Normal	-								
Scary Face	28	Normal	-	Hydro Pump	55	Water	120								
Slash	37	Normal	70												

#160 FERALIGATR

TYPE: Water

STATS	HP	Attack	Defense	Speed	SpAttack	SpDefense
	85	105	100	78	79	83

BREEDABLE MOVES

Thrash	Razor Wind	Ancientpower
Rock Slide	Crunch	Hydro Pump

ABLE TO LEARN
TM: 1, 2, 3, 5, 6, 8, 10, 13, 14, 15, 16, 17, 18, 20, 21, 23, 26, 27, 28, 31, 32, 33, 34, 35, 43, 44, 45, 49
HM: 1, 3, 4, 6

TECHNIQUES

Name	Level	Type	Power	Name	Level	Type	Power	Name	Level	Type	Power	Name	Level	Type	Power
Slash	38	Normal	70												
Screech	47	Normal	-												
Hydro Pump	58	Water	120												

#161 SENTRET

TYPE: Normal

STATS	HP	Attack	Defense	Speed	SpAttack	SpDefense
	35	46	34	20	35	45

BREEDABLE MOVES: Pursuit, Focus Energy, Reversal, Slash, Double-Edge

ABLE TO LEARN: TM: 1, 2, 3, 4, 6, 10, 11, 13, 17, 20, 21, 23, 27, 28, 30, 31, 32, 33, 34, 35, 39, 40, 41, 43, 44, 45, 46, 48, 49
HM: 1, 3

TECHNIQUES

Name	Level	Type	Power	Name	Level	Type	Power	Name	Level	Type	Power
Tackle	0	Normal	35	Fury Swipes	17	Normal	18	Amnesia	41	Psychic	-
Defense Curl	5	Normal	-	Slam	25	Normal	80				
Quick Attack	11	Normal	40	Rest	33	Psychic	-				

#162 FURRET

TYPE: Normal

STATS	HP	Attack	Defense	Speed	SpAttack	SpDefense
	85	76	64	90	45	55

BREEDABLE MOVES: Pursuit, Focus Energy, Reversal, Slash, Double-Edge

ABLE TO LEARN: TM: 1, 2, 3, 4, 6, 10, 11, 13, 15, 17, 20, 21, 23, 27, 28, 30, 31, 32, 33, 34, 35, 39, 40, 41, 43, 44, 45, 46, 48, 49
HM: 1, 3, 4

TECHNIQUES

Name	Level	Type	Power	Name	Level	Type	Power
Fury Swipes	18	Normal	18	Amnesia	48	Psychic	-
Slam	28	Normal	80				
Rest	38	Psychic	-				

#163 HOOTHOOT

TYPE: Normal/Flying

STATS	HP	Attack	Defense	Speed	SpAttack	SpDefense
	60	30	30	50	35	56

BREEDABLE MOVES: Mirror Move, Faint Attack, Supersonic, Wing Attack, Whirlwind

ABLE TO LEARN: TM: 3, 6, 10, 11, 13, 17, 20, 21, 27, 31, 32, 34, 35, 39, 42, 43, 44, 45, 46, 47, 50
HM: 2, 5

TECHNIQUES

Name	Level	Type	Power	Name	Level	Type	Power	Name	Level	Type	Power
Tackle	0	Normal	35	Peck	11	Flying	35	Take Down	28	Normal	90
Growl	0	Normal	-	Hypnosis	16	Psychic	-	Confusion	34	Psychic	50
Foresight	6	Normal	-	Reflect	22	Psychic	-	Dream Eater	48	Psychic	100

#164 NOCTOWL

TYPE: Normal/Flying

STATS	HP	Attack	Defense	Speed	SpAttack	SpDefense
	100	50	50	70	76	96

BREEDABLE MOVES: Mirror Move, Faint Attack, Supersonic, Wing Attack, Whirlwind

ABLE TO LEARN: TM: 3, 6, 10, 11, 13, 15, 17, 20, 21, 27, 31, 32, 34, 35, 39, 42, 43, 44, 45, 46, 47, 50
HM: 2, 5

TECHNIQUES

Name	Level	Type	Power	Name	Level	Type	Power
Reflect	25	Psychic	-	Dream Eater	57	Psychic	100
Take Down	33	Normal	90				
Confusion	41	Psychic	50				

#165 LEDYBA

TYPE: Bug/Flying

STATS	HP	Attack	Defense	Speed	SpAttack	SpDefense
	43	20	30	55	40	80

BREEDABLE MOVES: Bide, Psybeam, Light Screen

ABLE TO LEARN: TM: 1, 2, 3, 4, 6, 10, 11, 12, 13, 17, 19, 20, 21, 22, 27, 28, 32, 33, 34, 35, 39, 41, 44, 45, 46
HM: 5

TECHNIQUES

Name	Level	Type	Power	Name	Level	Type	Power	Name	Level	Type	Power	Name	Level	Type	Power
Tackle	0	Normal	35	Light Screen	22	Psychic	-	Baton Pass	29	Normal	-	Double-Edge	50	Normal	120
Supersonic	8	Normal	-	Reflect	22	Psychic	-	Swift	36	Normal	60				
Comet Punch	15	Normal	18	Safeguard	22	Normal	-	Agility	43	Psychic	-				

#166 LEDIAN

TYPE: Bug/Flying

STATS	HP	Attack	Defense	Speed	SpAttack	SpDefense
	55	35	50	85	55	110

BREEDABLE MOVES: Bide, Psybeam, Light Screen

ABLE TO LEARN: TM: 1, 2, 3, 4, 6, 10, 11, 12, 13, 15, 17, 19, 20, 21, 22, 27, 28, 32, 33, 34, 35, 39, 41, 44, 45, 46
HM: 5

TECHNIQUES

Name	Level	Type	Power	Name	Level	Type	Power	Name	Level	Type	Power
Light Screen	24	Psychic	-	Baton Pass	33	Normal	-	Double-Edge	60	Normal	120
Reflect	24	Psychic	-	Swift	42	Normal	60				
Safeguard	24	Normal	-	Agility	51	Psychic	-				

#167 SPINARAK

TYPE: Bug/Poison

STATS	HP	Attack	Defense	Speed	SpAttack	SpDefense
	40	60	40	30	40	40

BREEDABLE MOVES: Pursuit, Disable, Psybeam, Sonicboom, Baton Pass

ABLE TO LEARN: TM: 3, 6, 10, 11, 13, 17, 19, 20, 21, 22, 27, 28, 29, 32, 34, 35, 36, 44, 45, 46
HM: 5

TECHNIQUES

Name	Level	Type	Power	Name	Level	Type	Power	Name	Level	Type	Power	Name	Level	Type	Power
Poison Sting	0	Poison	15	Constrict	11	Normal	10	Fury Swipes	30	Normal	18	Psychic	53	Psychic	90
String Shot	0	Bug	-	Night Shade	17	Ghost	-	Spider Web	37	Bug	-				
Scary Face	6	Normal	-	Leech Life	23	Bug	20	Screech	45	Normal	-				

#168 ARIADOS

STATS	HP	Attack	Defense	Speed	SpAttack	SpDefense
	70	90	70	40	60	60

TYPE: Bug/Poison

BREEDABLE MOVES:

Pursuit	Psybeam	Baton Pass
Disable	Sonicboom	

ABLE TO LEARN TM: 3, 6, 10, 11, 13, 15, 17, 19, 20, 21, 22, 27, 28, 29, 32, 34, 35, 36, 44, 45, 46
HM: 5

TECHNIQUES

Name	Level	Type	Power	Name	Level	Type	Power	Name	Level	Type	Power	Name	Level	Type	Power
Leech Life	25	Bug	20	Screech	53	Normal	-								
Fury Swipes	34	Normal	18	Psychic	63	Psychic	90								
Spider Web	43	Bug	-												

#169 CROBAT

STATS	HP	Attack	Defense	Speed	SpAttack	SpDefense
	85	90	80	130	70	80

TYPE: Poison/Flying

BREEDABLE MOVES:

Pursuit	Faint Attack	Whirlwind
Gust	Quick Attack	

ABLE TO LEARN TM: 3, 6, 10, 11, 13, 15, 17, 19, 20, 21, 27, 32, 34, 35, 39, 43, 44, 45, 46, 47
HM: 2

TECHNIQUES

Name	Level	Type	Power	Name	Level	Type	Power	Name	Level	Type	Power	Name	Level	Type	Power
Wing Attack	30	Flying	60												
Mean Look	42	Normal	-												
Haze	55	Ice	-												

#170 CHINCHOU

STATS	HP	Attack	Defense	Speed	SpAttack	SpDefense
	75	38	38	67	56	56

TYPE: Water/Electric

BREEDABLE MOVES:

Screech	Flail
Supersonic	

ABLE TO LEARN TM: 3, 6, 7, 10, 13, 17, 18, 20, 21, 25, 27, 32, 34, 44, 45
HM: 3, 5, 6, 7

TECHNIQUES

Name	Level	Type	Power	Name	Level	Type	Power	Name	Level	Type	Power	Name	Level	Type	Power
Bubble	0	Water	20	Flail	13	Normal	-	Confuse Ray	29	Ghost	-				
Thunder Wave	0	Electric	-	Water Gun	17	Water	40	Take Down	37	Normal	90				
Supersonic	5	Normal	-	Spark	25	Electric	65	Hydro Pump	41	Water	120				

#171 LANTURN

STATS	HP	Attack	Defense	Speed	SpAttack	SpDefense
	125	58	58	67	76	76

TYPE: Water/Electric

BREEDABLE MOVES:

Screech	Flail
Supersonic	

ABLE TO LEARN TM: 3, 6, 7, 10, 13, 15, 17, 18, 20, 21, 25, 27, 32, 34, 35, 44, 45
HM: 3, 5, 6, 7

TECHNIQUES

Name	Level	Type	Power	Name	Level	Type	Power	Name	Level	Type	Power	Name	Level	Type	Power
Confuse Ray	33	Ghost	-												
Take Down	45	Normal	90												
Hydro Pump	53	Water	120												

#172 PICHU

STATS	HP	Attack	Defense	Speed	SpAttack	SpDefense
	20	40	15	60	35	35

TYPE: Electric

BREEDABLE MOVES:

Encore	Bide	Present
Doubleslap	Reversal	

ABLE TO LEARN TM: 1, 2, 3, 4, 6, 7, 10, 13, 17, 18, 20, 21, 23, 25, 27, 31, 32, 34, 35, 39, 40, 43, 44, 45
HM: 4, 5

TECHNIQUES

Name	Level	Type	Power	Name	Level	Type	Power	Name	Level	Type	Power	Name	Level	Type	Power
Thundershock	0	Electric	40	Thunder Wave	8	Electric	-								
Charm	0	Normal	-	Sweet Kiss	11	Normal	-								
Tail Whip	6	Normal	-												

#173 CLEFFA

STATS	HP	Attack	Defense	Speed	SpAttack	SpDefense
	70	45	48	35	60	65

TYPE: Normal

BREEDABLE MOVES:

Amnesia	Belly Drum	Mimic
Splash	Present	Metronome

ABLE TO LEARN TM: 1, 2, 3, 4, 6, 7, 9, 10, 11, 13, 16, 17, 18, 20, 21, 22, 23, 27, 29, 30, 31, 32, 34, 35, 38, 40, 42, 43, 44, 45, 50
HM: 5

TECHNIQUES

Name	Level	Type	Power	Name	Level	Type	Power	Name	Level	Type	Power	Name	Level	Type	Power
Pound	0	Normal	40	Sing	8	Normal	-								
Charm	0	Normal	-	Sweet Kiss	13	Normal	-								
Encore	4	Normal	-												

#174 IGGLYBUFF

STATS	HP	Attack	Defense	Speed	SpAttack	SpDefense
	90	30	15	15	40	20

TYPE: Normal

BREEDABLE MOVES:

Faint Attack	Perish Song
Present	

ABLE TO LEARN TM: 1, 2, 3, 4, 6, 7, 9, 10, 11, 13, 16, 17, 18, 20, 21, 22, 27, 29, 30, 31, 32, 34, 35, 38, 40, 42, 43, 44, 45, 50
HM: 5

TECHNIQUES

Name	Level	Type	Power	Name	Level	Type	Power	Name	Level	Type	Power	Name	Level	Type	Power
Sing	0	Normal	-	Pound	9	Normal	40								
Charm	0	Normal	-	Sweet Kiss	14	Normal	-								
Defense Curl	4	Normal	-												

#175 TOGEPI

TYPE: Normal

STATS	HP	Attack	Defense	Speed	SpAttack	SpDefense
	35	20	65	20	40	65

BREEDABLE MOVES

Mirror Move	Present	Future Sight
Peck	Foresight	

ABLE TO LEARN
TM: 2, 3, 4, 6, 7, 8, 9, 10, 11, 13, 17, 18, 20, 22, 27, 29, 30, 31, 32, 34, 35, 38, 39, 40, 42, 43, 44, 45
HM: 5

TECHNIQUES

Name	Level	Type	Power	Name	Level	Type	Power	Name	Level	Type	Power	Name	Level	Type	Power
Charm	0	Normal	-	Sweet Kiss	18	Normal	-	Double-Edge	38	Normal	120				
Growl	0	Normal	-	Encore	25	Normal	-								
Metronome	7	Normal	-	Safeguard	31	Normal	-								

#176 TOGETIC

TYPE: Normal/ Flying

STATS	HP	Attack	Defense	Speed	SpAttack	SpDefense
	55	40	85	40	80	105

BREEDABLE MOVES

Mirror Move	Present	Future Sight
Peck	Foresight	

ABLE TO LEARN
TM: 2, 3, 4, 6, 7, 8, 9, 10, 11, 13, 15, 17, 18, 20, 21, 22, 27, 29, 30, 31, 32, 34, 35, 38, 39, 40, 42, 43, 44, 45, 47
HM: 2, 5

TECHNIQUES

Name	Level	Type	Power	Name	Level	Type	Power	Name	Level	Type	Power	Name	Level	Type	Power
Metronome	7	Normal	-	Safeguard	31	Normal	-								
Sweet Kiss	18	Normal	-	Double-Edge	38	Normal	120								
Encore	25	Normal	-												

#177 NATU

TYPE: Psychic/ Flying

STATS	HP	Attack	Defense	Speed	SpAttack	SpDefense
	40	50	45	70	70	45

BREEDABLE MOVES

Haze	Quick Attack	Steel Wing
Faint Attack	Drill Peck	

ABLE TO LEARN
TM: 3, 6, 9, 10, 11, 13, 14, 15, 17, 19, 20, 21, 22, 27, 29, 32, 34, 35, 39, 42, 43, 44, 45, 46, 50
HM: 5

TECHNIQUES

Name	Level	Type	Power	Name	Level	Type	Power	Name	Level	Type	Power	Name	Level	Type	Power
Peck	0	Flying	35	Teleport	20	Psychic	-	Psychic	50	Psychic	90				
Leer	0	Normal	-	Future Sight	30	Psychic	80								
Night Shade	10	Ghost	-	Confuse Ray	40	Ghost	-								

#178 XATU

TYPE: Psychic/ Flying

STATS	HP	Attack	Defense	Speed	SpAttack	SpDefense
	65	75	70	95	95	70

BREEDABLE MOVES

Haze	Quick Attack	Steel Wing
Faint Attack	Drill Peck	

ABLE TO LEARN
TM: 3, 6, 9, 10, 11, 13, 14, 15, 17, 19, 20, 21, 22, 27, 29, 32, 34, 35, 39, 42, 43, 44, 45, 46, 50
HM: 2, 5

TECHNIQUES

Name	Level	Type	Power	Name	Level	Type	Power	Name	Level	Type	Power	Name	Level	Type	Power
Future Sight	35	Psychic	80												
Confuse Ray	50	Ghost	-												
Psychic	65	Psychic	90												

#179 MAREEP

TYPE: Electric

STATS	HP	Attack	Defense	Speed	SpAttack	SpDefense
	55	40	40	35	65	45

BREEDABLE MOVES

Screech	Safeguard	Body Slam
Thunderbolt	Take Down	Reflect

ABLE TO LEARN
TM: 1, 2, 3, 6, 7, 8, 10, 13, 17, 18, 20, 21, 23, 25, 27, 32, 34, 35, 39, 40, 41, 44, 45, 48
HM: 5

TECHNIQUES

Name	Level	Type	Power	Name	Level	Type	Power	Name	Level	Type	Power	Name	Level	Type	Power
Tackle	0	Normal	35	Thunder Wave	16	Electric	-	Thunder	37	Electric	120				
Growl	0	Normal	-	Cotton Spore	23	Grass	-								
Thundershock	9	Electric	40	Light Screen	30	Psychic	-								

#180 FLAAFFY

TYPE: Electric

STATS	HP	Attack	Defense	Speed	SpAttack	SpDefense
	70	55	55	45	80	60

BREEDABLE MOVES

Screech	Safeguard	Body Slam
Thunderbolt	Take Down	Reflect

ABLE TO LEARN
TM: 1, 2, 3, 6, 7, 8, 10, 13, 17, 18, 20, 21, 23, 25, 27, 32, 34, 35, 39, 40, 41, 44, 45, 48
HM: 4, 5

TECHNIQUES

Name	Level	Type	Power	Name	Level	Type	Power	Name	Level	Type	Power	Name	Level	Type	Power
Thunder Wave	18	Electric	-	Thunder	45	Electric	120								
Cotton Spore	27	Grass	-												
Light Screen	36	Psychic	-												

#181 AMPHAROS

TYPE: Electric

STATS	HP	Attack	Defense	Speed	SpAttack	SpDefense
	90	75	75	55	115	90

BREEDABLE MOVES

Screech	Safeguard	Body Slam
Thunderbolt	Take Down	Reflect

ABLE TO LEARN
TM: 1, 2, 3, 6, 7, 8, 10, 13, 17, 18, 20, 21, 23, 25, 27, 32, 34, 35, 39, 40, 41, 44, 45, 48
HM: 4, 5

TECHNIQUES

Name	Level	Type	Power	Name	Level	Type	Power	Name	Level	Type	Power	Name	Level	Type	Power
Thunderpunch	30	Electric	75												
Light Screen	42	Psychic	-												
Thunder	57	Electric	120												

#182 BELLOSSOM

TYPE: Grass

STATS	HP	Attack	Defense	Speed	SpAttack	SpDefense
	75	80	85	50	90	100

BREEDABLE MOVES: Synthesis, Flail, Razor Leaf, Swords Dance

ABLE TO LEARN TM: 3, 6, 10, 11, 12, 13, 15, 17, 19, 20, 21, 22, 27, 32, 34, 35, 44, 45
HM: 1, 5

TECHNIQUES

Name	Level	Type	Power	Name	Level	Type	Power	Name	Level	Type	Power	Name	Level	Type	Power
Solarbeam	55	Grass	120												

#183 MARILL

TYPE: Water

STATS	HP	Attack	Defense	Speed	SpAttack	SpDefense
	70	20	50	40	20	50

BREEDABLE MOVES: Supersonic, Amnesia, Belly Drum, Light Screen, Present, Future Sight, Foresight, Perish Song

ABLE TO LEARN TM: 1, 2, 3, 4, 6, 8, 10, 13, 14, 16, 17, 18, 20, 21, 23, 27, 33, 34, 35, 39, 40, 44, 45
HM: 3, 6, 7

TECHNIQUES

Name	Level	Type	Power	Name	Level	Type	Power	Name	Level	Type	Power	Name	Level	Type	Power
Tackle	0	Normal	35	Water Gun	10	Water	40	Double-Edge	28	Normal	120				
Defense Curl	3	Normal	-	Rollout	15	Rock	30	Rain Dance	36	Water	-				
Tail Whip	6	Normal	-	Bubblebeam	21	Water	65								

#184 AZUMARILL

TYPE: Water

STATS	HP	Attack	Defense	Speed	SpAttack	SpDefense
	100	50	80	50	50	80

BREEDABLE MOVES: Supersonic, Amnesia, Belly Drum, Light Screen, Present, Future Sight, Foresight, Perish Song

ABLE TO LEARN TM: 1, 2, 3, 4, 6, 8, 10, 13, 14, 15, 16, 17, 18, 20, 21, 23, 27, 33, 34, 35, 39, 40, 44, 45
HM: 3, 4, 6, 7

TECHNIQUES

Name	Level	Type	Power	Name	Level	Type	Power	Name	Level	Type	Power	Name	Level	Type	Power
Bubblebeam	25	Water	65												
Double-Edge	36	Normal	120												
Rain Dance	48	Water	-												

#185 SUDOWOODO

TYPE: Rock

STATS	HP	Attack	Defense	Speed	SpAttack	SpDefense
	70	100	115	30	30	65

BREEDABLE MOVES: Selfdestruct

ABLE TO LEARN TM: 1, 2, 3, 4, 6, 8, 9, 10, 11, 13, 17, 20, 21, 26, 27, 28, 31, 32, 33, 34, 35, 37, 40, 41, 44, 45, 46, 48
HM: 4

TECHNIQUES

Name	Level	Type	Power	Name	Level	Type	Power	Name	Level	Type	Power	Name	Level	Type	Power
Rock Throw	0	Rock	50	Low Kick	19	Fighting	50	Slam	46	Normal	80				
Mimic	0	Normal	-	Rock Slide	28	Rock	75								
Flail	10	Normal	-	Faint Attack	37	Dark	60								

#186 POLITOED

TYPE: Water

STATS	HP	Attack	Defense	Speed	SpAttack	SpDefense
	90	75	75	70	90	100

BREEDABLE MOVES: Haze, Mind Reader, Mist, Splash, Bubblebeam

ABLE TO LEARN TM: 1, 2, 3, 6, 8, 10, 13, 14, 15, 16, 17, 18, 20, 21, 26, 27, 29, 31, 32, 33, 34, 35, 40, 43, 44, 45, 46
HM: 3, 4, 6, 7

TECHNIQUES

Name	Level	Type	Power	Name	Level	Type	Power	Name	Level	Type	Power	Name	Level	Type	Power
Perish Song	35	Normal	-												
Swagger	51	Normal	-												

#187 HOPPIP

TYPE: Grass/Flying

STATS	HP	Attack	Defense	Speed	SpAttack	SpDefense
	35	35	40	50	35	55

BREEDABLE MOVES: Encore, Double-Edge, Amnesia, Growl, Pay Day, Confusion, Reflect

ABLE TO LEARN TM: 2, 3, 6, 10, 11, 12, 13, 17, 19, 20, 21, 22, 27, 32, 34, 35, 40, 44, 45, 46, 47, 48, 49, 50
HM: 5

TECHNIQUES

Name	Level	Type	Power	Name	Level	Type	Power	Name	Level	Type	Power	Name	Level	Type	Power
Splash	0	Normal	-	Tackle	10	Normal	35	Sleep Powder	17	Grass	-	Mega Drain	30	Grass	40
Synthesis	0	Grass	-	Poisonpowder	13	Poison	-	Leech Seed	20	Grass	-				
Tail Whip	5	Normal	-	Stun Powder	15	Grass	-	Cotton Spore	25	Grass	-				

#188 SKIPLOOM

TYPE: Grass/Flying

STATS	HP	Attack	Defense	Speed	SpAttack	SpDefense
	55	45	50	80	45	65

BREEDABLE MOVES: Encore, Double-Edge, Amnesia, Growl, Pay Day, Confusion, Reflect

ABLE TO LEARN TM: 2, 3, 6, 10, 11, 12, 13, 17, 19, 20, 21, 22, 27, 32, 34, 35, 40, 44, 45, 46, 47, 48, 49, 50
HM: 5

TECHNIQUES

Name	Level	Type	Power	Name	Level	Type	Power	Name	Level	Type	Power	Name	Level	Type	Power
Leech Seed	22	Grass	-												
Cotton Spore	29	Grass	-												
Mega Drain	36	Grass	40												

#189 JUMPLUFF

STATS	HP	Attack	Defense	Speed	SpAttack	SpDefense
TYPE: Grass/Flying	75	55	70	110	55	85

BREEDABLE MOVES

Encore	Amnesia	Pay Day	Reflect
Double-Edge	Growl	Confusion	

ABLE TO LEARN
TM: 2, 3, 6, 10, 11, 12, 13, 15, 17, 19, 20, 21, 22, 27, 32, 34, 35, 40, 44, 45
HM: 5

TECHNIQUES

Name	Level	Type	Power	Name	Level	Type	Power
Cotton Spore	33	Grass	-				
Mega Drain	44	Grass	40				

#190 AIPOM

STATS	HP	Attack	Defense	Speed	SpAttack	SpDefense
TYPE: Normal	55	70	55	85	40	55

BREEDABLE MOVES

Spite	Doubleslap	Slam
Pursuit	Counter	Beat Up

ABLE TO LEARN
TM: 1, 2, 3, 6, 7, 8, 10, 11, 13, 17, 20, 21, 23, 25, 27, 30, 31, 32, 33, 34, 35, 39, 40, 41, 42, 43, 44, 45, 46, 48, 49, 50
HM: 1, 4

TECHNIQUES

Name	Level	Type	Power	Name	Level	Type	Power	Name	Level	Type	Power
Scratch	0	Normal	40	Baton Pass	12	Normal	-	Screech	36	Normal	-
Tail Whip	0	Normal	-	Fury Swipes	19	Normal	18	Agility	46	Psychic	-
Sand-Attack	6	Ground	-	Swift	27	Normal	60				

#191 SUNKERN

STATS	HP	Attack	Defense	Speed	SpAttack	SpDefense
TYPE: Grass	30	30	30	30	30	30

BREEDABLE MOVES None

ABLE TO LEARN
TM: 3, 6, 10, 11, 12, 13, 17, 19, 20, 21, 22, 27, 32, 34, 35, 36, 44, 45
HM: 1, 5

TECHNIQUES

Name	Level	Type	Power	Name	Level	Type	Power
Absorb	0	Grass	20	Sunny Day	19	Fire	-
Growth	4	Normal	-	Synthesis	31	Grass	-
Mega Drain	10	Grass	40	Giga Drain	46	Grass	60

#192 SUNFLORA

STATS	HP	Attack	Defense	Speed	SpAttack	SpDefense
TYPE: Grass	75	75	55	30	105	85

BREEDABLE MOVES None

ABLE TO LEARN
TM: 3, 6, 10, 11, 12, 13, 15, 17, 19, 20, 21, 22, 27, 32, 34, 35, 36, 44, 45
HM: 1, 5

TECHNIQUES

Name	Level	Type	Power	Name	Level	Type	Power
Pound	-	Normal	40	Solarbeam	46	Grass	120
Growth	4	Normal	-	Razor Leaf	10	Grass	55
Sunny Day	19	Fire	-	Petal Dance	31	Grass	70

#193 YANMA

STATS	HP	Attack	Defense	Speed	SpAttack	SpDefense
TYPE: Bug/Flying	65	65	45	95	75	45

BREEDABLE MOVES

Reversal	Whirlwind
Leech Life	

ABLE TO LEARN
TM: 2, 3, 6, 10, 11, 13, 17, 19, 20, 21, 22, 27, 32, 34, 35, 39, 43, 44, 45, 46
HM: 5

TECHNIQUES

Name	Level	Type	Power	Name	Level	Type	Power	Name	Level	Type	Power
Tackle	0	Normal	35	Double Team	13	Normal	-	Supersonic	31	Normal	-
Foresight	0	Normal	-	Sonicboom	19	Normal	20	Swift	37	Normal	60
Quick Attack	7	Normal	40	Detect	25	Fighting	-	Screech	43	Normal	-

#194 WOOPER

STATS	HP	Attack	Defense	Speed	SpAttack	SpDefense
TYPE: Water/Ground	55	45	45	15	25	25

BREEDABLE MOVES

Ancientpower	Body Slam
Safeguard	

ABLE TO LEARN
TM: 1, 2, 3, 4, 6, 8, 10, 13, 17, 18, 20, 21, 23, 26, 27, 28, 31, 32, 33, 34, 35, 36, 37, 40, 44, 45
HM: 3, 5, 6

TECHNIQUES

Name	Level	Type	Power	Name	Level	Type	Power	Name	Level	Type	Power
Water Gun	0	Water	40	Amnesia	21	Psychic	-	Mist	51	Ice	-
Tail Whip	0	Normal	-	Earthquake	31	Ground	100	Haze	51	Ice	-
Slam	11	Normal	80	Rain Dance	41	Water	-				

#195 QUAGSIRE

STATS	HP	Attack	Defense	Speed	SpAttack	SpDefense
TYPE: Water/Ground	95	85	85	35	65	65

BREEDABLE MOVES

Ancientpower	Body Slam
Safeguard	

ABLE TO LEARN
TM: 1, 2, 3, 4, 6, 8, 10, 13, 15, 17, 18, 20, 21, 23, 26, 27, 28, 31, 32, 33, 34, 35, 36, 37, 40, 44, 45
HM: 3, 4, 5, 6

TECHNIQUES

Name	Level	Type	Power	Name	Level	Type	Power
Amnesia	23	Psychic	-	Mist	59	Ice	-
Earthquake	35	Ground	100	Haze	59	Ice	-
Rain Dance	47	Water	-				

98

#196 ESPEON

TYPE:	Psychic

STATS	HP	Attack	Defense	Speed	SpAttack	SpDefense
	65	65	60	110	130	95

BREEDABLE MOVES			
Charm			
Flail			

ABLE TO LEARN
TM: 2, 3, 6, 7, 9, 10, 11, 13, 15, 17, 18, 20, 21, 23, 27, 29, 30, 31, 32, 34, 35, 39, 42, 43, 44, 45, 50
HM: 1, 5

Name	Level	Type	Power	Name	Level	Type	Power	Name	Level	Type	Power	Name	Level	Type	Power
Sand-Attack	8	Ground	-	Swift	30	Normal	60	Psychic	47	Psychic	90				
Confusion	16	Psychic	50	Psybeam	36	Psychic	65	Morning Sun	52	Normal	-				
Quick Attack	23	Normal	40	Psych Up	42	Normal	-								

#197 UMBREON

TYPE:	Dark

STATS	HP	Attack	Defense	Speed	SpAttack	SpDefense
	95	65	110	65	60	130

BREEDABLE MOVES			
Charm			
Flail			

ABLE TO LEARN
TM: 2, 3, 6, 7, 9, 10, 11, 13, 15, 17, 18, 20, 21, 23, 27, 29, 30, 31, 32, 34, 35, 39, 42, 43, 44, 45, 50
HM: 1, 5

Name	Level	Type	Power	Name	Level	Type	Power	Name	Level	Type	Power	Name	Level	Type	Power
Sand-Attack	8	Ground	-	Confuse Ray	30	Ghost	-	Screech	47	Normal	-				
Pursuit	16	Dark	40	Faint Attack	36	Dark	60	Moonlight	52	Normal	-				
Quick Attack	23	Normal	40	Mean Look	42	Normal	-								

#198 MURKROW

TYPE:	Dark/Flying

STATS	HP	Attack	Defense	Speed	SpAttack	SpDefense
	60	85	42	91	85	42

BREEDABLE MOVES			
Mirror Move	Quick Attack	Whirlwind	
Wing Attack	Drill Peck		

ABLE TO LEARN
TM: 3, 6, 9, 10, 11, 13, 16, 17, 20, 21, 27, 30, 31, 32, 34, 35, 39, 42, 43, 44, 45, 46, 47, 50
HM: 2

Name	Level	Type	Power	Name	Level	Type	Power	Name	Level	Type	Power	Name	Level	Type	Power
Peck	0	Flying	35	Night Shade	26	Ghost	-								
Pursuit	11	Dark	40	Faint Attack	31	Dark	60								
Haze	16	Ice	-	Mean Look	41	Normal	-								

#199 SLOWKING

TYPE:	Water/Psychic

STATS	HP	Attack	Defense	Speed	SpAttack	SpDefense
	95	75	80	30	100	110

BREEDABLE MOVES			
Safeguard	Stomp		
Belly Drum	Future Sight		

ABLE TO LEARN
TM: 1, 2, 3, 6, 7, 8, 9, 10, 11, 13, 14, 15, 16, 17, 18, 20, 21, 23, 26, 27, 28, 29, 30, 31, 32, 33, 34, 35, 38, 39, 42, 44, 45, 49, 50
HM: 3, 4, 5, 6

Name	Level	Type	Power	Name	Level	Type	Power	Name	Level	Type	Power	Name	Level	Type	Power
Swagger	43	Normal	-												
Psychic	48	Psychic	90												

#200 MISDREAVUS

TYPE:	Ghost

STATS	HP	Attack	Defense	Speed	SpAttack	SpDefense
	60	60	60	85	85	85

BREEDABLE MOVES			
Screech			
Destiny Bond			

ABLE TO LEARN
TM: 2, 3, 6, 7, 9, 10, 11, 13, 17, 18, 20, 21, 25, 27, 29, 30, 32, 34, 35, 39, 40, 42, 44, 45, 46, 50
HM: 5

Name	Level	Type	Power	Name	Level	Type	Power	Name	Level	Type	Power	Name	Level	Type	Power
Growl	0	Normal	-	Confuse Ray	12	Ghost	-	Pain Split	36	Normal	-				
Psywave	0	Psychic	-	Mean Look	19	Normal	-	Perish Song	46	Normal	-				
Spite	6	Ghost	-	Psybeam	27	Psychic	65								

#201 UNOWN

TYPE:	Psychic

STATS	HP	Attack	Defense	Speed	SpAttack	SpDefense
	48	72	48	48	72	48

BREEDABLE MOVES			
None			

ABLE TO LEARN
TM: None
HM: None

Name	Level	Type	Power	Name	Level	Type	Power	Name	Level	Type	Power	Name	Level	Type	Power
Hidden Power	0	Normal	-												

#202 WOOBBUFFET

TYPE:	Psychic

STATS	HP	Attack	Defense	Speed	SpAttack	SpDefense
	190	33	58	33	33	58

BREEDABLE MOVES			
None			

ABLE TO LEARN
TM: None
HM: None

Name	Level	Type	Power	Name	Level	Type	Power	Name	Level	Type	Power	Name	Level	Type	Power
Counter	0	Fighting	-	Destiny Bond	0	Ghost	-								
Mirror Coat	0	Psychic	-												
Safeguard	0	Normal	-												

#203 GIRAFARIG

TYPE: Normal/Psychic

STATS	HP	Attack	Defense	Speed	SpAttack	SpDefense
	70	80	65	85	90	65

ABLE TO LEARN TM: 2, 3, 6, 7, 8, 9, 10, 11, 13, 17, 20, 21, 23, 25, 26, 27, 29, 30, 31, 32, 34, 35, 39, 42, 44, 45, 46, 50
HM: 4

BREEDABLE MOVES: Take Down, Amnesia, Beat Up, Foresight, Future Sight

TECHNIQUES

Name	Level	Type	Power	Name	Level	Type	Power	Name	Level	Type	Power
Tackle	0	Normal	35	Stomp	13	Normal	65	Psybeam	41	Psychic	65
Growl	0	Normal	-	Agility	20	Psychic	-	Crunch	54	Dark	80
Confusion	7	Psychic	50	Baton Pass	30	Normal	-				

#204 PINECO

TYPE: Bug

STATS	HP	Attack	Defense	Speed	SpAttack	SpDefense
	50	65	90	15	35	35

ABLE TO LEARN TM: 2, 3, 4, 6, 8, 10, 11, 12, 13, 17, 19, 20, 21, 22, 27, 32, 34, 35, 40, 44, 45
HM: 4

BREEDABLE MOVES: Flail, Swift, Pin Missile, Reflect

TECHNIQUES

Name	Level	Type	Power	Name	Level	Type	Power	Name	Level	Type	Power
Tackle	0	Normal	35	Take Down	15	Normal	90	Explosion	36	Normal	250
Protect	0	Normal	-	Rapid Spin	22	Normal	20	Spikes	43	Ground	-
Selfdestruct	8	Normal	200	Bide	29	Normal	-	Double-Edge	50	Normal	120

#205 FORRETRESS

TYPE: Bug/Steel

STATS	HP	Attack	Defense	Speed	SpAttack	SpDefense
	75	90	140	40	60	60

ABLE TO LEARN TM: 2, 3, 4, 6, 8, 10, 11, 12, 13, 15, 17, 19, 20, 21, 22, 27, 32, 34, 35, 37, 40, 44, 45
HM: 4

BREEDABLE MOVES: Flail, Swift, Pin Missile, Reflect

TECHNIQUES

Name	Level	Type	Power	Name	Level	Type	Power	Name	Level	Type	Power
Explosion	39	Normal	250								
Spikes	49	Ground	-								
Double-Edge	59	Normal	120								

#206 DUNSPARCE

TYPE: Normal

STATS	HP	Attack	Defense	Speed	SpAttack	SpDefense
	100	70	70	45	65	65

ABLE TO LEARN TM: 2, 3, 4, 6, 7, 8, 9, 10, 11, 13, 17, 18, 20, 21, 22, 23, 25, 27, 28, 31, 32, 34, 35, 40, 42, 44, 45, 46, 50
HM: 4

BREEDABLE MOVES: Rock Slide, Bide, Bite, Ancientpower, Rage

TECHNIQUES

Name	Level	Type	Power	Name	Level	Type	Power	Name	Level	Type	Power
Rage	0	Normal	20	Spite	18	Ghost	-	Take Down	38	Normal	90
Defense Curl	5	Normal	-	Pursuit	26	Dark	40				
Glare	13	Normal	-	Screech	30	Normal	-				

#207 GLIGAR

TYPE: Ground/Flying

STATS	HP	Attack	Defense	Speed	SpAttack	SpDefense
	65	75	105	85	35	65

ABLE TO LEARN TM: 2, 3, 6, 8, 10, 11, 13, 17, 20, 21, 23, 27, 32, 34, 35, 36, 37, 39, 43, 44, 45, 46, 49
HM: 1, 4

BREEDABLE MOVES: Counter, Razor Wind, Wing Attack, Metal Claw

TECHNIQUES

Name	Level	Type	Power	Name	Level	Type	Power	Name	Level	Type	Power
Poison Sting	0	Poison	15	Quick Attack	20	Normal	40	Screech	44	Normal	-
Sand-Attack	6	Ground	-	Faint Attack	28	Dark	60	Guillotine	52	Normal	-
Harden	13	Normal	-	Slash	36	Normal	70				

#208 STEELIX

TYPE: Steel/Ground

STATS	HP	Attack	Defense	Speed	SpAttack	SpDefense
	75	85	200	30	55	65

ABLE TO LEARN TM: 2, 3, 4, 5, 6, 8, 10, 11, 13, 15, 17, 20, 21, 23, 24, 26, 27, 28, 31, 32, 34, 35, 37, 40, 44, 45
HM: 1, 5

BREEDABLE MOVES: Flail, Rock Slide

TECHNIQUES

Name	Level	Type	Power	Name	Level	Type	Power	Name	Level	Type	Power
Bind	10	Normal	15	Rage	27	Normal	20	Crunch	49	Dark	80
Rock Throw	14	Rock	50	Sandstorm	36	Rock	-				
Harden	23	Normal	-	Slam	40	Normal	80				

#209 SNUBBULL

TYPE: Normal

STATS	HP	Attack	Defense	Speed	SpAttack	SpDefense
	60	80	50	30	40	40

ABLE TO LEARN TM: 1, 2, 3, 5, 6, 7, 8, 10, 11, 13, 17, 18, 20, 21, 25, 27, 30, 31, 32, 33, 34, 35, 36, 40, 41, 43, 44, 45, 46, 48
HM: 4

BREEDABLE MOVES: Heal Bell, Crunch, Faint Attack, Leer, Present, Metronome, Reflect, Lick

TECHNIQUES

Name	Level	Type	Power	Name	Level	Type	Power	Name	Level	Type	Power
Tackle	0	Normal	35	Charm	8	Normal	-	Roar	26	Normal	-
Scary Face	0	Normal	-	Bite	13	Dark	60	Rage	34	Normal	20
Tail Whip	4	Normal	-	Lick	19	Ghost	20	Take Down	43	Normal	90

#210 GRANBULL

TYPE: Normal

STATS	HP	Attack	Defense	Speed	SpAttack	SpDefense
	90	120	75	45	60	60

BREEDABLE MOVES: Heal Bell, Crunch, Faint Attack, Leer, Present, Metronome, Reflect, Lick

ABLE TO LEARN: TM: 1, 2, 3, 5, 6, 7, 8, 10, 11, 13, 15, 17, 18, 20, 21, 25, 27, 30, 31, 32, 33, 34, 35, 36, 40, 41, 43, 44, 45, 46, 48
HM: 4

Name	Level	Type	Power	Name	Level	Type	Power	Name	Level	Type	Power	Name	Level	Type	Power
Roar	28	Normal	-												
Rage	38	Normal	20												
Take Down	51	Normal	90												

#211 QWILFISH

TYPE: Water/Poison

STATS	HP	Attack	Defense	Speed	SpAttack	SpDefense
	65	95	75	85	55	55

BREEDABLE MOVES: Haze, Flail, Supersonic, Bubblebeam

ABLE TO LEARN: TM: 2, 3, 4, 6, 10, 13, 14, 16, 17, 18, 20, 21, 27, 32, 34, 35, 36, 39, 40, 44, 45
HM: 3, 6, 7

Name	Level	Type	Power	Name	Level	Type	Power	Name	Level	Type	Power	Name	Level	Type	Power
Tackle	0	Normal	35	Minimize	10	Normal	-	Take Down	37	Normal	90				
Poison Sting	0	Poison	15	Water Gun	19	Water	40	Hydro Pump	46	Water	120				
Harden	10	Normal	-	Pin Missile	28	Bug	14								

#212 SCIZOR

TYPE: Bug/Steel

STATS	HP	Attack	Defense	Speed	SpAttack	SpDefense
	70	130	100	65	55	80

BREEDABLE MOVES: Counter, Razor Wind, Reversal, Safeguard, Baton Pass, Light Screen

ABLE TO LEARN: TM: 2, 3, 6, 8, 10, 11, 13, 15, 17, 20, 21, 27, 32, 34, 35, 37, 39, 43, 44, 45, 46, 47, 49
HM: 1, 4

Name	Level	Type	Power	Name	Level	Type	Power	Name	Level	Type	Power	Name	Level	Type	Power
Focus Energy	6	Normal	-	Agility	24	Psychic	-	Swords Dance	42	Normal	-				
Pursuit	12	Dark	40	Metal Claw	30	Steel	50	Double Team	48	Normal	-				
False Swipe	18	Normal	40	Slash	36	Normal	70								

#213 SHUCKLE

TYPE: Bug/Rock

STATS	HP	Attack	Defense	Speed	SpAttack	SpDefense
	20	10	230	5	10	230

BREEDABLE MOVES: Sweet Scent

ABLE TO LEARN: TM: 2, 3, 4, 6, 8, 10, 11, 13, 17, 20, 21, 26, 27, 28, 31, 32, 34, 35, 36, 37, 40, 44, 45
HM: 4, 5

Name	Level	Type	Power	Name	Level	Type	Power	Name	Level	Type	Power	Name	Level	Type	Power
Constrict	0	Normal	10	Encore	14	Normal	-	Rest	37	Psychic	-				
Withdraw	0	Water	-	Safeguard	23	Normal	-								
Wrap	9	Normal	15	Bide	28	Normal	-								

#214 HERACROSS

TYPE: Bug/Fighting

STATS	HP	Attack	Defense	Speed	SpAttack	SpDefense
	80	125	75	85	40	95

BREEDABLE MOVES: Harden, Bide, Flail

ABLE TO LEARN: TM: 2, 3, 6, 8, 10, 11, 13, 17, 20, 21, 26, 27, 32, 34, 35, 43, 44, 45, 46, 49
HM: 1, 4

Name	Level	Type	Power	Name	Level	Type	Power	Name	Level	Type	Power	Name	Level	Type	Power
Tackle	0	Normal	35	Endure	12	Normal	-	Take Down	35	Normal	90				
Leer	0	Normal	-	Fury Attack	19	Normal	15	Reversal	44	Fighting	-				
Horn Attack	6	Normal	65	Counter	27	Fighting	-	Megahorn	54	Bug	120				

#215 SNEASEL

TYPE: Dark/Ice

STATS	HP	Attack	Defense	Speed	SpAttack	SpDefense
	55	95	55	115	35	75

BREEDABLE MOVES: Spite, Counter, Bite, Foresight, Reflect

ABLE TO LEARN: TM: 1, 2, 3, 6, 8, 9, 10, 13, 14, 16, 17, 18, 20, 21, 23, 27, 28, 30, 31, 32, 33, 34, 35, 39, 40, 42, 43, 44, 45, 46, 49, 50
HM: 1, 3, 4

Name	Level	Type	Power	Name	Level	Type	Power	Name	Level	Type	Power	Name	Level	Type	Power
Scratch	0	Normal	40	Screech	17	Normal	-	Agility	41	Psychic	-				
Leer	0	Normal	-	Faint Attack	25	Dark	60	Slash	49	Normal	70				
Quick Attack	9	Normal	40	Fury Swipes	33	Normal	18	Beat Up	57	Dark	-				

#216 TEDDIURSA

TYPE: Normal

STATS	HP	Attack	Defense	Speed	SpAttack	SpDefense
	60	80	50	40	50	50

BREEDABLE MOVES: Counter, Crunch, Focus Energy, Seismic Toss, Take Down

ABLE TO LEARN: TM: 1, 2, 3, 4, 5, 6, 7, 8, 10, 11, 13, 17, 20, 21, 26, 27, 28, 31, 32, 33, 34, 35, 39, 40, 41, 44, 45, 46, 48, 49
HM: 1, 4

Name	Level	Type	Power	Name	Level	Type	Power	Name	Level	Type	Power	Name	Level	Type	Power
Scratch	0	Normal	40	Fury Swipes	15	Normal	18	Slash	36	Normal	70				
Leer	0	Normal	-	Faint Attack	22	Dark	60	Snore	43	Normal	40				
Lick	8	Ghost	20	Rest	29	Psychic	-	Thrash	50	Normal	90				

#217 URSARING

TYPE: Normal

STATS	HP	Attack	Defense	Speed	SpAttack	SpDefense
	90	130	75	55	75	75

BREEDABLE MOVES: Counter, Crunch, Focus Energy, Seismic Toss, Take Down

ABLE TO LEARN TM: 1, 2, 3, 4, 5, 6, 7, 8, 10, 11, 13, 15, 17, 20, 21, 26, 27, 28, 31, 32, 33, 34, 35, 39, 40, 41, 44, 45, 46, 48, 49
HM: 1, 4

TECHNIQUES

Name	Level	Type	Power
Slash	39	Normal	70
Snore	49	Normal	40
Thrash	59	Normal	90

#218 SLUGMA

TYPE: Fire

STATS	HP	Attack	Defense	Speed	SpAttack	SpDefense
	40	40	40	20	70	40

BREEDABLE MOVES: Acid Armor

ABLE TO LEARN TM: 3, 4, 6, 8, 10, 11, 13, 17, 20, 21, 26, 27, 31, 32, 34, 35, 38, 40, 44, 45
HM: 4

TECHNIQUES

Name	Level	Type	Power	Name	Level	Type	Power	Name	Level	Type	Power
Smog	0	Poison	20	Harden	22	Normal	-	Rock Slide	43	Rock	75
Ember	8	Fire	40	Amnesia	29	Psychic	-	Body Slam	50	Normal	85
Rock Throw	15	Rock	50	Flamethrower	36	Fire	95				

#219 MAGCARGO

TYPE: Fire/Rock

STATS	HP	Attack	Defense	Speed	SpAttack	SpDefense
	50	50	120	30	80	80

BREEDABLE MOVES: Acid Armor

ABLE TO LEARN TM: 3, 4, 6, 8, 10, 11, 13, 15, 17, 20, 21, 26, 27, 31, 32, 34, 35, 38, 40, 44, 45
HM: 4

TECHNIQUES

Name	Level	Type	Power
Rock Slide	48	Rock	75
Body Slam	60	Normal	85

#220 SWINUB

TYPE: Ice/Ground

STATS	HP	Attack	Defense	Speed	SpAttack	SpDefense
	50	50	40	50	30	30

BREEDABLE MOVES: Rock Slide, Bite, Ancientpower, Body Slam, Take Down

ABLE TO LEARN TM: 2, 3, 5, 6, 8, 10, 13, 14, 16, 17, 18, 20, 21, 26, 27, 31, 32, 34, 35, 40, 43, 44, 45
HM: 4

TECHNIQUES

Name	Level	Type	Power	Name	Level	Type	Power
Tackle	0	Normal	35	Take Down	28	Normal	90
Powder Snow	10	Ice	40	Mist	37	Ice	-
Endure	19	Normal	-	Blizzard	46	Ice	120

#221 PILOSWINE

TYPE: Ice/Ground

STATS	HP	Attack	Defense	Speed	SpAttack	SpDefense
	100	100	80	50	60	60

BREEDABLE MOVES: Rock Slide, Bite, Ancientpower, Body Slam, Take Down

ABLE TO LEARN TM: 2, 3, 5, 6, 8, 10, 13, 14, 15, 16, 17, 18, 20, 21, 26, 27, 31, 32, 34, 35, 40, 43, 44, 45
HM: 4

TECHNIQUES

Name	Level	Type	Power
Fury Attack	33	Normal	15
Mist	42	Ice	-
Blizzard	56	Ice	120

#222 CORSOLA

TYPE: Water/Rock

STATS	HP	Attack	Defense	Speed	SpAttack	SpDefense
	55	55	85	35	65	85

BREEDABLE MOVES: Amnesia, Mist, Rock Slide, Safeguard

ABLE TO LEARN TM: 2, 3, 4, 6, 8, 9, 10, 11, 13, 17, 18, 20, 21, 26, 27, 29, 31, 32, 34, 35, 37, 40, 44, 45
HM: 3, 4, 6

TECHNIQUES

Name	Level	Type	Power	Name	Level	Type	Power	Name	Level	Type	Power
Tackle	0	Normal	35	Recover	19	Normal	-	Mirror Coat	37	Psychic	-
Harden	7	Normal	-	Bubblebeam	25	Water	65	Ancientpower	43	Rock	60
Bubble	13	Water	20	Spike Cannon	31	Normal	20				

#223 REMORAID

TYPE: Water

STATS	HP	Attack	Defense	Speed	SpAttack	SpDefense
	35	65	35	65	65	35

BREEDABLE MOVES: Screech, Octazooka, Haze, Supersonic, Aurora Beam

ABLE TO LEARN TM: 3, 6, 10, 13, 15, 17, 18, 20, 21, 27, 31, 32, 34, 35, 39, 40, 44, 45, 46
HM: 3, 6

TECHNIQUES

Name	Level	Type	Power	Name	Level	Type	Power	Name	Level	Type	Power
Water Gun	0	Water	40	Psybeam	22	Psychic	65	Ice Beam	44	Ice	95
Lock-On	11	Normal	-	Aurora Beam	22	Ice	65	Hyper Beam	55	Normal	150
Bubblebeam	22	Water	65	Focus Energy	33	Normal	-				

#224 OCTILLERY

TYPE: Water

STATS	HP	Attack	Defense	Speed	SpAttack	SpDefense
	75	105	75	45	105	75

BREEDABLE MOVES: Screech, Octazooka, Haze, Supersonic, Aurora Beam

ABLE TO LEARN: TM: 3, 6, 10, 13, 15, 17, 18, 20, 21, 27, 31, 32, 34, 35, 39, 40, 44, 45, 46
HM: 3, 6

TECHNIQUES

Name	Level	Type	Power
Focus Energy	38	Normal	-
Ice Beam	54	Ice	95
Hyper Beam	70	Normal	150

#225 DELIBIRD

TYPE: Ice/Flying

STATS	HP	Attack	Defense	Speed	SpAttack	SpDefense
	45	55	45	75	65	45

BREEDABLE MOVES: Aurora Beam, Rapid Spin, Quick Attack, Splash, Future Sight

ABLE TO LEARN: TM: 2, 3, 6, 10, 13, 14, 16, 17, 18, 20, 21, 27, 31, 32, 34, 35, 39, 43, 44, 45, 46
HM: 2

TECHNIQUES

Name	Level	Type	Power
Present	0	Normal	-

#226 MANTINE

TYPE: Water/Flying

STATS	HP	Attack	Defense	Speed	SpAttack	SpDefense
	65	40	70	70	80	140

BREEDABLE MOVES: Haze, Slam, Twister, Hydro Pump

ABLE TO LEARN: TM: 2, 3, 6, 10, 13, 14, 16, 17, 18, 20, 21, 27, 31, 32, 34, 35, 39, 44, 45
HM: 3, 6, 7

TECHNIQUES

Name	Level	Type	Power	Name	Level	Type	Power	Name	Level	Type	Power
Tackle	0	Normal	35	Bubblebeam	18	Water	65	Wing Attack	40	Flying	60
Bubble	0	Water	20	Take Down	25	Normal	90	Confuse Ray	49	Ghost	-
Supersonic	10	Normal	-	Agility	32	Psychic	-				

#227 SKARMORY

TYPE: Steel/Flying

STATS	HP	Attack	Defense	Speed	SpAttack	SpDefense
	65	80	140	70	40	70

BREEDABLE MOVES: Pursuit, Drill Peck, Whirlwind

ABLE TO LEARN: TM: 3, 6, 10, 11, 13, 17, 20, 21, 27, 31, 32, 34, 35, 37, 39, 43, 44, 45, 46, 47
HM: 1, 2

TECHNIQUES

Name	Level	Type	Power	Name	Level	Type	Power	Name	Level	Type	Power
Leer	0	Normal	-	Swift	19	Normal	60	Steel Wing	49	Steel	70
Peck	0	Flying	35	Agility	25	Psychic	-				
Sand-Attack	13	Ground	-	Fury Attack	37	Normal	15				

#228 HOUNDOUR

TYPE: Dark/Fire

STATS	HP	Attack	Defense	Speed	SpAttack	SpDefense
	45	60	30	65	80	50

BREEDABLE MOVES: Rage, Spite, Pursuit, Counter, Reversal, Beat Up, Fire Spin

ABLE TO LEARN: TM: 2, 3, 5, 6, 8, 10, 11, 13, 17, 20, 21, 22, 23, 27, 30, 31, 32, 34, 35, 36, 38, 39, 42, 43, 44, 45, 46, 50
HM: None

TECHNIQUES

Name	Level	Type	Power	Name	Level	Type	Power	Name	Level	Type	Power
Leer	0	Normal	-	Smog	13	Poison	20	Flamethrower	35	Fire	95
Ember	0	Fire	40	Bite	20	Dark	60	Crunch	43	Dark	80
Roar	7	Normal	-	Faint Attack	27	Dark	60				

#229 HOUNDOOM

TYPE: Dark/Fire

STATS	HP	Attack	Defense	Speed	SpAttack	SpDefense
	75	90	50	95	110	80

BREEDABLE MOVES: Rage, Spite, Pursuit, Counter, Reversal, Beat Up, Fire Spin

ABLE TO LEARN: TM: 2, 3, 5, 6, 8, 10, 11, 13, 15, 17, 20, 21, 22, 23, 27, 30, 31, 32, 34, 35, 36, 38, 39, 42, 43, 44, 45, 46, 50
HM: None

TECHNIQUES

Name	Level	Type	Power
Faint Attack	30	Dark	60
Flamethrower	41	Fire	95
Crunch	52	Dark	80

#230 KINGDRA

TYPE: Water/Dragon

STATS	HP	Attack	Defense	Speed	SpAttack	SpDefense
	75	95	95	85	95	95

BREEDABLE MOVES: Aurora Beam, Octazooka, Disable, Flail, Splash, Dragon Rage

ABLE TO LEARN: TM: 2, 3, 6, 10, 13, 14, 15, 16, 17, 18, 20, 21, 24, 27, 32, 34, 35, 39, 44, 45
HM: 3, 6, 7

TECHNIQUES

Name	Level	Type	Power
Agility	40	Psychic	-
Hydro Pump	51	Water	120

#231 PHANPY

TYPE: Ground

STATS	HP	Attack	Defense	Speed	SpAttack	SpDefense
	90	60	60	40	40	40

BREEDABLE MOVES: Focus Energy | Body Slam | Ancientpower

ABLE TO LEARN — TM: 2, 3, 4, 5, 6, 8, 10, 11, 13, 17, 20, 21, 26, 27, 31, 32, 34, 35, 37, 40, 44, 45
HM: 4

TECHNIQUES

Name	Level	Type	Power	Name	Level	Type	Power	Name	Level	Type	Power	Name	Level	Type	Power
Tackle	0	Normal	35	Flail	17	Normal	-	Endure	41	Normal	-				
Growl	0	Normal	-	Take Down	25	Normal	90	Double-Edge	49	Normal	120				
Defense Curl	9	Normal	-	Rollout	33	Rock	30								

#232 DONPHAN

TYPE: Ground

STATS	HP	Attack	Defense	Speed	SpAttack	SpDefense
	90	120	120	50	60	60

BREEDABLE MOVES: Focus Energy | Body Slam | Ancientpower

ABLE TO LEARN — TM: 2, 3, 4, 5, 6, 8, 10, 11, 13, 15, 17, 20, 21, 26, 27, 31, 32, 34, 35, 37, 40, 44, 45
HM: 4

TECHNIQUES

Name	Level	Type	Power	Name	Level	Type	Power
Fury Attack	25	Normal	15	Earthquake	49	Ground	100
Rollout	33	Rock	30				
Rapid Spin	41	Normal	-				

#233 PORYGON2

TYPE: Normal

STATS	HP	Attack	Defense	Speed	SpAttack	SpDefense
	85	80	90	60	105	95

BREEDABLE MOVES: None

ABLE TO LEARN — TM: 3, 6, 7, 9, 10, 11, 13, 14, 15, 16, 17, 18, 20, 21, 23, 25, 27, 29, 32, 34, 35, 39, 40, 42, 44, 46, 50
HM: 5

TECHNIQUES

Name	Level	Type	Power	Name	Level	Type	Power	Name	Level	Type	Power
Agility	9	Psychic	-	Defense Curl	24	Normal	-	Zap Cannon	44	Electric	100
Psybeam	12	Psychic	65	Lock-On	32	Normal	-				
Recover	20	Normal	-	Tri Attack	36	Normal	80				

#234 STANTLER

TYPE: Normal

STATS	HP	Attack	Defense	Speed	SpAttack	SpDefense
	73	95	62	85	85	65

BREEDABLE MOVES: Spite | Bite | Reflect | Disable | Light Screen

ABLE TO LEARN — TM: 2, 3, 5, 6, 9, 10, 11, 13, 17, 18, 20, 21, 26, 27, 29, 31, 32, 34, 35, 39, 42, 43, 44, 45, 46, 50
HM: 5

TECHNIQUES

Name	Level	Type	Power	Name	Level	Type	Power	Name	Level	Type	Power
Tackle	0	Normal	35	Stomp	23	Normal	65	Confuse Ray	49	Ghost	-
Leer	8	Normal	-	Sand-Attack	31	Ground	-				
Hypnosis	15	Psychic	-	Take Down	40	Normal	90				

#235 SMEARGLE

TYPE: Normal

STATS	HP	Attack	Defense	Speed	SpAttack	SpDefense
	55	20	35	75	20	45

BREEDABLE MOVES: None

ABLE TO LEARN — TM: None
HM: None

TECHNIQUES

Name	Level	Type	Power	Name	Level	Type	Power	Name	Level	Type	Power	Name	Level	Type	Power
Sketch	0	Normal	-	Sketch	31	Normal	-	Sketch	61	Normal	-	Sketch	91	Normal	-
Sketch	11	Normal	-	Sketch	41	Normal	-	Sketch	71	Normal	-				
Sketch	21	Normal	-	Sketch	51	Normal	-	Sketch	81	Normal	-				

#236 TYROGUE

TYPE: Fighting

STATS	HP	Attack	Defense	Speed	SpAttack	SpDefense
	35	35	35	35	35	35

BREEDABLE MOVES: Rapid Spin | Hi Jump Kick | Mind Reader | Mach Punch

ABLE TO LEARN — TM: 2, 3, 6, 8, 10, 11, 13, 17, 20, 21, 27, 31, 32, 34, 35, 39, 43, 44, 45, 46
HM: 4

TECHNIQUES

Name	Level	Type	Power	Name	Level	Type	Power	Name	Level	Type	Power	Name	Level	Type	Power
Tackle	0	Normal	35												

#237 HITMONTOP

TYPE: Fighting

STATS	HP	Attack	Defense	Speed	SpAttack	SpDefense
	50	95	95	70	35	110

BREEDABLE MOVES: Rapid Spin | Hi Jump Kick | Mind Reader | Mach Punch

ABLE TO LEARN — TM: 2, 3, 6, 8, 10, 11, 13, 17, 20, 21, 27, 28, 31, 32, 34, 35, 39, 43, 44, 45, 46
HM: 4

TECHNIQUES

Name	Level	Type	Power	Name	Level	Type	Power	Name	Level	Type	Power	Name	Level	Type	Power
Rolling Kick	0	Fighting	60	Quick Attack	19	Normal	40	Agility	37	Psychic	-				
Focus Energy	7	Normal	-	Rapid Spin	25	Normal	20	Detect	43	Fighting	-				
Pursuit	13	Dark	40	Counter	31	Fighting	-	Triple Kick	49	Fighting	10				

#238 SMOOCHUM

TYPE: Ice/Psychic

STATS	HP	Attack	Defense	Speed	SpAttack	SpDefense
	45	30	15	65	85	65

BREEDABLE MOVES: Meditate

ABLE TO LEARN TM: 1, 3, 6, 9, 10, 12, 13, 14, 16, 17, 18, 20, 21, 27, 29, 30, 31, 32, 33, 34, 35, 42, 44, 45, 46, 50
HM: None

Name	Level	Type	Power	Name	Level	Type	Power	Name	Level	Type	Power	Name	Level	Type	Power
Pound	0	Normal	40	Powder Snow	13	Ice	40	Mean Look	33	Normal	-	Blizzard	49	Ice	120
Lick	0	Ghost	20	Confusion	21	Psychic	50	Psychic	37	Psychic	90				
Sweet Kiss	9	Normal	-	Sing	25	Normal	-	Perish Song	45	Normal	-				

#239 ELEKID

TYPE: Electric

STATS	HP	Attack	Defense	Speed	SpAttack	SpDefense
	45	63	37	95	95	55

BREEDABLE MOVES: Karate Chop, Rolling Kick, Barrier, Meditate

ABLE TO LEARN TM: 1, 2, 3, 6, 7, 10, 13, 17, 18, 20, 21, 25, 27, 29, 31, 32, 33, 34, 35, 39, 41, 43, 44, 45, 46, 48
HM: 5

Name	Level	Type	Power	Name	Level	Type	Power	Name	Level	Type	Power	Name	Level	Type	Power
Quick Attack	0	Normal	40	Light Screen	17	Psychic	-	Thunderbolt	41	Electric	95				
Leer	0	Normal	-	Swift	25	Normal	60	Thunder	49	Electric	120				
Thunderpunch	9	Electric	75	Screech	33	Normal	-								

#240 MAGBY

TYPE: Fire

STATS	HP	Attack	Defense	Speed	SpAttack	SpDefense
	45	75	37	83	70	55

BREEDABLE MOVES: Screech, Barrier, Karate Chop, Mega Punch

ABLE TO LEARN TM: 1, 2, 3, 6, 8, 10, 11, 13, 17, 20, 23, 27, 29, 31, 32, 34, 35, 38, 41, 43, 44, 45, 46, 48
HM: None

Name	Level	Type	Power	Name	Level	Type	Power	Name	Level	Type	Power	Name	Level	Type	Power
Ember	0	Fire	40	Fire Punch	19	Fire	75	Flamethrower	37	Fire	95				
Leer	7	Normal	-	Smokescreen	25	Normal	-	Confuse Ray	43	Ghost	-				
Smog	13	Poison	20	Sunny Day	31	Fire	-	Fire Blast	49	Fire	120				

#241 MILTANK

TYPE: Normal

STATS	HP	Attack	Defense	Speed	SpAttack	SpDefense
	95	80	105	100	40	70

BREEDABLE MOVES: Reversal, Present, Seismic Toss

ABLE TO LEARN TM: 1, 2, 3, 4, 6, 7, 8, 10, 11, 12, 13, 14, 15, 16, 17, 18, 20, 21, 23, 25, 26, 27, 30, 31, 32, 33, 34, 35, 37, 40, 41, 44, 45, 48
HM: 3, 4

Name	Level	Type	Power	Name	Level	Type	Power	Name	Level	Type	Power	Name	Level	Type	Power
Tackle	0	Normal	35	Stomp	13	Normal	65	Rollout	34	Rock	30				
Growl	4	Normal	-	Milk Drink	19	Normal	-	Body Slam	43	Normal	85				
Defense Curl	8	Normal	-	Bide	26	Normal	-	Heal Bell	53	Normal	-				

#242 BLISSEY

TYPE: Normal

STATS	HP	Attack	Defense	Speed	SpAttack	SpDefense
	255	10	10	55	75	135

BREEDABLE MOVES: Heal Bell, Metronome, Present

ABLE TO LEARN TM: 1, 2, 3, 4, 6, 7, 8, 10, 11, 13, 14, 15, 16, 17, 18, 20, 21, 22, 23, 25, 27, 29, 30, 31, 32, 34, 35, 37, 38, 40, 42, 44, 45
HM: 4, 5

Name	Level	Type	Power	Name	Level	Type	Power	Name	Level	Type	Power	Name	Level	Type	Power
Growl	4	Normal	-	Doubleslap	13	Normal	15	Egg Bomb	28	Normal	100	Double-Edge	47	Normal	120
Tail Whip	7	Normal	-	Minimize	18	Normal	-	Defense Curl	33	Normal	-				
Softboiled	10	Normal	-	Sing	23	Normal	-	Light Screen	40	Psychic	-				

#243 RAIKOU

TYPE: Electric

STATS	HP	Attack	Defense	Speed	SpAttack	SpDefense
	90	85	75	115	115	100

BREEDABLE MOVES: None

ABLE TO LEARN TM: 2, 3, 5, 6, 7, 8, 9, 10, 11, 13, 15, 17, 18, 20, 21, 23, 25, 27, 28, 31, 32, 34, 35, 37, 39, 43, 44
HM: 1, 4, 5

Name	Level	Type	Power	Name	Level	Type	Power	Name	Level	Type	Power	Name	Level	Type	Power
Bite	0	Dark	60	Roar	21	Normal	-	Reflect	51	Psychic	-				
Leer	0	Normal	-	Quick Attack	31	Normal	40	Crunch	61	Dark	80				
Thundershock	11	Electric	40	Spark	41	Electric	65	Thunder	71	Electric	120				

#244 ENTEI

TYPE: Fire

STATS	HP	Attack	Defense	Speed	SpAttack	SpDefense
	115	115	85	100	90	75

BREEDABLE MOVES: None

ABLE TO LEARN TM: 2, 3, 5, 6, 8, 9, 10, 11, 13, 15, 17, 18, 20, 21, 22, 23, 27, 28, 31, 32, 34, 35, 37, 38, 39, 43, 44
HM: 1, 4, 5

Name	Level	Type	Power	Name	Level	Type	Power	Name	Level	Type	Power	Name	Level	Type	Power
Bite	0	Dark	60	Roar	21	Normal	-	Flamethrower	51	Fire	95				
Leer	0	Normal	-	Fire Spin	31	Fire	15	Swagger	61	Normal	-				
Ember	11	Fire	40	Stomp	41	Normal	65	Fire Blast	71	Fire	120				

105

#245 SUICUNE

TYPE: Water

STATS	HP	Attack	Defense	Speed	SpAttack	SpDefense
	100	75	115	85	90	115

BREEDABLE MOVES: None

ABLE TO LEARN: TM: 2, 3, 5, 6, 8, 9, 10, 11, 13, 14, 15, 16, 17, 18, 20, 21, 23, 27, 28, 31, 32, 34, 35, 37, 39, 43, 44
HM: 1, 3, 6, 7

TECHNIQUES

Name	Level	Type	Power	Name	Level	Type	Power	Name	Level	Type	Power	Name	Level	Type	Power
Bite	0	Dark	60	Roar	0	Normal	-	Mist	51	Ice	-				
Leer	0	Normal	-	Gust	31	Flying	40	Mirror Coat	61	Psychic	-				
Water Gun	0	Water	40	Bubblebeam	41	Water	65	Hydro Pump	71	Water	120				

#246 LARVITAR

TYPE: Rock/Ground

STATS	HP	Attack	Defense	Speed	SpAttack	SpDefense
	50	64	50	41	45	50

BREEDABLE MOVES: Pursuit, Focus Energy, Outrage, Ancient Power, Stomp

ABLE TO LEARN: TM: 2, 3, 6, 10, 11, 13, 15, 17, 18, 20, 21, 26, 27, 28, 31, 32, 34, 35, 37, 43, 44, 45
HM: None

TECHNIQUES

Name	Level	Type	Power	Name	Level	Type	Power	Name	Level	Type	Power	Name	Level	Type	Power
Bite	0	Dark	60	Screech	15	Normal	-	Scary Face	36	Normal	-	Hyper Beam	57	Normal	150
Leer	0	Normal	-	Rock Slide	22	Rock	75	Crunch	43	Dark	80				
Sandstorm	8	Rock	-	Thrash	29	Normal	90	Earthquake	50	Ground	100				

#247 PUPITAR

TYPE: Rock/Ground

STATS	HP	Attack	Defense	Speed	SpAttack	SpDefense
	70	84	70	51	65	70

BREEDABLE MOVES: Pursuit, Focus Energy, Outrage, Ancientpower, Stomp

ABLE TO LEARN: TM: 1, 2, 3, 5, 6, 8, 10, 11, 13, 17, 18, 20, 21, 23, 24, 26, 27, 28, 31, 32, 34, 35, 37, 38, 43, 44, 45, 48, 49, 50
HM: 1, 3

TECHNIQUES

Name	Level	Type	Power	Name	Level	Type	Power	Name	Level	Type	Power	Name	Level	Type	Power
Scary Face	38	Normal	-	Hyper Beam	65	Normal	150								
Crunch	47	Dark	80												
Earthquake	56	Ground	100												

#248 TYRANITAR

TYPE: Rock/Dark

STATS	HP	Attack	Defense	Speed	SpAttack	SpDefense
	100	134	110	61	95	100

BREEDABLE MOVES: Pursuit, Focus Energy, Outrage, Ancientpower, Stomp

ABLE TO LEARN: TM: 1, 2, 3, 5, 6, 8, 10, 11, 13, 15, 17, 18, 20, 21, 23, 24, 26, 27, 28, 31, 32, 34, 35, 37, 38, 43, 44, 45, 48, 49, 50
HM: 1, 3, 4

TECHNIQUES

Name	Level	Type	Power	Name	Level	Type	Power	Name	Level	Type	Power	Name	Level	Type	Power
Earthquake	61	Ground	100												
Hyper Beam	75	Normal	150												

#249 LUGIA

TYPE: Psychic/Flying

STATS	HP	Attack	Defense	Speed	SpAttack	SpDefense
	106	90	130	110	90	154

BREEDABLE MOVES: None

ABLE TO LEARN: TM: 2, 3, 5, 6, 7, 8, 10, 11, 13, 14, 15, 16, 17, 18, 19, 20, 21, 23, 24, 25, 26, 27, 29, 30, 31, 32, 34, 35, 37, 39, 42, 43, 44, 47, 50

TECHNIQUES

Name	Level	Type	Power	Name	Level	Type	Power	Name	Level	Type	Power	Name	Level	Type	Power
Aeroblast	0	Flying	100	Recover	33	Normal	-	Swift	66	Normal	60	Future Sight	99	Psychic	80
Safeguard	11	Normal	-	Hydro Pump	44	Water	120	Whirlwind	77	Normal	-				
Gust	22	Flying	40	Rain Dance	55	Water	-	Ancientpower	88	Rock	60				

#250 HO-OH

TYPE: Fire/Flying

STATS	HP	Attack	Defense	Speed	SpAttack	SpDefense
	106	130	90	90	110	154

BREEDABLE MOVES: None

ABLE TO LEARN: TM: 3, 5, 6, 7, 8, 9, 10, 11, 13, 15, 17, 18, 19, 20, 22, 24, 25, 26, 27, 29, 30, 31, 32, 34, 35, 37, 38, 39, 42, 43, 44, 47, 50
HM: 2, 4, 5

TECHNIQUES

Name	Level	Type	Power	Name	Level	Type	Power	Name	Level	Type	Power	Name	Level	Type	Power
Sacred Fire	0	Fire	100	Recover	33	Normal	-	Swift	66	Normal	60	Future Sight	99	Psychic	80
Safeguard	11	Normal	-	Fire Blast	44	Fire	120	Whirlwind	77	Normal	-				
Gust	22	Flying	40	Sunny Day	55	Fire	-	Ancientpower	88	Rock	60				

#251 CELEBI

TYPE: Psychic/Grass

STATS	HP	Attack	Defense	Speed	SpAttack	SpDefense
	100	100	100	100	100	100

BREEDABLE MOVES: None

ABLE TO LEARN: TM: 3, 6, 9, 10, 11, 12, 13, 15, 17, 18, 19, 20, 21, 22, 27, 29, 30, 31, 32, 34, 35, 37, 39, 40, 42, 43, 44, 50
HM: 5

TECHNIQUES

Name	Level	Type	Power	Name	Level	Type	Power	Name	Level	Type	Power	Name	Level	Type	Power
Leech Seed	0	Grass	-	Recover	0	Normal	-	Future Sight	30	Psychic	80				
Confusion	0	Psychic	50	Safeguard	10	Normal	-	Baton Pass	40	Normal	-				
Heal Bell	0	Normal	-	Ancientpower	20	Rock	60	Perish Song	50	Normal	-				

Pokémon STADIUM 2

POKéMON REFERENCE TABLES

HOLD ITEMS

Item	Use
Amulet Coin	Raises money gained in battle
Berserk Gene	Doubles attack and confuses
Blackbelt	Raises power of Fighting attacks
Blackglasses	Raises power of Dark attacks
Bright Powder	Reduces opponent's accuracy
Charcoal	Raises power of Fire attacks
Cleanse Tag	Reduces wild Pokémon encounters
Dragon Fang	Raises power of Dragon attacks
Everstone	Prevents evolution
Exp. Share	Gives exp. to a Pokémon, even if that Pokémon did not fight in the battle
Focus Band	Pokémon has a chance of surviving an attack that would make it faint
Hard Stone	Raises power of Rock attacks
Leftovers	Restores some HP every round
Light Ball	Doubles Special Attack for Pikachu
Lucky Egg	Increases amount of exp. gained
Lucky Punch	Raises Chansey's critical hit ratio
Magnet	Raises power of Electric attacks

Item	Use
Metal Coat	Raises power of Steel attacks
Metal Powder	Raises Ditto's Defense
Miracle Seed	Raises power of Grass attacks
Mystic Water	Raises power of Water attacks
Nevermeltice	Raises power of Ice attacks
Pink Bow	Raises power of Normal attacks
Poison Barb	Raises power of Poison attacks
Quick Claw	Occasionally attacks first, ignoring speed
Scope Lens	Raises chance of a critical hit
Sharp Beak	Raises power of Flying attacks
Silverpowder	Raises power of Bug attacks
Smoke Ball	Gives 100% chance to run from wild Pokémon
Soft Sand	Raises power of Ground attacks
Spell Tag	Raises power of Ghost attacks
Stick	Raises power of Farfetch'd attacks
Thick Club	Doubles Cubone and Marowak's Attack
Twistedspoon	Raises power of Psychic attacks

TECHNICAL MACHINES REFERENCE

TM	Use	Type	Power	Acc	PP	Location	Effect
01	Dynamicpunch	Fighting	100	50	5	Cianwood City Gym	Confuses opponent 100%
02	Headbutt	Normal	70	100	15	Ilex Forest	30% Flinch, Hit trees out of combat
03	Curse	N/A	-	-	10	Celadon City Pokémon Mansion at Nite	If used by a Ghost type, reduces own HP by half and cuts foe's HP each round. If used by a non Ghost, lowers Speed and raises Attack and Defense by 1
04	Rollout	Rock	30	90	20	Route 35	Attacks five times, doubling in power each time
05	Roar	Normal	-	100	20	Route 32	Ends battle against wild Pokémon, forces Trainers to switch Pokémon
06	Toxic	Poison	-	85	10	Fuchsia City Gym	Deals increasing damage to your opponent each round—1/16, 2/16, 3/16, etc.
07	Zap Cannon	Electric	100	50	5	Manager in Power Plant	100% Paralyze if it hits
08	Rock Smash	Fighting	20	100	15	Route 36	Reduces enemy Defense by 1, Breaks cracked rocks out of combat
09	Psych Up	Normal	-	100	10	Trade an Abra from Red/Blue	Any beneficial stat effects used by opponent's Pokémon benefit your Pokémon as well
10	Hidden Power	Normal	-	100	15	In house northwest of Lake of Rage	Type (any) and Power (from 31 to 70) varies depending on the Pokémon it is taught to
11	Sunny Day	Fire	-	100	5	Celadon City Dept. Store, Girl in Radio Tower	Fire attacks inflict 50% more damage. Water attacks inflict 50% less. Solarbeam becomes a single-turn attack. Thunder accuracy is lowered to 50%. Grass recovery moves, Morning Sun, and Moonlight, are doubled in effectiveness
12	Sweet Scent	Normal	-	100	20	Ilex Forest Gate	Reduces enemy Evade by 1, Attracts wild Pokémon out of combat
13	Snore	Normal	40	100	15	Moomoo Farm (sick Miltank), Dark Cave	Flinch 30%, can only be used while asleep
14	Blizzard	Ice	120	70	5	Goldenrod City Game Corner	Freeze 10%
15	Hyper Beam	Normal	150	90	5	Celadon City Game Corner	Attacks first turn, recharges second.
16	Icy Wind	Ice	55	95	15	Mahogany Town Gym	Reduces enemy Speed by 1
17	Protect	Normal	-	100	10	Celadon City Dept. Store	Always goes first, blocks enemy attack with 100% effectiveness, but success rate drops if used continuously
18	Rain Dance	Water	-	100	5	Celadon City Dept. Store Slowpoke Well	Water attacks inflict 50% more damage, Fire attacks inflict 50% less. Thunder becomes 100% accurate, cuts effectiveness of Grass recovery moves, Morning Sun, and Moonlight, by 50%
19	Giga Drain	Grass	60	100	5	Celadon City Gym	Heals half the damage dealt
20	Endure	Normal	-	100	10	Burnt Tower	Always goes first, will survive any attack with 1 HP remaining, but success rate drops if used continuously
21	Frustration	Normal	-	100	20	Woman in Goldenrod City Dept. Store	Power depends on how much your Pokémon dislikes you, up to a maximum power of 102
22	Solarbeam	Grass	120	100	10	Route 27	Charges first turn, attacks second
23	Iron Tail	Steel	100	75	15	Olivine City Gym	30% Reduces enemy Defense by 1
24	Dragonbreath	Dragon	60	100	20	Dragon's Den	30% Paralyze
25	Thunder	Electric	120	70	10	Goldenrod City Game Corner	30% Paralyze
26	Earthquake	Ground	100	100	10	Victory Road	Deals 2x damage to Pokémon using Dig

Item	Use	Type	Power	Acc	PP	Location	Effect
27	Return	Normal	-	100	20	Woman in Goldenrod City Dept. Store	Power depends on how much your Pokémon likes you, up to a maximum power of 102
28	Dig	Ground	60	100	10	National Park	Digs first turn, attacks second, mostly invulnerable during Dig
29	Psychic	Psychic	90	100	10	Mr. Psychic in Saffron City	10% Reduce enemy Special Defense by 1
30	Shadow Ball	Ghost	80	100	15	Ecruteak City Gym	20% Reduce enemy Special Defense by 1
31	Mud-Slap	Ground	20	100	10	Violet City Gym	Reduces enemy Accuracy by 1
32	Double Team	Normal	-	100	15	Celadon City Game Corner	Raises Evade by 1
33	Ice Punch	Ice	75	100	15	Goldenrod City Dept. Store	10% Freeze
34	Swagger	Normal	-	90	15	Lighthouse	Increases enemy Attack by 2, confuses enemy
35	Sleep Talk	Normal	-	100	10	Near Director under Goldenrod City	Attacks with a random learned technique, only usable while asleep
36	Sludge Bomb	Poison	90	100	10	Route 43 after defeating Team Rocket	30% Poison
37	Sandstorm	Rock	-	100	10	Route 27	Inflicts 1/8 total HP damage to both Pokémon, does not affect Rock, Ground or Steel
38	Fire Blast	Fire	120	85	5	Goldenrod City Game Corner	10% Burn
39	Swift	Normal	60	100	20	Lower level Union Cave	Attacks first, hits through moves that increase evasion
40	Defense Curl	Normal	-	100	40	Mount Mortar	Raises Defense by 1, doubles power of Rollout if used next turn
41	Thunderpunch	Electric	75	100	15	Goldenrod City Dept. Store	10% Paralyze
42	Dream Eater	Psychic	100	100	15	Viridian City	Heals half of damage dealt, only works on sleeping foes
43	Detect	Fighting	-	100	5	North of Lake of Rage	Always goes first, protects against any attack, success rate drops if used continuously
44	Rest	Psychic	-	100	10	Ice Path	Fully heals HP and falls asleep
45	Attract	Normal	-	100	15	Goldenrod City Gym	Prevents enemy from attacking 50% of the time, only works on opposite sex Pokémon
46	Thief	Dark	40	100	10	Team Rocket HQ	Steals any items carried by Pokémon
47	Steel Wing	Steel	70	90	25	Mount Silver, Rock Tunnel	10% Raises Defense by 1
48	Fire Punch	Fire	75	100	15	Goldenrod City Dept. Store	10% Burn
49	Fury Cutter	Bug	10	95	20	Azalea Town Gym	Power doubles with successive hits, until miss
50	Nightmare	Ghost	-	100	15	Route 31, bring mail to waiting man	Cuts opponents HP by 1/4 each round, only works on sleeping Pokémon

HIDDEN MACHINES REFERENCE

HM	Use	Type	Power	Acc	PP	Location	Effect
01	Cut	Normal	50	95	30	Ilex Forest	Out of combat cuts trees
02	Fly	Flying	70	95	15	Cianwood City, after gym fight	Flies first turn, attacks second. Can be used out of battle to fly to any visited city
03	Surf	Water	95	100	15	Ecruteak City, Dance Theater	Out of combat can surf on water
04	Strength	Normal	80	100	15	Olivine City, Sailor	Out of combat pushes boulders
05	Flash	Normal	-	70	20	Sprout Tower elder	Reduces enemy Accuracy by 1, out of combat lights dark areas
06	Whirlpool	Water	15	70	15	Team Rocket HQ, given by Lance	Traps opponent in fight for 2-5 rounds, out of combat can be used to remove whirlpools from the water
07	Waterfall	Water	80	100	15	Ice Path	Out of combat can be used to climb waterfalls

TECHNIQUES REFERENCE

Name	Type	Power	Acc	PP	Notes
Absorb	Grass	20	100	20	Restores half of the damage dealt to opponent
Acid	Poison	40	100	30	10% Reduces Defense by 1
Acid Armor	Poison	-	100	40	Raises Defense by 2
Aeroblast	Flying	100	95	5	Increased chance of critical hitting
Agility	Psychic	-	100	30	Raises Speed by 2
Amnesia	Psychic	-	100	20	Raises Special Defense by 2
Ancientpower	Rock	60	100	5	10% Raises all abilities by 1
Aurora Beam	Ice	65	100	20	10% Reduces Attack by 1
Barrage	Normal	15	85	20	Attacks 2-5 times
Barrier	Psychic	-	100	30	Raises Defense by 2
Baton Pass	Normal	-	100	40	Switches out Pokémon and confers all positive status effects on the Pokémon swapped in
Beat Up	Dark	10	100	10	Power is 10 base, plus 10 per member of your team, not counting status affected Pokémon (sleep, etc). Damage affected by the Special Attack of all members of your team
Belly Drum	Normal	-	100	10	Maximizes Attack, cuts HP in half
Bide	Normal	-	100	10	Waits for 2-3 turns, and then returns double the amount of damage received
Bind	Normal	15	75	20	Traps opponent and inflicts damage for 2-5 rounds
Bite	Dark	60	100	25	30% Flinch
Body Slam	Normal	85	100	15	30% Paralyze
Bone Club	Ground	65	85	20	10% Flinch
Bone Rush	Ground	25	80	10	Attacks 2-5 times
Bonemerang	Ground	50	90	10	Attacks twice
Bubble	Water	20	100	30	10% Reduces Speed by 1

Name	Type	Power	Acc	PP	Notes
Bubblebeam	Water	65	100	20	10% Reduces Speed by 1
Charm	Normal	-	100	20	Reduces Attack by 2
Clamp	Water	35	75	10	Traps opponent for 2-5 turns
Comet Punch	Normal	18	85	15	Attacks 2-5 times
Confuse Ray	Ghost	-	100	10	Confuses
Confusion	Psychic	50	100	25	10% Confuses
Constrict	Normal	10	100	35	10% Reduces Speed by 1
Conversion	Normal	-	100	30	Changes Pokémon's type to that of the last attack used against you
Cotton Spore	Grass	-	85	40	Reduces Speed by 2
Counter	Fighting	-	100	20	Always attacks second, returns twice the damage received
Crabhammer	Water	90	85	10	Increased chance of a critical hit
Cross Chop	Fighting	100	80	5	Increased chance of a critical hit
Crunch	Dark	80	100	15	20% Reduces Special Defense by 1
Destiny Bond	Ghost	-	100	5	If Pokémon faints, opponent faints as well
Disable	Normal	-	55	20	Disables last move used against you for several turns
Dizzy Punch	Normal	70	100	10	20% Confuses
Double Kick	Fighting	30	100	30	Attacks twice
Double Team	Normal	-	100	15	Raises Evade by 1
Double-Edge	Normal	120	100	15	Recoil damages user by 1/4 of damage dealt
Doubleslap	Normal	15	85	10	Attacks 2-5 times
Dragon Rage	Dragon	40	100	10	Deals 40 damage
Drill Peck	Flying	80	100	20	-
Egg Bomb	Normal	100	75	10	-
Ember	Fire	40	100	25	10% Burn
Encore	Normal	-	100	5	Forces opponent to use last used move 2-6 more times
Explosion	Normal	250	100	5	Faints user
Extremespeed	Normal	80	100	5	Attacks first
Faint Attack	Dark	60	100	20	Always hits
False Swipe	Normal	40	100	40	Cannot reduce opponent's HP below 1
Fire Spin	Fire	15	70	15	Traps opponent for 2-5 turns
Fissure	Ground	-	30	5	One hit K.O.
Flail	Normal	-	100	15	Power depends on how low your Pokémon's HP is
Flame Wheel	Fire	60	100	25	10% Burn, releases user and target from Freeze
Flamethrower	Fire	95	100	15	10% Burn
Focus Energy	Normal	-	100	30	Increases chance of critical hit for next attack
Foresight	Normal	-	100	40	Ignores any Evade modifiers opponent has used, and allows Normal and Fighting attacks to hit Ghosts
Fury Attack	Normal	15	85	20	Attacks 2-5 times
Fury Swipes	Normal	18	80	15	Attacks 2-5 times
Future Sight	Psychic	80	90	15	Attacks opponent two turns later, user can still use attacks during those rounds
Glare	Normal	-	75	30	Paralyze
Growl	Normal	-	100	40	Reduces Attack by 1
Growth	Normal	-	100	40	Raises Special Attack by 1
Guillotine	Normal	-	30	5	One-hit K.O.
Gust	Flying	40	100	35	-
Harden	Normal	-	100	30	Raises Defense by 1
Haze	Ice	-	100	30	Removes all stat affecters from both Pokémon
Heal Bell	Normal	-	100	5	Heals all status ailments for your entire team
Hi Jump Kick	Fighting	85	90	20	If it misses, recoil deals 1/8 damage to user
Horn Attack	Normal	65	100	25	-
Horn Drill	Normal	-	30	5	One hit K.O.
Hydro Pump	Water	120	80	5	-
Hyper Fang	Normal	80	90	15	10% Flinch
Hypnosis	Psychic	-	60	20	Puts opponent to sleep
Ice Beam	Ice	95	100	10	10% Freeze
Jump Kick	Fighting	70	95	25	If it misses, recoil deals 1/8 to user
Karate Chop	Fighting	50	100	25	Increased chance of a critical hit
Kinesis	Psychic	-	80	15	Reduces Accuracy by 1
Leech Life	Bug	20	100	15	Heals half of damage dealt
Leech Seed	Grass	-	90	10	Absorbs 1/8 of opponent's HP every round
Leer	Normal	-	100	30	Reduces Defense by 1
Lick	Ghost	20	100	30	30% Paralyze
Light Screen	Psychic	-	100	30	Cuts damage from special attacks in half for five rounds. Remains even if Pokémon are switched
Lock-On	Normal	-	100	5	Next attack has 100% accuracy
Lovely Kiss	Normal	-	75	10	Puts opponent to sleep
Low Kick	Fighting	50	90	20	30% Flinch
Mach Punch	Fighting	40	100	30	Attacks first
Magnitude	Ground	Varies	100	30	Has a random power from 10 to 150, typically 70
Mean Look	Normal	-	100	5	Prevents opponent from fleeing while user is still the active Pokémon
Meditate	Psychic	-	100	40	Raises Attack by 1
Mega Drain	Grass	40	100	10	Heals half of damage dealt
Mega Kick	Normal	120	75	5	-
Mega Punch	Normal	80	85	20	-
Megahorn	Bug	120	85	10	-

Name	Type	Power	Acc	PP	Notes
Metal Claw	Steel	50	95	35	10% Raises Attack by 1
Metronome	Normal	-	100	10	Uses a completely random move
Milk Drink	Normal	-	100	10	Heals half of Max HP, out of battle shares 1/5 of HP with a team member
Mimic	Normal	-	100	10	Copies last move used by enemy
Mind Reader	Normal	-	100	5	Next attack is 100% accurate
Minimize	Normal	-	100	20	Raises Evade by 1
Mirror Coat	Psychic	-	100	20	Always attacks second, returns double the damage if hit with a special attack
Mirror Move	Flying	-	100	20	Attacks with the last attack used against you
Mist	Ice	-	100	30	Protects against stat-lowering attacks
Moonlight	Normal	-	100	5	Refills HP, more at Nite
Morning Sun	Normal	-	100	5	Refills HP, double HP restored while sunny
Night Shade	Ghost	-	100	15	Deals damage equal to the Pokémon's level
Octazooka	Water	65	85	10	50% Reduces Accuracy by 1
Outrage	Dragon	90	100	15	Attacks 2-3 turns, then user is confused
Pain Split	Normal	-	100	20	Averages the HP between your Pokémon and the opponent's Pokémon
Pay Day	Normal	40	100	20	Gives money (Pokémon's level X number of times used X 2)
Peck	Flying	35	100	35	-
Perish Song	Normal	-	100	5	In three turns, both Pokémon faint, will fail if Pokémon are switched
Petal Dance	Grass	70	100	20	Attacks 2-3 turns, then user is confused
Pin Missile	Bug	14	85	20	Attacks 2-5 times
Poison Gas	Poison	-	55	40	Poisons
Poison Sting	Poison	15	100	35	30% Poisons
Poisonpowder	Poison	-	75	35	Poisons
Pound	Normal	40	100	35	-
Powder Snow	Ice	40	100	25	10% Freeze
Present	Normal	-	90	15	Deals 40, 80, or 120 damage, or heals opponent 80
Psybeam	Psychic	65	100	20	10% Confuses
Psywave	Psychic	Varies	80	15	Power is 1 to 1.5 times Pokémon's level
Pursuit	Dark	40	100	20	If opponent switches out, deals double damage
Quick Attack	Normal	40	100	30	Attacks first
Rage	Normal	20	100	20	Power raises each time Pokémon is hit by opponent while using Rage
Rapid Spin	Normal	20	100	40	Escapes from trapping moves and Leech Seed
Razor Leaf	Grass	55	95	25	Increased chance of critical hit
Razor Wind	Normal	80	75	10	Increased chance of critical hit
Recover	Normal	-	100	20	Refills half of user's HP
Reflect	Psychic	-	100	20	Halves damage from Physical attacks for 5 rounds. Effect stays even if Pokémon are switched out
Reversal	Fighting	-	100	15	The lower the user's HP, the higher the power of this technique
Rock Slide	Rock	75	90	10	30% Flinch
Rock Throw	Rock	50	90	15	-
Rolling Kick	Fighting	60	85	15	30% Flinch
Sacred Fire	Fire	100	95	5	50% Burn, can be used while Frozen
Safeguard	Normal	-	100	25	Protects against status attacks for 5 turns, effect remains even if Pokémon are switched out
Sand-Attack	Ground	-	100	15	Reduces Accuracy by 1
Scary Face	Normal	-	90	10	Reduces Speed by 2
Scratch	Normal	40	100	35	-
Screech	Normal	-	85	40	Reduces Defense by 2
Seismic Toss	Fighting	-	100	20	Deals damage equal to Pokémon's level
Selfdestruct	Normal	200	100	5	User faints
Sharpen	Normal	-	100	30	Raises Attack by 1
Sing	Normal	-	55	15	Puts opponent to sleep
Sketch	Normal	-	100	1	Replaces Sketch with opponent's last used move
Skull Bash	Normal	100	100	15	Charges first turn, attacks second, raises Defense by 1
Sky Attack	Flying	140	90	5	Charges first turn, attacks second, increased chance of a critical hit
Slam	Normal	80	75	20	-
Slash	Normal	70	100	15	Increased chance of a critical hit
Sleep Powder	Grass	-	75	15	Puts opponent to sleep
Sludge	Poison	65	100	20	30% Poisons
Smog	Poison	20	70	20	40% Poisons
Smokescreen	Normal	-	100	20	Reduces Accuracy by 1
Softboiled	Normal	-	100	10	Refills half of HP, can be used out of battle to heal team member by 1/5
Sonicboom	Normal	20	90	20	Deals 20 damage
Spark	Electric	65	100	20	30% Paralyze
Spider Web	Bug	-	100	10	Prevents opponent from fleeing, during a trainer battle, prevents trainer from switching Pokémon
Spike Cannon	Normal	20	100	15	Attacks 2-5 times
Spikes	Ground	-	100	20	If opponent switches Pokémon, the switched-in Pokémon takes 1/8 of its maximum HP in damage
Spite	Ghost	-	100	10	Reduces PP of opponent's last used move by 2-5
Splash	Normal	-	100	40	Does nothing
Spore	Grass	-	100	15	Puts opponent to sleep
Stomp	Normal	65	100	20	30% Flinch
String Shot	Bug	-	95	40	Reduces Speed by 1

Name	Type	Power	Acc	PP	Notes
Struggle	Normal	50	100	1	All Pokémon gain this move when they exhaust their PP. Deals recoil damage of 1/4 to using Pokémon
Stun Spore	Grass	-	75	30	Paralyzes
Submission	Fighting	80	80	25	Recoil damages Pokémon by 1/4 of damage dealt
Substitute	Normal	-	100	10	Creates a substitute Pokémon using 1/4 of maximum HP. Substitute absorbs damage and blocks status-affecting moves
Super Fang	Normal	-	90	10	Cuts opponent's HP in half
Supersonic	Normal	-	55	20	Confuses
Sweet Kiss	Normal	-	75	10	Confuses
Swords Dance	Normal	-	100	30	Raises Attack by 2
Synthesis	Grass	-	100	5	Refills HP, effectiveness depends on time of day
Tackle	Normal	35	95	35	-
Tail Whip	Normal	-	100	30	Reduces Defense by 1
Take Down	Normal	90	85	20	Recoil damages user by 1/4
Teleport	Psychic	-	100	20	Escapes from wild Pokémon fights, out of battle, teleports to last used Pokémon Center
Thrash	Normal	90	100	20	Attacks 2-3 turns, user is confused
Thunder Wave	Electric	-	100	20	Paralyzes
Thunderbolt	Electric	95	100	15	10% Paralyzes
Thundershock	Electric	40	100	30	10% Paralyzes
Transform	Normal	-	100	10	Transforms Pokémon into opponent's Pokémon, but all moves have a PP of 5
Tri Attack	Normal	80	100	10	20% Freeze, Paralyze, or Burn
Triple Kick	Fighting	10	90	10	Attacks 3 times in one round, power increases by 10 each time
Twineedle	Bug	25	100	20	Attacks twice, 20% Poisons
Twister	Dragon	40	100	20	20% Flinch
Vicegrip	Normal	55	100	30	-
Vine Whip	Grass	35	100	10	-
Vital Throw	Fighting	70	100	10	Attacks second, attack will always hit
Water Gun	Water	40	100	25	-
Whirlwind	Normal	-	100	20	Ends fights with wild Pokémon, in trainer battles, forces opponent to switch Pokémon
Wing Attack	Flying	60	100	35	-
Withdraw	Water	-	100	40	Raises Defense by 1
Wrap	Normal	15	85	20	Traps opponent for 2-5 turns

POKéMON PAGE INDEX

POKéMON TYPE COMBAT CHART

★ More Effective
👎 Less Effective
⊘ No Effect

DEFENDING POKéMON TYPE

ATTACK TYPE	Normal	Fire	Water	Electric	Grass	Ice	Fighting	Poison	Ground	Flying	Psychic	Bug	Rock	Ghost	Dragon	Dark	Steel
Normal													👎	⊘			👎
Fire	👎	👎			★	★						★	👎		👎		★
Water	★		👎		👎				★				★		👎		
Electric			★	👎	👎				⊘	★					👎		
Grass		👎	★		👎			👎	★	👎		👎	★		👎		👎
Ice		👎	👎		★	👎			★	★					★		👎
Fighting	★					★		👎		👎	👎	👎	★	⊘		★	★
Poison					★			👎	👎				👎	👎			⊘
Ground		★		★	👎			★		⊘		👎	★				★
Flying				👎	★		★					★	👎				👎
Psychic							★	★			👎					⊘	👎
Bug	👎				★		👎	👎		👎	★			👎		★	👎
Rock		★				★	👎		👎	★		★					👎
Ghost	⊘										⊘			★		👎	👎
Dragon															★		👎
Dark							👎				★			★		👎	👎
Steel		👎	👎	👎		★							★				👎